CHOICES FOR
SELF-MANAGING SCHOOLS

Choices for Self-Managing Schools

Autonomy and Accountability

edited by

Brian Fidler, Sheila Russell and Tim Simkins

British Educational Management and Administration Society

Paul Chapman
Publishing Ltd

Copyright © 1997 BEMAS (British Educational Management and Administration Society)

Paul Chapman Publishing Ltd
144 Liverpool Road
London N1 1LA

British Library Cataloguing in Publication Data
Choices for self-managing schools. – (BEMAS series in
   education management)
   1. School management and organization – Great Britain
   I. Fidler, Brian   II. Russell, Sheila   III. Simkins, Tim
   371.2'00941

ISBN 1 85396 338 0

Typeset by Dorwyn Ltd, Rowlands Castle, Hants
Printed and bound in Great Britain

A B C D E F G H   9 8 7

Contents

Contributors

Kath Aspinwall has taught in primary schools, further and higher education in Sheffield, Rotherham and Jamaica. Currently she lectures in education management at Sheffield Hallam University. Her principal interests are in personal and professional development of people in organisations, using evaluation for developmental purposes and in organisational learning.

Hugh Busher is Lecturer in Educational Management at Sheffield University. Formerly at Leeds and Loughborough Universities he has an extensive research and publication background in teacher development and the leadership and management of schools and has recently helped to develop an LEA/HEI partnership HEADLAMP scheme for headteacher training.

Brian Fidler teaches and researches at the University of Reading where he is senior lecturer and course leader for the MSc Managing School Improvement. He was editor with Geoff Bowles of *Effective Local Management of Schools*, Longman, in 1989 and his most recent BEMAS book was *Strategic Planning for School Improvement*, Pitman, in 1996. He is editor of *School Leadership and Management* the international journal of leadership and school development. He is also treasurer of BEMAS.

Valerie Hall is a senior lecturer in human resource management at the National Development Centre for Educational Management and Policy at the University of Bristol. She currently directs the taught doctor of education (Ed.D) programme at the University of Bristol, the first of its kind in Europe. She has taught in schools, colleges and universities for over thirty years. During the past twenty years she has been involved in a number of research projects, including the POST Project looking at the selection of secondary heads, the CROSH project (changing role of the secondary head) and the SMT Project (senior management teams in secondary schools). Her latest book *Dancing on the Ceiling: A Study of Women Managers in Education* describes her study of education management from a gender perspective.

Keith Hodgkinson is Senior Lecturer and Director of the PGCE Primary course at Loughborough University. He has published widely on aspects of primary and secondary education and teacher training especially on history teaching and information technology in education.

David Hopkins is Professor of Education and Chair (designate) of the School of Education at the University of Nottingham. He is a long time consultant to the OECD on School Improvement and Teacher Quality and has consulted in some twenty countries on School Development issues. He is currently co-director of the 'Improving the Quality of Education for All' (IQEA) project and of the ESRC 'Improving Schools' project. Some of his recent books include *A Teachers' Guide to Classroom Research*, Cassell, 1993 and *School Improvement in an Era of Change*, Cassell, 1994. He is an international mountain guide and has climbed many of the world's great mountain ranges.

Chris James is Professor of Education Management in the University of Glamorgan Business School. He has research interests in professional knowledge and its acquisition and in the management of educational organisations. He has published in medical education, nurse education, teacher education and education management. He lives in Bath with his wife and their four children.

Hugh Jenkins is Head of the Anglia Business School, Anglia Polytechnic University. After teaching he became a senior manager in LEAs and industry. A doctor of philosophy of the University of Birmingham, he has been visiting professor in Canada and Australia and was recently made a Fellow of the Commonwealth Council for Educational Administration.

Mike Pedler is an independent writer and consultant and a partner in the Learning Company Project. Previously with Proctor and Gamble and the Workers' Educational Association, he spent 17 years at Sheffield Business School and is Visiting Professor in the Department of Health Studies at the University of York. He has written and co-authored a number of books and articles on learning, management development and organisational development.

Peter Phillips is presently Headmaster of West Monmouth School, Pontypool, his second headship. He has worked in five secondary schools in the maintained sector and acted as a consultant to the University of Glamorgan Education Management course for many years. Within educational management his main area of interest is educational marketing.

Sylvia Reid is Senior Lecturer in the School of Professional Education and Development at Leeds Metropolitan University. Her research interests include appraisal, mentoring and managing creativity.

Kathryn Riley is Professor of Educational Management at the Roehampton Institute, London. She has wide experience in education and local government, as senior officer, elected member, school governor and senior teacher. She has written and researched nationally and internationally on issues of management, leadership, quality, equality and performance in the public sector and education and on central/local government relations.

David Rowles, who provided illustrative material for the two case studies in Chapter 2.1, is Principal Research Officer in educational management at the

Roehampton Institute, London, where he has worked extensively on teacher appraisal and the new arrangements for school inspection. Previously he was Senior Inspector for schools in the London Borough of Merton, concentrating on management issues and the professional development of staff. He serves on two governing bodies, for one of which he is chair.

Sheila Russell is a Visiting Fellow at Leeds Metropolitan University. Formerly an LEA Senior Inspector she now is involved in research into the relationship between school self-review, school inspection and school improvement. Her most recent publication is *Collaborative School Self-Review*, Lemos & Crane, 1996.

Tim Simkins is Head of the Centre for Education Management and Administration at Sheffield Hallam University. His main interests are in planning and resource management in education, in which areas he teaches and researches and has undertaken consultancy work in many parts of the world. He is currently vice-chair of the British Educational Management and Administration Society and chair of its Publications Committee.

Preface

This is the first book in a new series to be published by BEMAS in conjunction with Paul Chapman Publishing. The aim of the series is to provide all those working in education with an opportunity to reflect on the major issues confronting those managing our schools, and who are involved with those managing schools. The unique characteristic of BEMAS books in this series is the powerful linking of practice, research and theory, but with the emphasis sharply on school improvement.

The theme of this book is most apposite. Over many years BEMAS publications have mapped, analysed and commented on the progress of the Government's educational policies, since the Education Reform Act of 1988. For example, *Effective Local Management of Schools: a strategic approach* (1989) provided what was then a seminal analysis of the key management implications for schools of moving away from local authority and control towards self-management, while *Implementing Educational Reform: the early lessons* (1992) brought together some important writing on the consequences of the Education Reform Act as they were emerging in practice. This volume is a natural successor to these. After nearly ten years of evolving experience, it is time to take stock of progress and to explore the options which are available to those who manage schools in an era of greater autonomy, but also, in many ways, of greater constraint in terms of accountability demands and resource pressures.

In order to do this, the editors have brought together a team of writers who are able to provide a broad and informed perspective on the issues and dilemmas which are involved and – an important concern of BEMAS in particular – to link theory and practice. The book explores in detail the choices available to schools in relation to specific areas of management, such as curriculum and resource management. Beyond this, however, it addresses much more fundamental issues: what kinds of values should underpin the strategic vision of schools as they face an increasingly challenging environment, and how might these values be expressed through, for example, leadership and the management of school culture? These are important indeed fundamental questions, and it is a key part of BEMAS' mission to facilitate their wide discussion and debate. This book is a contribution to this process.

Hugh Busher and Harry Tomlinson
Series Editors
on behalf of the British Educational Management and Administration Society

Introduction

In 1989 the British Educational Management and Administration Society published a book entitled *Effective Local Management of Schools*, edited by Brian Fidler and Geoff Bowles. It proved to be one of the most successful titles in the Society's series. It addressed the key issue of local management arising from the 1988 Education Reform Act in a way which no other book did, particularly through its carefully focused linking of management theory with the description of practice. However, since the book was published in 1989 the world has changed. First, LMS is no longer the only model of school autonomy in Britain, although it is still the dominant one, and most schools have now adapted their management practices, often pragmatically and to varying extents, to take up the opportunity to define their own direction under whichever administrative scheme they are managed. Secondly, however, as the experience of LMS and GMS has grown, the limits of autonomy have also become clearer. The tension between the freedom to develop in an autonomous way and the need to be accountable through a range of mechanisms to a variety of stakeholders, is increasingly commented upon. Indeed, many of the most important developments over the past five years have been concerned to constrain or direct the ways in which schools can choose to develop. Such developments include national curriculum and testing requirements, reporting, inspection and its associated expectations about school planning and documentation, teacher appraisal, increasingly tight budgetary settlements and the need to respond to parental choice in many areas.

Thus the number and speed of assimilation of the various changes passed down by central government has given most schools little time to place them within a longer term context. The realisation of the potential for autonomous development, therefore, has in many cases trailed behind the adaptation necessary to show that the school is being managed responsibly. With financial and other pressures on schools looking set to intensify, many heads who thought they had survived the changes now recognise that a period of reflection and choice is essential to plan effectively for their future.

The aim of this book is to provide some of the essential ideas and concepts which underlie the management of autonomous schools in a way which is accessible to those responsible for the management of such schools, to students of education management and to others who are interested in the management

consequences of policy change generally. It aims to present theoretical frameworks which are valuable for conceptualising management and managing, and
to demonstrate how these frameworks are valuable in articulating, analysing
and developing practice. The book's specific objectives are:

- to provide an overview of the key aspects of management as they relate to
  autonomous schools;
- to show how theory and practice are related in each of these aspects;
- to consider, through the examination of these aspects, how the tension
  between autonomy and accountability may be managed.

The book comprises four parts. Part 1, *Context and Concepts*, introduces the
context within which schools operate and describes the key dimensions of
autonomy under various arrangements as well as mapping the main constraints within which this autonomy must be exercised. It recaps on recent
changes imposed on schools and outlines some trends which have emerged in
response to them. It explores the concepts of autonomy and accountability and
tensions between the two, considering how the ways in which values are
incorporated into organisational culture provide a basis for making important
choices about how to manage publicly-funded value-laden institutions for the
education of the young. Finally, it considers the implications of current trends
in thinking about school effectiveness and planned school improvement for the
management of change.

Part 2, *The Components of Management*, takes an essentially functional
approach to management. Each chapter explores one particular aspect of management which is significant for the effective management of the autonomous
school. It maps the main areas of freedom and constraint which are open to
school managers in the area, and the key tensions which result; it presents
some key theoretical frameworks for articulating and analysing issues in the
area; it summarises recent research evidence on how these tensions are being
addressed in practice; and it provides examples of this practice in the form of
'cameos'.

Part 3 of the book, *Looking Towards the Future*, explores ways in which the
functional aspects of management can be integrated, using a number of key
themes from current management thinking which address the issue of how
organisations can ensure direction in an increasingly turbulent environment.
The three themes chosen for extended discussion in this part are strategic
leadership, the effective management of the core activities of the school,
namely teaching and learning, and the concept of the learning organisation.
The aim of this section is not be to be prescriptive, but to enable readers to
'reframe' their thinking about school management in ways which are appropriate to their own schools and in particular to suggest new ways of thinking
about the autonomy/accountability dilemma.

Finally, in Part 4 the editors provide an overview which draws together the
main themes of the book and identifies the main areas of choice for heads,
governors and other key leaders and managers for the future.

We envisage that this book may be used in one of two ways. First, particular chapters may be used as free-standing analyses of particular aspects of the management of 'autonomous' schools. The chapters in Part 2 in particular will give readers an insight into the recent experience of self-management in the United Kingdom, the kinds of conceptual frameworks which might be used to analyse this experience, and the major management choices which this experience highlights. They also provide up-to-date résumés of recent writing on the major themes which they explore.

Secondly, readers may wish to consider the implications of school self-management more broadly. This may be done by studying in particular Parts 1, 3 and 4 of the book. The chapters in these parts reflect in some depth on the meaning of school autonomy and the importance of values, culture and leadership in the new context of the self-managing school. These chapters may be read as an extended, and hopefully stimulating, essay on the current state of play in the field of school management and on possibilities for the future.

Finally, we hope that many will read the book as a whole. The more wide-ranging chapters might be seen as the wholemeal bread which sandwiches a variety of fillings. Each component is nourishing, but taken together they are likely to be most tasty and interesting!

We have enjoyed working together on this book, and it has been the stimulus for many fruitful discussions. This book is a truly joint venture and the ordering of names on the cover is strictly alphabetical, and does not indicate any order of precedence.

The editors wish to thank all the contributors for the wisdom, creativity and hard work which went into their chapters, and the forbearance with which they responded to editorial suggestions.

Acknowledgements

We also wish to thank the following authors and publishers for permission to reproduce the case studies in Chapter 2.6:

R. Levačić, *Local Management of Schools: analysis and practice*, Open University Press, 1995.
H. Thomas and J. Martin, *Managing Resources for School Improvement: creating a cost-effective school*, Routledge, 1996.

PART 1
CONTEXT AND CONCEPTS

1.1

A Changing Context

SHEILA RUSSELL

VALUES AND SYSTEMS

This chapter records some of the influences on the management of the provision of education in England and Wales since the 1944 Education Act and outlines some of the constraints and freedoms that affect the choices schools may make at the end of the century.

It is the values and political culture of a society in its historical setting that determine choices about the purpose and institutional arrangements of its education system. Hence an analysis of the government and control of education must take account of the social and political order existing at the time, which Ranson (1994) suggests can be modelled by

- the organising principles – the values, beliefs and ideas which are dominant;
- the constitutive system – the form of government: policy, tasks, authority and organisation;
- the social power – the interest groups, resources and power.

The way education is governed 'reveals conceptions about its role: in relations between public and private, in promoting the common good, and in the development of the capacities and powers of citizens within the community' (Ranson, 1994, p. 12). Ranson identifies three overlapping periods since 1945, the age of professionalism (1945–75), the period of corporatism (1970–81) and lastly the period of consumerism (1979–the present), when education moved into the market-place.

In each of these periods the dominant values of the time drove the different systems that emerged, although other oppositional forces were and are also present. The descriptions of the three ages are useful frames through which to observe the forces shaping the education debate in different periods of recent history. Each philosophy still has its influence, through structures and legislation that remain in place, and through attitudes that determine how the key actors on the education scene view themselves and their roles. Particularly over the last decade the philosophies of consumer choice, and the associated need for variety of provision, have dominated a profound reworking of the education system, and changes have been made which have affected every area of provision. Since 1988 'The relationship between central and local authority, school structures, funding and resourcing, curriculum, pedagogy, assessment, relationships with parents, early years and post-16, modes of inspection, ancillary services, higher education and teacher training have all been subject to scrutiny, criticism and legislation' (Tomlinson, 1994, p. 1). In setting out the context where self-managing schools can make choices it is necessary to recognise the philosophical as well as the legislative sources of the freedoms and constraints. Both leave a strong legacy to schools.

The age of professionalism

The basis of provision of education in England and Wales in this century has been a shifting set of partnerships, involving key groups whose influence and power has varied at different times. The 1944 Education Act created a new system which nevertheless maintained a continuity with pre-war provision, and which managed to reconcile conflicting interests through a prolonged three-year drafting stage, involving wide-ranging discussion with those representing churches, with education professionals and with the wider public.

The Act provided for free, compulsory schooling for young people between 5 and 15, through an education system which rested on a triangle of power informally shared between central government, represented by a Minister of Education, the local education authorities (LEAs), and the organised teaching profession. Bogdanor (1979) argues that this set of interdependent relationships was essential to the success of the system, providing necessary checks and balances. The myth of the post-war period was that decisions about education were generally taken over lunch at a London club, by Sir William Alexander, the Secretary of the Association of Education Committees, Sir Ronald Gould, General Secretary of the National Union of Teachers, and the Permanent Secretary for the Department of Education, and it was in keeping with the spirit of the times that this was seen to be a good thing. No one group had a monopoly of power and there was a continuing debate about the distribution of resources, and about the organisation and content of education, in order for decisions to be made. In the period of economic growth and prosperity which followed the second world war there were sufficient resources to fund an expansion of education provision, underpinned by a consensus of political commitment to the welfare state.

From 1945 to 1975 the prime purpose of education was seen as the development of the personal qualities and capacities of each individual, and teachers were recognised as professionals with a responsibility to analyse a child's needs and to choose the curriculum and methods to meet them. Many education professionals are still inspired by the principle of education as a force for individual development, and have developed their practice as educators through 'child-centred' techniques.

The 1944 Act's provision of a tripartite system, with allocation to secondary education based on an intelligence test at 11, was gently challenged through the *ad hoc* growth of a 'comprehensive' school movement throughout the late 1950s; indeed by 1964 nearly 10 per cent of pupils of secondary school age in England and Wales were being educated in comprehensive schools. There was a national expectation of equal educational opportunities for all children, whatever type of school they attended, and when in 1965 the Labour Government made a commitment to abolish selection at 11+ this was seen to be an acceptable extension of education policy (Chitty, 1992).

The age of corporatism

Throughout the 1970s an increasing stress was placed on the economic function of education, mirroring the start of a national economic decline. A new emphasis on realism, relevance and vocational preparation emerged, and there was a new urgency about the provision of 'human capital' to contribute to industrial and technological growth. As Prime Minister in 1976, James Callaghan launched 'The Great Debate' in his speech at Ruskin College, expressing concern that 'teachers lack experience, knowledge and understanding of trade and industry' (DES, 1977). As efficiency and productivity became overriding priorities, central government sought to establish its influence over the education system through extending its steering capacity, relying on a new emphasis on rational planning, and on control of LEA activities through its demands for information, and through grants related to evidence of planning and the meeting of objectives. An essential mechanism for this type of central steering was embodied in the Education (Grants and Awards) Act of 1984, which provided for the government to allocate sums of money to LEAs for particular purposes, with LEAs having to contribute their share (at least 25 per cent) of these educational support grants. The legacy of this period is seen in the way in which education administrators have learned to see strategic planning as a way of managing scarce resources, with principles of equity and efficiency as drivers.

THE REFORM AGENDA

The transition to Ranson's third period of 'consumerism' was signalled by the election in 1979 of a Conservative government with a manifesto declaring its commitment to the rights of the individual, a government led by those who espoused the philosophy that the institution of a 'social market' would more effectively restructure and improve the education system than any application of rational planning principles. The argument as it applies to public services is cogently summarised by a former Controller of the Audit Commission:

> Successful public sector agencies need to adopt the same characteristics as successful private sector concerns. They need to be responsive to their customers and constantly in search of efficiency gains and quality improvements. These desirable characteristics cannot be imposed from the top down. They are created by the operation of market systems which impose competitive pressure.
>
> (Davies, 1992, p. 9)

Successive Conservative governments since 1979 have introduced legislation to reform and restructure public services with twin concerns of first improving the efficiency of public spending, through introducing a value-for-money approach which stresses the monitoring of outputs at least as strongly as concern for the amount of financial input, and secondly decentralising decision making, in order to make services more directly responsive to the needs of those who use them. As it has affected the education system the main features of the strategy are

- centralisation – a national curriculum and a national assessment system, enabling performance monitoring against national standards;
- devolution – delegation of school budgets with an emphasis on efficiency and choice of services, and an increase in the power of parent and co-opted community members of governing bodies;
- marketisation – an increase in the diversity of provision, the types of school available and their accessibility to parents through enhanced rights of choice – 'you have a right to a place in the school you want unless it is full to capacity with pupils who have a stronger claim' (DES, 1991, p. 10).

Although driven by an ideology of marketisation the changes also evidence a high degree of central control; the government did not rely totally on a consumerist conviction that all that was needed was devolution and a free market for those using the services, and this tension is evident in the introduction of a strong degree of control over what is taught and how it is to be assessed. In the 1988 legislation a framework was set up for controlling and measuring the outputs of the education system, through the establishment of a common national curriculum and the setting of attainment targets for pupils to reach at different key stages of education. A concern for 'standards of achievement' measured by examination success and attainment in terms of the national curriculum targets has been one motivator of the reforms. There is a recognition that education is a public good, and echoes of the corporatist view that standards of success must be set to measure the effective use of public moneys. As a government minister claimed 'The education reforms we have put in place have all been directed at ensuring we have a sound framework in place for raising standards of attainment' (Squire, 1995).

Yet the changes were also based on a belief that greater self-government for schools, in financial terms, would secure greater value for money, at a time when it was intended to keep public spending under restraint, and that devolution of powers would secure an improved quality of education that would meet the needs of 'clients'. Consultants to the government summarised one view of the management approach needed to deliver the reforms:

> The underlying philosophy of financial delegation to schools stems from the application of the principles of good management. Good management requires the identification of management units for which objectives can be set and resources allocated; the unit is then required to manage itself within those resources in a way which seeks to achieve the objectives; the performance of the unit is monitored and the unit is

held to account for its performance and for its use of funds. These concepts are just as applicable in the public sector as they are in the private sector.

(Coopers & Lybrand, 1988, p. 7)

The government proclaimed its belief in schools' good stewardship of their resources, expecting that the schemes of local management to be introduced after the 1988 Act would enable governing bodies and headteachers to plan their use of resources, including their use of staff, to good effect in accordance with their own priorities. They also envisaged that schools would become more responsive to their clients – to parents, pupils, the local community and employers (DES, 1988).

In order to provide a mechanism for this 'responsiveness' to client need, opportunities had to be created for parental choice between schools, and greater differences between schools had to be introduced in the interests of 'diversity' of choice. The 1988 Education Reform Act therefore provided for open enrolment through removing the right of LEAs to set planned admission limits, provided for a greater variety of schools by introducing grant-maintained (GM) schools and City Technology Colleges, and gave greater powers to governing bodies through the introduction of schemes for Local Management of Schools.

Davies (1992, p. 39) argues that a number of important elements must be in place if public services are to enter a positive cycle of self-improvement through a successful social market. These are:

- a rational financial framework;
- clearly defined outputs;
- a purchaser/provider split;
- market testing and competing providers;
- contracts;
- customer choice;
- a strong and realistic customer voice;
- comparative data on performance;
- strong lay management;
- independent inspection and audit.

While many of these features were put in place by legislation up to and including 1988 those features most strongly related to accountability were missing, namely comparative data on performance and independent inspection and audit. The Citizen's Charter, as interpreted in the Parent's (sic) Charter, promised 'annual written reports on your child's progress; regular reports by independent inspectors on the strengths and weaknesses of your school and published tables so that you can compare the performance of local schools' (DES, 1991, p. 1). These promises required new legislation in the Education Acts of 1992 and 1993 to take the reforms one stage further by introducing an external inspection service through the Office for Standards in Education (Ofsted), regular public reports on schools, and a procedure for dealing with those schools that were found to be 'failing to provide an acceptable standard of education'.

Underlying the reforms and much of the language used to introduce them there seemed to be a profound mistrust of professionals, of LEAs and of teachers. The government claimed, according to Ranson (1994, p. 69) that 'The whole purpose of education had been distorted by a mistaken preoccupation with social engineering and egalitarianism: education is intrinsically individual and inequality of achievement inescapable.' LEAs were particularly distrusted. The 1993 Act in particular undermined LEA power by establishing a Funding Agency for Schools (FAS) which, when the percentage of schools that are GM within the primary or secondary phase in any LEA exceeds 10 per cent, works jointly with LEA to administer funding, and which assumes total responsibility for that phase in that area when the percentage reaches 75 per cent. As Morris (1992), pointed out at the time there is a problem when the funding body takes on the functions of the local authority in parallel with or in substitution for that authority.

There has been a breakdown in the consensus apparently present in the 'age of professionalism', and an overturning of the system of checks and balances inherent in the pre-1979 partnership between central government, LEAs and teaching organisations. Yet the last decade has seen the emergence of new forms of partnership, wherein many of the values and principles of previous ages still operate and motivate decisions. The tensions inherent in the legislation have had to be resolved through management at school level. Ball argues (1993, p. 64) that 'the reforms and the forms of control they embody can be represented by three clusters: the curriculum, the market and management. In particular the market and management are tied closely together in the reworking of orientation and purpose in schools. Management plays a key role in delivering other changes.'

In this volume we examine the way that managers have taken on their role in delivering the changes, and what options are open to them in using devolved powers in a system driven by a belief in the virtue of the market, and a desire for demonstrable efficiency in the use of public money. As the Conservative government reaches the end of its third successive term of office, there are some signs of a renewal of consensus, strongly motivated by a concern for overall standards, fuelled possibly by the increased amount of information available about the performance of schools. In the *Improving Schools* initiative launched in 1995, the DFEE has reverted to a position, which it perhaps never really abandoned, of working for the collective interests of schools. At the same time the Labour Party's crusade to raise standards is based on the belief that managers should set targets, and on the expectation that different stakeholder groups will act in partnership with each other.

Opportunities for parental choice

As we have seen the offer of 'choice' to consumers of education carried with it the implication that there should be different 'offers' to choose between. The 1944 Act and subsequent progress towards a system of comprehensive schools encouraged and required by successive Labour governments had produced by the end of the 1970s a variety of maintained schools, the majority of which were comprehensive, mixed and non-denominational. There was some local choice between the county schools, mainly mixed and comprehensive, and the schools which admitted pupils in accordance with a specified religious denomination (usually voluntary schools), by sex or, less commonly, on the basis of their academic or other abilities. Moves towards broadening the diversity of provision commenced in 1979 when the government repealed the 1976 Act which had imposed on LEAs the duty to make plans to implement the comprehensive principle. These moves were continued in the Education Act of 1980 through provision of state funding for some pupils to attend independent schools, with the introduction of the Assisted Places scheme. In addition, the 1980 Act affirmed the right of parents to choose the schools their children were to attend, and gave them the right to appeal against LEA allocation of places. Parental rights were recognised, too, in the 1981 Act, which linked the LEAs' responsibilities for the education of pupils with special needs to their parents' rights to be consulted.

The 1988 Education Reform Act and further legislation in the Education Act of 1993 promoted the idea of GM schools in order to add a new dimension to the ability of parents to exercise choice within the publicly provided sector of education. GM schools are existing institutions which have balloted parents on the question of 'opting-out' of local authority control and where a majority of parents have voted in favour of such a change. They have largely preserved their existing character in terms of admission policies and are bound, as state schools, to teach the national curriculum. By 1996 there were just over 1,100 GM schools in England and Wales (just under 5 per cent of the total number of state schools).

City Technology Colleges (CTCs) were set up to offer parents another type of choice. Such colleges were proposed in 1986, and the 1988 Act further formalised their status. For parents of pupils in urban areas, these colleges provide an education which has a specific emphasis on science and technology (or, in one case, the performing arts). They are legally independent of LEA control, partly funded by private sector, and must provide education for different ability groups although they can select those pupils who are deemed to have the right 'attitude' to benefit from the special provision. Only 15 such colleges have been established.

In a further attempt to increase the range of provision in 1993 the government launched a scheme for 'specialist' or sponsored schools, which are state maintained schools with some of the characteristics of CTCs. The scheme is open to schools that can raise sponsorship of £100,000 to support education in languages or technology. If the school's proposal is accepted the government matches this with £100,000 of capital funding, and extra annual funding of £100 per pupil. By summer 1996 151 schools had been designated specialist Technology Colleges and 30 had been designated Language Colleges.

There is also the option for any school to introduce a level of selection into its admissions procedures. Schools are informed that 'the introduction of a limited amount of selection in a secondary school involving the selection of about 10 per cent (and this figure was increased to 15 per cent in 1996) of pupils on the basis of ability or aptitude in one or more of music, art, drama and sport will not in general lead to a significant change in the character of the schools as a whole' (DFE, 1993, paragraph 47). A white paper (DFEE, 1996c) proposes that all GM schools should be able to select up to 50 per cent of their pupils without the need to publish statutory proposals, and that LEA schools should be able to select up to 20 per cent of their pupils by ability or aptitude without central approval. There is clearly scope for the range of different types and varieties of secondary provision to increase without further primary legislation.

At the end of the twentieth century, then, pupils of compulsory school age in England and Wales may be educated in county schools, voluntary schools, grant-maintained schools, City Technology Colleges, Pupil Referral Units, in-dependent schools, hospitals or at home. For parents the key distinctions are in terms of first, the cost, if any, of a school place and secondly, the admissions policies, and how they are applied, for instance through interview, e ntrance examination or the application of other criteria. Increasingly it is the popu-larity of a school that enables it to select pupils, and this is becoming equally as important as the stated character of the school. A popular school will become a better resourced school as allocation of funds is to a large extent directly related to age-weighted pupil numbers. Popular schools in crowded areas are able to recruit selectively on the basis of their perception of the commitment of parents to the education of their children. These factors combine to create differences between schools which, though not related to any statutory distinc-tion, are a direct result of legislation based on a market philosophy.

Some of the most substantial changes to the education system in recent years have been in pre-5 and post-16 education, where an adherence to the notion of the market-place has had an even greater effect on development than in the compulsory sector. Sixth form and further education colleges have been se-vered from LEA control and are funded by new funding councils. There is still a great variety of provision post-16, and a variety of qualifications. Output-related funding, the consideration of learning credits (Sharron and Williams, 1996) and the variety of routes to qualifications, have brought this sector firmly into a competitive market environment.

A voucher scheme for nursery education, piloted in 1996, is designed to promote choice for parents, diversity of provision and high standards. Nursery vouchers are exchangeable for three terms of nursery provision from a vali-dated provider. All providers must endorse a set of learning outcomes, agree to be inspected and publish information for parents. Should the scheme be con-tinued parents will be able to make their choices for children, even at this young age, on the basis of an institution's performance on nationally agreed learning outcomes (DFEE, 1996b).

KEY DIMENSIONS OF FREEDOM AND CONSTRAINT FOR SELF-MANAGING SCHOOLS

For school managers the key distinctions between types of school subsume those of concern to parents, but have other dimensions which specifically relate to their freedom to plan, to implement and resource plans, to prove their accountability and to determine their client group and the type of curriculum they offer. Figure 1.1.1 sets out some of the controls and constraints on these dimensions of freedom under the headings of:

- governance;
- curriculum;
- staffing;
- admissions;
- public information;
- finance.

The governing body

The notion of governors as the 'board of directors' of the business known as a school was taken as a model for school management in the early 1980s. The board includes representatives of shareholders (community), consumers (parents) and providers (LEA and teachers). From that time the LEA representatives were no longer viewed as the best representatives of community interest, and Sir Keith Joseph as Secretary of State for Education heralded moves to re-establish governing bodies as a force for good in the life of individual schools and the communities that they served and to give them independence from the LEA. Nevertheless the types of school can be differentiated by the nature and representativeness of the governing body; some contain members who have been elected or nominated on the basis of a democratic responsibility to others in the community. One of the key criticisms of grant-maintained schools has been that they no longer have a democratically elected governing body, but a majority of 'first' or 'foundation' governors who are selected by the governing body itself. Similar arrangements are made for the replacement of governors of CTCs. Although governing bodies of all schools have many similar powers and responsibilities, it seems that in some kinds of schools they are explicitly expected to put their school's success first, and to see survival in the market-place as their principal concern.

The 1993 Act makes provision for all governing bodies of maintained schools to become incorporated bodies in law, thus providing some legal protection for individual members from the extreme consequences of personal liability, and detaching the governing body further from the LEA (Morris, Reid and Fowler, 1993) and, incidentally, reducing the difference between a grant-maintained and county or voluntary school.

Curriculum and testing

Under the 1988 Reform Act each governing body of a maintained school, with the LEA if appropriate, has the duty to ensure that curriculum satisfies legal

Type	Governance	Curriculum	Staffing	Admissions	Public information	Finance
LEA maintained and voluntary controlled	May be elected, nominated, co-opted, ex-officio.	National curriculum and governor approved school curriculum.	Governors appoint and dismiss, LEA is employer, salaries determined by Secretary of State.	LEA decides admissions limit and arrangements, decisions subject to appeal, schools may select up to 10% of intake by ability or aptitude.	Examination results at 16 and 18 made public in performance tables, indicators must be published in prospectuses and annual reports.	School formula share of LEA Potential Schools Budget, together with any income from other sources. Capital works from DFEE grant funded projects, applied for by LEA.
LEA voluntary aided	May be elected, nominated, co-opted, appointed, ex-officio.	National curriculum and governor approved school curriculum.	Governors are the employer, salaries determined by Secretary of State.	Governors decide admissions arrangements, decisions subject to appeal, schools may select up to 10% of intake by ability or aptitude.	Examination results at 16 and 18 made public in performance tables, indicators must be published in prospectuses and annual reports.	School formula share of LEA Potential Schools Budget, together with any income from other sources. Capital works from own foundation and applications to DFEE for special projects.
GM	May be elected (the minority), selected (first/foundation), represent sponsors, ex-officio.	National curriculum and governor approved school curriculum.	Governors are the employer, salaries determined by Secretary of State but may apply for exemption.	Proposal for GM status must include admissions policy, character of school may later be changed, may select an agreed percentage by aptitude or ability.	Examination results at 16 and 18 made public in performance tables, indicators must be published in prospectuses and annual reports.	Day-to-day costs from Annual Maintenance Grant (AMG). Formula allocation for some capital grant. May bid for Special Purposes Grant and further capital grant.
CTC	May be nominated, or co-opted (including parents).	Specialist emphasis in school curriculum.	Governors are the employer, salaries determined by governors.	Interview to assess suitability and commitment.	Examination results at 16 and 18 made public in performance tables, indicators must be published in prospectuses and annual reports.	Own or lease premises, DFEE pays running costs. Industrial sponsorship.
Independent	Nominated, according to foundation of school.	May choose school curriculum.	Governors are the employer, salaries determined by school.	Fee-paying, often selected by entrance examination.	Examination results at 16 and 18 made public in performance tables.	Own premises and pay own running costs, may take pupils on government funded assisted places scheme.

Figure 1.1.1 Dimensions of control and constraint

requirements, that it complies with the national curriculum. Lawton (1992) reflects that the introduction of the national curriculum could have been a means of achieving a new consensus, building on the activity of Her Majesty's Inspectors (HMI) in publicising an 'entitlement' curriculum based on areas of experience rather than a list of subjects. Instead, critics argue, the national curriculum is devised so that knowledge itself is 'carefully regulated and determined by central government and is largely based on a late nineteenth century curriculum with distinct cultural barriers between academic, practical and technical learning' (Tomlinson, 1994, p. 4). Despite the fact that the introduction of a nationally regulated curriculum was one of the most heatedly debated aspects of reform (Havilland, 1988; Chitty and Simon, 1993) concern in recent years has centred more on the extent of the curriculum and teacher and pupil overload than on the principle of central direction. Although neither independent schools nor CTCs are required to follow the national curriculum, in practice their curricula are strongly influenced by it and by the attainment targets and programmes of study associated with it.

Although the revised national curriculum orders introduced in 1995 have allayed some concern about the curriculum, there is still debate about the purpose of national key stage testing and assessment, from which pupils in the independent sector are exempt. Black (1994) warns of the complex interactions that ensue from combining formative and summative functions of assessment into the same system.

Staffing

One of the anomalies for county and voluntary controlled schools is that the governors are responsible for determining the number of teaching and non-teaching staff, for their development, their appraisal and for any disciplinary action, yet the schools are not the employer. The governors can select who they wish to employ, nevertheless the LEA has formal responsibility for appointing and dismissing staff. The situation is clearer for GM schools, voluntary aided schools and CTCs, which have full powers of employment. However the influence of the School Teachers' Pay and Conditions Act of 1991 is felt in all these schools. This Act established the School Teachers' Review Body to examine and report annually to the Prime Minister on the remuneration of teachers. The 1991 Act makes provision for GM schools to apply for exemption from a pay and conditions order laid down by the Secretary of State, but in practice few take up this option.

The governing body has the power and duty to decide about the award of above scale payments, and may relate pay to performance. Hargreaves (1994) believes that this power should be used to reward excellent teachers. In practice some schools, whether county or GM, have found it possible to use their powers creatively, as in this description of the arrangements for the senior management team of one county secondary school:

I have paid them 1 point more than the highest allowance, in order for them to forego these conditions [of service]. I have been told it is illegal but as yet no one has used the law to force me to change it. The unions have objected but they are powerless to do anything about it.

(Bleischer, 1995, p. 41)

Although this represents an explicit use of teachers' pay regulations to reinforce a certain style of management, it also illustrates clearly the opportunities afforded within the present system for some form of performance related remuneration.

Admissions

Choice between schools is governed to a considerable extent by the admission criteria that come into operation when demand for places exceeds the number available. The DFE (1993) recognises that popular schools will have to find ways of limiting their admissions, and the law requires that LEAs (for county schools) and governing bodies (for aided and grant-maintained schools) must make public each year clear arrangements and policies for admissions. In each case there is provision for parents to appeal, if their child is refused a place at a particular school. In the case of grant-maintained and aided schools it is the governing body that must set up the arrangements for appeal.

Not all changes in admission arrangements are seen as causing a significant change in the character of a school, and there has been strong encouragement (Squire, 1995) for schools to use the flexibility to select by aptitude in particular subjects. Both LEA maintained and GM schools are able to use some form of selection when oversubscribed through refusing to admit pupils with problems who have been excluded from neighbouring schools. Conversely schools with falling rolls will tend to take in an increasing proportion of less motivated and less able youngsters, may have an unstable school population with large turnover, and spend more time on short term coping strategies. Such a situation can lead to low expectations and deteriorating examination results. Ball, Bowe and Gerwitz (1994) reported that none of the secondary schools in their study of three adjacent LEAs could afford to ignore the market-place, and that awareness that there is a degree of volatility and fashion in parental choice gives rise to a sense of anxiety, particularly in a system of year-on-year funding linked to student numbers.

Publication of performance measures

The updated Parent's Charter (DFE, 1994) informs parents that there are five key documents which give them information to keep track of their child's progress, to find out how the school is being run and to compare all local schools. These are:

- a report about the child;

- regular reports from independent inspectors;
- performance tables for all local schools;
- a prospectus or brochure about individual schools;
- an annual report from the school's governors.

All schools are required to provide information about examination results at GCSE and A level for secondary school performance tables, and these tables include results for independent schools. Schools are also judged by the reports of Ofsted, which are made public. Performance tables for primary schools based on results of pupils at the age of 11 were opposed by headteachers, but were introduced in 1996.

Regulations govern what schools must include in their prospectus and annual report to parents. Schools are encouraged to set out their aims and values and their approach to teaching. They market themselves through their prospectuses, and 'good' Ofsted reports are freely quoted, indeed even edited extracts from less good reports can play their part in enhancing the reputation of a school.

Concern about the public and comparative nature of information has centred on 'contextualisation' and the risk that like is not being compared with like. Both main political parties are committed to investigating and implementing the use of 'value-added' measures to compare school performance (Labour Party, 1995; DFE, 1995). All schools are expected to use quantified data about performance to set targets for improvement (DFEE, 1996a).

Finance

The government controls local authority expenditure through block grant, setting standard spending assessments (SSAs) for each area. Each LEA allocates a share of its education budget to schools through the potential schools budget (PSB), and under a Local Management of Schools scheme the governing bodies have powers to spend on:

- teaching and non-teaching staff, supply cover, incentive allowances, recruitment, dismissal;
- books, materials, cleaning, grounds maintenance, caretaking, meals;
- advisory support, technical and financial support, internal audit;
- buildings repairs and maintenance, rent and rates, energy and water, insurance.

The governing body has to report annually to parents about the expenditure of the delegated budget and other monies, and the power to manage a delegated budget can only be removed if the budget is not used for the purposes of the school in a satisfactory manner, or if a school is considered to be in need of 'special measures' as the result of an Ofsted inspection. In a white paper (DFEE, 1996c) the government proposed to raise to 95 per cent that percentage of the PSB that must be allocated by LEAs to schools, suggesting that this would be equivalent to a further £200 per pupil to be managed directly by schools.

The annual maintenance grant to a GM school is linked in level to that of other local schools through a formula. In addition GM schools receive finance to cover those services which would have been provided centrally by an LEA and make bids for grants for capital projects The financial management of GM schools is monitored by the FAS, which arranges for value-for-money studies to be undertaken.

Without exception all schools have felt the effects of funding constraints in the past decade, although Levacic (1995, p. 141) judges that 'Whether schools actually experienced cuts in real funding per pupil depended on which LEA they were maintained by and which sector they were in.' Hargreaves (1994, p. 19) advocates funding by national formula 'to replace the present highly diverse and inequitable patterns of per capita spending according to local whim'. Geographical and sector differences are more significant than the differences between LEA and GM schools, and as Local Schools Information (1994, p. 18) point out in commenting on the potential advantages of opting out 'there is actually very little extra money now especially when all the new costs are taken into account.' The exploration of a Common Funding Formula, which would operate across the country and even out local differences of funding for education, continues, but is beset by technical difficulties, and would if introduced require a transitional period to phase in new budget allocations.

IMPLICATIONS OF THE CHANGES FOR MANAGEMENT

Critics of the reforms have two major concerns; the first relates to the effect on the education system as a whole of the introduction of decentralisation and competition. Education has some of the characteristics of a 'public good', and these features are tacitly acknowledged in the system of free compulsory education that was introduced in the 1944 Act. In expanding consumer choice and influence at the expense of providers, and in relying on individual self-interest as the 'hidden hand' to improve quality and rational use of resources (Jonathan, 1990), the government has deliberately eroded the authority of that element of the system which provides the 'engine of social democratic order – local government' (Ranson 1994, p. 72). Put at its simplest what is of concern to society collectively, as distinct from the individual parent, is the quality of provision for all – what happens to pupils in the ineffective school on the road to closure? As Jonathan wrote, somewhat prophetically,

> When market conditions are introduced throughout the state system, the private schooling dilemma of affluent parents in publicly under-resourced areas becomes universalised to all parents. The immediate losers, this time, are of course those who are lacking in cultural rather than economic capital, but the long-term losers may arguably include us all.

(1990, p. 126)

and the former Chief Inspector for Schools questioned overall effectiveness of the market philosophy: 'It is surely a triumph of hope over experience to expect that such self-interested, isolated, fragmented decisions, made in thousands of separate institutions, will add up to a sensible, effective and efficient national schools system' (Bolton, 1993, p. 8).

Maden (1996) refers to Sir Peter Newsam's findings that in London in 1995 more than three-quarters of children in the top 25 per cent of the ability range are in half the schools, including the selective independent schools. He found that the 'other half' comprises schools where very few, if any, pupils are of high ability, and where examination success reported in league tables will be low. Maden asserts that good quality education for all children is denied when ghettoes are allowed to flourish.

The second major concern about the reforms is the nature of management freedoms and is articulated by critics such as Ball (1993, 1994) and Watkins (1993). As Le Metais (1995, p. 9) records, 'the detailed statutory definition of the school's principal objectives (in terms of the national curriculum and its assessment) and the constraints of the budget reduce much "decision making" to operational rather than policy levels'. Thus teachers' professionalism is reduced and the freedom to manage is reduced to a bureaucratic managerialism preoccupied with inputs and outputs. Macpherson (1996, p. 140) reports that international case studies of restructures of educational systems have shown that 'decentralisation of pedagogical, administrative and governance powers to locally managed schools, with simultaneous recentralisation of key curricular, assessment and budgetary (i.e. control) functions has led to a consensus of cynicism amongst professionals and a sense of low policy legitimacy among other stakeholders'. This type of concern resonates with the apparent powerlessness and sense of disillusion felt by many in the profession in England and Wales, and has to be taken account of by those who endeavour to give renewed value to teachers' professional judgements within a predominately customer-oriented system.

What choices do schools have in their response to these concerns? Many professionals have taken on aspects of the reforms described in this chapter with energy and optimism, albeit tempered by some of the reservations of the previous paragraphs. Downes (1988, p. 162), an early practitioner of local financial management, set out his hopes for the new system in these words: 'it offers us a freedom and flexibility in the state system which we have never had before and which we desperately need. In the long run I sincerely believe it offers us a better future.' He links this to the needs of the child: 'let us hope that we shall be able to offer him or her an education which is more efficient, more effective, more tailored to his or her needs . . . and no less humane.'

Ranson (1994) recognises what the reforms have achieved, as well as setting out his vision of what might be done in the future. He argues (p. 105) for 'a new moral and political order that responds to the needs of a society undergoing a historic transition'. Any programme of reforms needs to build on what the 1988 Act has set up, to strengthen the authority and quality of schools and colleges, but to encourage them to see themselves as more than inward-looking islands of learning. A deeper version of partnership would recognise the power of parents as much in the 'voice' they have about the running of the educational system, as about 'choice' through entry or exit to the services of a single institution (Hirschman, 1970). The National Commission on Education's accounts (1996) of successful schools in disadvantaged areas, and research (Macbeath *et al.*, 1996) into collaborative school self-evaluation provide illustrations of how this might come about, as well as showing how the skills and professionalism of teachers can be valued within school-based management.

Ranson is an advocate for the continuing role of the LEA in this process, and argues that its strategic role should be complemented by a framework of community councils and institutional governing bodies with delegated decision making powers. In this way there could be some responsiveness to changing circumstances and efficiency in use of resources, and a conscious attempt to provide for the needs of the whole community. Newsam (1996) poses the question starkly. Rather than asking 'what is best for our school?', he suggests we should ask 'what can our schools do, *in association with others*, to ensure that the quality of education in our country's schools is as good as that in France, Germany, Japan?' (emphasis added). Management with this underlying purpose will need to build on the knowledge that schools make a difference to achievement; to enhance the professionalism of teachers; and begin to reinterpret partnership.

REFERENCES

Ball, S. J. (1993) Self-Management and Entrepreneurial Schooling in England and Wales in J. Smyth (ed) *A Socially Critical View of the Self-Managing School,* Falmer, London.

Ball, S. J. (1994) *Education Reform: a critical and post-structural approach,* Open University Press, Buckingham.

Ball, S. J., Bowe, R. and Gerwitz, S., (1994) Market Forces and Parental Choice in S. Tomlinson (ed) *Educational Reform and its Consequences,* IPPR, Rivers Oram, London.

Black, P. (1994) Alternative Education Policies: Assessment and Testing in S. Tomlinson (ed) *Educational Reform and its Consequences,* IPPR, Rivers Oram, London.

Bleischer, N. (1995) Bigger is Best, *Managing Schools Today,* Vol. 5, no. 3, pp. 40–3

Bogdanor, V. (1979) Power and Participation, *Oxford Review of Education,* Vol. 5, no. 2, pp. 157–68.

Bolton, E. (1993) Imaginary Gardens with Real Toads in C. Chitty and B. Simon (eds) *Education Answers Back: Critical Responses to Government Policy,* Lawrence and Wishart, London.

Chitty, C.(1992) *The Education System Transformed,* Baseline Books, Manchester.

Chitty, C. and Simon, B. (1993) *Education Answers Back: Critical Responses to Government Policy,* Lawrence & Wishart, London.

Coopers and Lybrand (1988) *Local Management of Schools,* HMSO, London.

Davies, H. (1992) *Fighting Leviathan: Building Social Markets that Work*, Social Market Foundation, London.

DES (1977) *Education in Schools* (Green Paper), HMSO, London.

DES (1988) *The Local Management of Schools: Circular 7/88*, DES, London.

DES (1991) *The Parents' Charter: You and Your Child's Education*, DES, London.

DFE (1993) *Admissions to Maintained Schools: Circular 6/93*, DFE, London.

DFE (1994) *Our Children's Education: The Updated Parent's Charter*, DFE, London.

DFE (1995) *Value Added in Education*, DFE, London.

DFEE (1996a) *Setting Targets to Raise Standards: A Survey of Good Practice*, DFEE, London.

DFEE (1996b) *Nursery education scheme: the next steps*, DFEE, London.

DFEE (1996c) *Self Government for Schools*, HMSO, London.

Downes, P. (1988) *Local Financial Management in Schools*, Blackwell, Oxford.

Hargreaves, D. (1994) *The Mosaic of Learning: Schools and Teachers for the Next Century*, Demos, London.

Havilland, J. (1988) *Take Care, Mr Baker!*, Fourth Estate, London.

Hirschman, A. O. (1970) *Exit, Voice and Loyalty: responses to decline in firms, organizations and states*, Harvard University Press, Cambridge, MA.

Jonathan, R. (1990) State Education Service or Prisoner's Dilemma: the 'Hidden Hand' as Source of Education Policy, *British Journal of Educational Studies*, Vol. 38, no. 2, pp. 116–32.

Labour Party (1995) *Excellence for Everyone*, Labour Party, London.

Lawton, D., (1992) *Education and Politics in the 1990s*, Falmer, London.

Le Metais, J. (1995) *Legislating for Change: School Reforms in England and Wales 1979–1994*, NFER, Slough.

Levacic, R (1995) *Local Management of Schools: Analysis and Practice*, Open University Press, Buckingham.

Local Schools Information (1994) *Guide to the Issue of Opting Out*, LSI, London.

Macbeath, J., Boyd B., Rand J. and Bell, S (1996) *Schools Speak for Themselves*, NUT, London.

Macpherson, R. J. S. (1996) Accountability: Towards Reconstructing a 'Politically Incorrect' Policy Issue, *Education Management and Administration*, Vol. 24, no. 2, pp. 139–50.

Maden, M. (1996) *Divided cities: dwellers in different zones, inhabitants of different planets*, Times Educational Supplement/Greenwich Lecture 9 May.

Morris, R. (1992) Week By Week, *Education*, Vol. 80, no. 20, p. 383.

Morris R., Reid, E. and Fowler J. (1993) *Education Act 1993: A critical guide*, Association of Metropolitan Authorities, London.

National Commission on Education (1996) *Success Against the Odds*, Routledge, London.

Newsam, P. (1996) What now for inner London? *Times Educational Supplement*, 22 March.

Ranson, S. (1994) *Towards the Learning Society*, Cassell, London.

Sharron, H. and Williams, C. (1996) Sixteen-plus learning vouchers back on agenda, *Managing Schools Today*, Vol. 5, no. 6, pp. 6–7.

Squire, R. (1995) *Address to the Secondary Heads Association*, 18 October, DFEE Press Office, London.

Tomlinson, S. (1994) Educational Reforms – Ideologies and Visions in S. Tomlinson (ed) *Educational Reform and its Consequences*, IPPR, Rivers Oram, London.

Watkins, P. (1993) Pushing Crisis and Stress down the line: the self managing school, in J. Smyth (ed) *A Socially Critical View of the Self-Managing School*, Falmer, London.

1.2

Autonomy and Accountability

TIM SIMKINS

WHAT KIND OF AUTONOMY?

The educational reforms of recent years have generated a plethora of terms in relation to the idea of school autonomy. In addition to the term autonomy itself, we have had 'self-managing schools', 'school- or site-based management', 'local financial management', 'local management of schools', delegation, devolution, decentralisation and restructuring. Some terms have been preferred at particular times in the history of reform; and some have been preferred in some countries rather than others. Are they all different ways of describing essentially the same concept, or are there important differences between them?

All the terms imply the *redistribution of power* within a school system in ways which enhance the importance of the individual school *vis-à-vis* the wider school systems, national and local, and undoubtedly such redistribution has been part of the reform experience in England and Wales and elsewhere over the past ten years. Indeed, it has been the central value underpinning the establishment of locally managed and grant-maintained schools within the state school system. However, in many ways the concept of organisational autonomy in school management is an unhelpful one. First, it suggests a degree of freedom which few if any organisations in the modern world can achieve. Secondly, certainly in England and Wales, it overemphasises one aspect of what, as Chapter 1.1 demonstrates, has been a multifaceted reform process aspects of which have had very different concerns. And thirdly, it reifies the school as an organisation over and above the individuals and groups both inside and outside who have a stake in, and influence over, the purposes and processes of schooling.

We need, therefore, to consider school autonomy in a wider context and to ask deeper questions about it. The most important of these are:

- *who* is empowered and who is disempowered by the reforms?
- *in respect to what* are their powers increased or decreased?

- under what forms of *control and constraint* must these powers be exercised?

This chapter will attempt to provide a framework for addressing these questions.

POWER IN THE SCHOOL SYSTEM

A useful way of exploring this issue is to distinguish between 'criteria power' and 'operational power' (Winstanley *et al.*, 1995). Criteria power refers to the ability of organisational stakeholders to define the aims and purposes of the service, design the overall system within which it is provided, set or influence the performance criteria which providers must satisfy, and evaluate their performance in relation to these criteria. Operational power, in contrast, refers to the ability of stakeholders to provide the service itself or to decide how it is provided, and to change the way in which it is delivered, through the allocation of limited resources or by using relevant knowledge and skills. In other words, criteria power is concerned with determining purposes and frameworks relating to the 'what' and 'why' of service provision, while operational power is concerned with the 'how' of service delivery.

Using this framework, we can identify a number of ways in which the nature and distribution of power in education has changed over recent years:

- *central government*, previously limited in power in relation to major aspects of educational policy and practice, has considerably increased its criteria power, so that it is now the key actor in relation to both the determination of policy objectives nationally and the establishment of operational frameworks through which these policies are carried out;
- *LEAs* have perhaps been the main losers, finding themselves squeezed between an increasingly powerful central government drawing criteria power to itself and developments in relation to local management and grant-maintained status which have transferred operational power to the level of the school or removed schools from the LEA's orbit entirely;
- *teachers* have lost criteria power, as the influence of the teacher unions on national policy has been all but removed while, at school level, the National Curriculum and testing have limited teachers' freedom in the classroom and LM and GM, through enhancing the power of governing bodies and head-teachers, has rendered the role of 'ordinary' teachers in the development of school policy more problematic;
- *parents* have seen their operational power increased both through the ability, which is unevenly distributed geographically and socially, to exercise choice about the school which their child attends and through representation on school governing bodies;
- *pupils* remain largely disempowered within the system, depending on the willingness of other parties – such as parents when choosing schools or governors, heads and teachers when determining school policy – to recognise, and take account of, their interests.

This analysis emphasises two important points about the reforms. The first, already referred to in Chapter 1.1, is something of a paradox, namely their simultaneous decentralising and centralising tendencies. Thus, while a number of parties may have had their *operational* power increased – particularly governors and heads – criteria power has been drawn much more firmly into the centre. In other words, school autonomy is exercised within a much firmer framework of central control. Thus central government defines the aims and purposes of the service through the national curriculum and testing; it increasingly specifies the parameters of good practice through the process of school inspection; it determines the broad basis on which schools will be funded through the approval of funding formulae; and it sets performance parameters for the system through the publication of performance indicators and inspection reports. Viewed in this context, increased school autonomy, while significant, is severely constrained. The prime areas of freedom lie partly on the edges of the 'what' – determining aspects of the character of the school and of policy beyond those established centrally – but primarily with the 'how' of school management: the organisation of the school, its pupils and its curriculum, the teaching and learning process, the deployment of resources in the pursuit of its objectives and the ways in which it manages its relations with the outside world.

Secondly, the reforms have significantly changed the formal pattern of power at the level of the school itself, with teachers seeing their power reduced while school governors, senior managers (especially heads) and parents have all had their power increased significantly. How these shifts in power actually work out in practice, however, depends very much on local circumstances and in particular on the ability and willingness of the various parties to make effective use of the potential they now have to influence policy and practice at the level of the school. The outcomes of such processes will have a major influence on how school self-management works in practice.

CHANGING PATTERNS OF ACCOUNTABILITY

The world of power relationships in which schools now operate is extremely complicated. For every area of increased power, there seems to be a corresponding area in which additional external controls and constraints have been imposed. A key issue here for schools, as for other public sector organisations, is that of accountability.

Accountability is a complex issue and it can take many forms (Kogan, 1986). In its pure form accountability of party A to party B requires three things: first, an expectation that A will act in ways which are consistent with the legitimate requirements of B; secondly, that A will render some form of account to B for their performance; and thirdly, that B may exercise sanctions over A if A fails to conform to B's expectations. This might be termed the 'hard' form of accountability. In many areas, however, while there may be a clear understanding that party B has a legitimate right to influence the behaviour of A, this is not accompanied by any means of ensuring compliance or punishing non-compliance. This might be called 'soft' accountability and its effectiveness will depend on the degree to which party B is able to use the influence strategies available to it to convince party A that compliance will be worthwhile.

It can be argued that the dominating Government concern which underlay the reforms was a concern that pre-existing accountability mechanisms within the school system were too soft, and consequently that new control mechanisms had to be established.

The challenge to professional control

Traditionally in education, primary responsibility for determining the core activities of the service has been seen as the domain of the professionals. The *professional* model of accountability is based on the assumption that quality in the educational system is best ensured by granting autonomy to teachers, advisers and others who have been trained in, and have access to, relevant bodies of professional knowledge and whose professional ethic leads them to act always in the interest of their 'client' – the pupil or student. The yardstick of quality under this model is good practice which is defined by the profession and moderated by processes of peer review, such as professional networks of information and exchange, LEA inspection and advisory teams and HMI. At the level of the school it is embodied in concepts of 'collegial' governance through which responsibility for policy and its implementation rests with the teaching staff acting together in the interests of the pupils.

As Chapter 1.1 suggested, it can be argued that this approach to accountability dominated educational practice at least to the end of the 1970s, and it has been the increasingly emphatic challenge to it which has characterised the policy debate of the last twenty years (Ranson, 1994). Indeed, within policy circles there is now a widespread view that professional accountability is so soft that it is tantamount to an absence of any real accountability at all, or, in a less extreme view, that professional accountability alone is insufficient to ensure that the educational provision responds adequately to the complex demands of a modern economy and society. Such suspicion of professional autonomy is not, of course, confined to education: it can be found in the health and social services and elsewhere, although it is perhaps in education that the dominant role of the professional has come under greatest challenge, not least in the view of many because of the inability of the unions to take a concerted lead on professional matters and the absence of a national body such as a General Teaching Council. Pressures have grown, therefore, to find other accountability mechanisms which can reduce professional power and increase the influence of other stakeholders in the educational system. The education reforms emphasised three of these: government regulation, community empowerment through governing bodies, and the marketisation of the school system through increased parental choice and the encouragement of increased competition between schools.

State control: the role of central government

Education – at least in the public sector – is clearly a legitimate concern of the political process and hence of representative bodies established to express the public interest. In this country, since the 1944 Education Act, formal political responsibility for education has been shared between central government, the local education authorities and school governing bodies, although in practice the latter had little power until the 1980s. Of course, the authority of each level of representative government derives from a rather different definition of political legitimacy, and there have always been areas of ambiguity, overlap and tension between their powers and aspirations, not least when different political groups have been in control at the different levels. Nevertheless, prior to the 1980s, the relationship between their respective powers and responsibilities remained fairly stable. The Education Acts of the 1980s, however, together with other legislation such as that on compulsory competitive tendering, have shifted the balance decisively away from the local authorities. Powers of governance now lie primarily with the other two legal 'partners', namely central government and governing bodies.

First, a multitude of powers now lie directly with central government. It was common prior to the recent legislation to argue that the Secretary of State's powers were primarily indirect and negative: he or she could steer change through some powers of resource control and the ability to refuse permission for particular developments. He or she had very few positive powers, however, and had little involvement in particular in curriculum matters. The position was changing to some extent prior to the 1988 Act with the increasing use of direct funding to encourage developments such as Technical and Vocational Education Initiative, but the major sea change came with the 1988 Act. For the first time the broad pattern of educational provision was to be managed within a framework established centrally.

Central government now exercises its powers in four main ways:

- it is using legislation and regulation to determine much more broadly than in the past the *content* of education through national curriculum and testing;
- it has used legislation to influence profoundly the *organisation of the system* and the position of individual schools within it: it determines the types of schools that there shall be, the terms on which each shall be funded, and the ways in which they shall be governed and held to account;
- it has used legislation and regulation to redistribute *rights and responsibilities* within the system, determining the powers of school governing bodies, of parents and of key quangoes in the schools sector, such as Ofsted and the Funding Agency for (grant-maintained) Schools;
- it has sought to influence the discourse about *school purposes and performance* through the publication of information about the performance of individual schools and through the process of inspection with its associated sanctions for schools deemed to be 'failing'.

Viewed from this perspective, one of the areas of choice facing the individual school is the response to the regulatory framework within which it must operate. What position will be taken on the character and governance of the school, given the range of opportunities provided for in legislation? To what degree and in what ways will it develop its curriculum provision in ways which respond to the values, priorities and needs of those whom it serves, given the framework provided by the National Curriculum and testing requirements? And how will it establish and present its own unique character both internally and to the world outside, given the standardised frameworks provided by the process of inspection and by the legal requirements to present certain kinds of information in particular ways? These are fundamental questions: the ways in which the school tackles them will go a long way in providing the basis upon which other choices can be built.

The school in the community: empowered governing bodies

Of equal significance to the increase in the powers of central government have been the changes in the constitution of school governing bodies and their real empowerment through the implementation of LMS and GMS. The empowerment of governing bodies has been an evolutionary process, dating back at least to the 1970s and one in which a number of LEAs played a major part. However, the reforms of the late 1980s saw a radical move forward. The granting to governing bodies of responsibility for personnel matters, for the management of block budgets running to millions of pounds in many cases, and for the management of premises has redefined the local government of education profoundly. Power has been transferred towards the specific stakeholder groups represented on governing bodies and away from the wider local community as represented by the local education authority.

Governing bodies can conceive their roles in a number of ways. Writing before the reforms, Kogan *et al.* (1984) suggested four such roles:

- the *supportive* governing body which looks beyond the school to generate political and other support for the school's activities;
- the *mediating* governing body which promotes a consensus between the various local stakeholder interests, hearing and testing different viewpoints in an attempt to ensure that the school system is operating smoothly;
- the *advisory* governing body which provides a sounding board for professionals within the school and provides advice where required;
- the *accountable* governing body which expects the professionals to render an account to it and makes judgements about the performance of the school in relation to policies and expectations established nationally and locally.

None of the governing bodies in Kogan *et al.*'s study played an accountable role. 'They were not seen in this way by appointing authorities, by schools, or indeed by the majority of their own membership, and lacked the authority, resources and, for the most part, inclination for such a role' (Kogan *et al.*,

1984, p. 164). The clear expectation now, of course, is that this should be the primary role played by all governing bodies, and they have been provided with the powers and authority to play it. However, the granting of *de jure* powers and responsibilities does not, in itself, guarantee that these will be fully exercised *de facto*. Indeed, the evidence suggests that despite the expectations placed upon them by the Government and others, it is still relatively unusual for governing bodies to exercise the accountable role in its full sense. The majority are continuing to play one or more of the other roles, whose potential value of course does not decrease as a result of the higher profile given to the accountability role.

In reality, therefore, even in relation to the accountable role, the way in which a governing body conceives and plays its role is a matter of considerable choice. How far, for example, should governors initiate policy and how far should they act as validators of policies that are designed primarily by the head and the staff of the school? The factors which will influence the role which a governing body actually plays include the types of individuals who are elected and co-opted to it, their expectations about what they should do and how they should behave, and the kinds of pressures which the governors face from inside and outside the school.

Schools in the market: parents as customers

Unlike the models of accountability considered so far, the market model is not concerned with the rearrangement of roles and power *within* the school system. Rather it is concerned to establish a competitive environment within which schools are compelled to respond to the wishes of their 'customers' through the operation of market forces. According to this model, accountability relationships can be established directly with those who use public services without the need for other groups, such as the government, community representatives or professionals, to interpret their needs for them. The purest expression of this model in education occurs in those areas, such as the private schools sector, where services are supplied at full cost to those who are able or willing to pay. Such an approach to accountability requires a number of conditions for it to work effectively, namely:

- a number of *supplier organisations* with the capacity to meet customer requirements on a competitive basis;
- individuals, who can act as *customers* in the market for services;
- an *information system,* which informs potential customers about the nature and quality of the services on offer;
- a *resource-based link* between customers and suppliers so that changing patterns of demand result in changes in the flow of resources to suppliers.

Where these conditions exist, it is argued, there is no need for any socially or institutionally agreed measure of educational quality to be established because quality is equated with customer satisfaction and those schools which attract pupils and hence prosper in the market will be self-evidently of high quality.

As Chapter 1.1 describes, the educational reforms contain elements which reflect all of these requirements. First, there has been an attempt to establish a diversity of institutional provision through the establishment of Grant Maintained Schools and City Technology Colleges as well as locally managed LEA schools and through the relaxing of regulations relating to schools' ability to change their character, in particular, to take some of their pupils on the basis of selection. Second, schools have been placed firmly in the market-place by linking resources to enrolment through the operation of formula budgeting and by increasing parental choice through the implementation of open enrolment. Third, requirements have been established that certain kinds of information, such as details of schools' policies and provision, their examination and test results and their inspection reports, are published in order, it is argued, to facilitate processes of choice.

However, despite these developments, the market, like that in other areas of public provision, remains a 'quasi-market' (Le Grand and Bartlett, 1993) with two highly significant characteristics. First, the market operates under a high degree of regulation. As has already been seen, the Secretary of State delimits (for the state sector of education at least) what products shall be available in the market (through the national curriculum and through curriculum policies in post-16 education), who shall be allowed to enter the market and on what terms (through the power to approve or disapprove local reorganisation proposals and applications for grant-maintained status), what 'prices' shall be charged (through placing constraints on funding formulae), and what information shall be made available to customers. The consequences of powers such as these are considerable: relatively minor changes can have considerable effect on the terms on which institutions compete so that some are advantaged – intentionally or unintentionally – in relation to others.

Secondly, the nature of market varies from area to area: different 'local competitive arenas' (Woods, *et al.*, 1996) vary enormously in the nature and degree of competition which are placed upon schools within them. For some schools – for example, some primary schools in rural areas – parental choice and competition may have little meaning. For others – for example, some comprehensive schools in urban areas – they may literally be a matter of life and death. Schools in different market circumstances, therefore, will face different degrees of market pressure and constraint and this will affect their attitude to the management of their external relationships, and particularly their conception of 'marketing'. Some, no doubt will find the market pressures so strong that their freedom of movement is severely limited. For others, though, their response to the 'market-place' will be a major indicator of the choices which they make about the kind of school they wish to be (Bagley, *et al.*, 1996). For example, are they seeking to develop and project a distinctive character, and if so what and how? How big do they wish to be? And what kind of pupil intake do they wish to have?

Two important points need to be made concerning such choices. First, the degree of choice a school has in these areas depends on the nature of its local arena and the school's position within it; and secondly, each has implications for other schools within the arena. Choices in these areas, therefore, cannot be made without also taking a view about the kind of relationships which are to be developed with other schools. In particular how far should the school accept market pressures and attempt to achieve competitive success within its local arena; and how far should attempts be made to reduce the pressures of competition by seeking collaborative strategies with other schools in the area? In some areas and at some times there may be little choice about such matters; at others real choices will exist which raise fundamental questions about the school's values.

METAPHORS FOR CHANGE

It can be seen, therefore, that the professional model of accountability has been challenged from three directions: increased central government control, increased community participation through governing bodies, and increased marketisation of the school system through enhanced parental choice. Taken together they have established quite new frameworks of discourse about education policy (Ball, 1990). Beyond this, however, each of these major changes in patterns of accountability provides important choices at the level of the school: choices about the kind of organisation it should be and the relations that it should have with its key stakeholders. These choices can perhaps be best expressed, as Glatter (1991) argues, through a number of images of the school which underlie different aspects of the reform.

First, the school might be viewed as a *local outlet* for a range of curricular products largely specified by the distant central office of the Department for Education and Employment. Viewed in this way the prime purpose of the school is to deliver a product – the national curriculum – in ways which meet local needs and expectations while maintaining the essential integrity of the product. Secondly, it might be viewed as a *participatory community*. From this perspective, the empowerment of governing bodies is seen as a means through which stakeholders drawn both from within the school and, more important, from the wider local community can enable the school to develop in ways which reflect and respond to local priorities and concerns. Finally, the school may be viewed as a *separate business* operating in a competitive market whose purpose is to provide products and services which individual consumers, i.e. parents, value and to market these in ways which will ensure that parents choose this school over others for their children.

Each of these images is, in fact, a metaphor which illuminates particular aspects of the complex world which schools now inhabit and emphasises some power relationships over others. Each embodies an important truth and important policy values in relation to the place of the individual school within the broader system. Such metaphors are extremely powerful in informing and guiding our thinking as Morgan (1986, p. 12) argues: 'Our theories and explanations of organizational life are based on metaphors that lead us to see and understand organizations in distinctive yet partial ways. . . . For the use of metaphor implies *a way of thinking* and *a way of seeing* that pervade how we understand our world generally.' Thus metaphors may either constrain our thinking – if we are imprisoned in one image of the organisation to the exclusion of others – or they can liberate us.

> By using different metaphors to understand the complex and paradoxical character of organizational life, we are able to manage and design organizations in ways that we may not have thought possible before. . . . While some of the metaphors tap familiar ways of thinking, others develop insights and perspectives that will be rather new.
>
> (Morgan, 1986, p. 13)

For those responsible for governing and managing schools, therefore, an understanding of such metaphors and their implications increases the power to choose the kinds of school that they wish to create. In particular, it helps to sharpen up thinking about desirable roles and relationships. For example, are governors local guardians of nationally determined expectations of schooling, representatives of the wider community which they serve, or are they a board of directors whose prime concern is to ensure the success of the institution in the market-place? Are parents loyal clients dependent on the professional expertise of teachers to do the best for their children, customers who can best influence schools by shopping around and exercising the option of 'exit' if they are dissatisfied, or partners or citizens who are expected, and expect, to influence the school through the exercise of informal or formal 'voice' (Hirschman, 1970)? And are senior staff leading professionals aspiring to develop a shared educational enterprise through building collegial relationships with colleagues or executives managing the human resources of the institution towards organisational goals established at the top of the institution or outside it? These are profound questions. The ways in which schools resolve them will help to determine the character of the education system for years to come.

BALANCING THE PRESSURES: THE INTERNAL ARENA OF THE SCHOOL

So far we have outlined three modes of accountability: central government control, community participation and market pressures. As Table 1.2.1 shows, each mode empowers different key actors, embodies different mechanisms of influence, and embodies different success criteria. The problems which such diverse and competing pressures place on public sector 'human service organisations', are well described by Kouzes and Mico (1979). Schools and similar organisations are potentially in a state of continuous tension between the various legitimate demands which are placed upon them, and their management involves a balancing act which is often far more complex than private sector organisations typically encounter. This complexity is increased when we add two further internal 'domains' to which Kouzes and Mico draw attention:

Table 1.2.1   Five modes of accountability

Accountability Mode	Key Actors	Influence Mechanisms	Success Criteria	Examples from Reforms
Government Control	Central government	Legislation and regulation; inspection	Policy conformance	National curriculum and testing
Community Participation	Community representatives	Governance	Satisfaction of interests	Residual powers of LEAs, empowerment of governing bodies
Market Pressure	Consumers	Choice	Competitive success	Parental choice
Managerial Control	Managers	Hierarchy	Organisational effectiveness and efficiency	Appraisal; performance related pay
Professional	Professionals	Peer Review	Good practice; meeting individual client needs	None

those of the professionals and of the managers. These are the groups whose actions will determine how decisions taken within the school will balance – or not – the competing external pressures; but in doing so they will bring their own values and expectations to the decision-making process. For this reason they, too, have been included in Table 1.2.1.

We have already referred to the external challenges to the professional domain within schools. We now need to note an additional challenge: the increased emphasis given to *managerial control* in the school system. Those who argue for an increase in the power of 'management' in educational organisations contend that this is necessary in order to subordinate professional autonomy and judgement to broader 'corporate' purposes. This cannot be achieved by the 'collegial' methods of shared responsibility favoured by professionals – such methods are often more rhetoric than reality anyway. It is necessary to establish clear organisational goals, agree means for achieving them, monitor progress, and then support the whole process by a suitable system of incentives. Only in this way can it be ensured that the organisation is effective in the accomplishment of its goals and efficient in its use of resources.

The development of such systems may be accomplished in a variety of ways. The 'hard' approach is to set up clearly defined, hierarchical structures of managerial accountability, design performance indicators to enable success or failure to be clearly identified, and to use staff appraisal and performance-related pay to reward those who perform well. Softer approaches are less concerned with such techniques: their emphasis is on the establishment of a strong achievement-oriented culture within which all members of the organisation are encouraged to accept responsibility for ensuring quality of performance. These more sympathetic approaches, too, however, essentially subordinate the role of the professional *qua* professional to that of the manager who must take the lead in defining the organisation's mission and shaping the beliefs and behaviour of organisational members to the desired culture. Hierarchy remains, albeit in a less stark form.

The rise of the manager in education, as elsewhere in the public sector, is often linked to the rise of 'managerialism' – a set of beliefs about how organisations should be run (Pollitt, 1993; Newman and Clarke, 1994). These beliefs include the following:

- that the prime purpose of all organisational activity is to maximise the effectiveness and efficiency of the organisation as a whole;
- that it is the task of 'management' to ensure that this occurs;
- 'management' is a separate and distinct organisational function, with its own knowledge base which should be carried out by those with clearly defined managerial roles and authority;
- that the techniques for achieving better management are knowable: indeed they are known and generally applicable – they can often be found in best practice in the private sector;
- that to enable these techniques to be applied effectively managers must be given the 'freedom to manage': this implies delegation of power within managerial hierarchies and may also imply the disempowerment of other groups such as political representatives and workers, including professional workers.

Many aspects of the recent changes suggest an increasing trend towards managerialism within the school system. For example, an increasing emphasis is being given to managerial roles in schools: the crucial importance placed on the headteacher is clearly central here, but a broader indicator is the priority given by the Teacher Training Agency to the continuing professional development of those holding formal managerial responsibilities within schools – heads of department and subject leaders and 'aspiring headteachers' for example. More explicitly 'managerial' processes and techniques are also receiving greater emphasis. Examples include the development of mission statements, school development plans, and marketing strategies, an emphasis on the achievement of clearly defined short-term targets and the use of quantified performance indicators to monitor these, and the introduction of particular managerial approaches drawn from industry such as Total Quality Management and Investors in People. At the level of individuals, staff appraisal, more flexible salary structures and performance-related pay for senior staff also provide considerable opportunities for the extension of 'managerialist' approaches.

There is undoubtedly a tension between the 'corporatist' and 'individualist' approaches to thinking about school purposes which the managerial and professional perspectives respectively imply.

In the corporatist conception, effectiveness is an aggregative concept relating to the achievement of broad objectives demonstrated through such indicators as aggregated measures of examination success expressed in league tables and in parental choice of school. In the individualist conception, effectiveness lies in the degree to which the complex needs of each child are identified and met and his or her learning maximised. In the days before the reforms it was possible – indeed common – for school managers to share with teachers the individualist conception of effectiveness; as the implementation of the reforms unfolds this is becoming more difficult.

(Simkins, 1994, p. 27)

Difficult, but not impossible. A key issue for schools in the future will be the degree to which they wish to adopt more 'managerialist' approaches to their management. The pressures are considerable. Headteachers now have far wider responsibilities than was the case ten years ago, and the range of powers now exercised at the level of the school give a quite new meaning to the tension between the roles of 'leading professional' and 'chief executive' to which Meredydd Hughes first drew attention (Hughes, 1985). Approaches which sufficed when many managerial responsibilities were exercised by the LEA will not do now. On the other hand, the advance of fully-fledged managerialism is not inevitable. Ways can still be found of balancing professional values with the demands of effective and efficient management. Traditional models of professional accountability can be protected, for example, through ideas such as self-evaluation and collaborative planning; but changing circumstances mean that such approaches are now not enough. There is a need constantly to balance attention to the 'core business' of the school – its pupils and the curriculum – with attention to more corporate concerns relating to the demands of external stakeholders and the survival of the school in its particular 'market-place'.

Underlying all of these issues are fundamental questions about the determination of guiding values in the school system. Value tensions can occur in all kinds of ways. For example, a teacher may feel that compliance with certain curriculum requirements deriving from the central government regulation would be inconsistent with his judgement of what is best for his pupils; a headteacher may feel that she has to take decisions as a 'manager' in the interests of 'efficiency' which are not consistent with her professional duty to her colleagues or pupils; in a governing body conflict may arise because a chair of governors feels that the headteacher is usurping the governors' legitimate policy-making role; or decisions by head or governors about individual pupils with particular difficulties or needs may be coloured by their potential impact on the school's image in the 'market-place'.

These tensions are never fully resolved because they embody competing concepts of legitimacy within any area of public service. They are worked out in practice through legislative frameworks which place duties and constraints on the organisations and individuals involved, through organisational structures which create frameworks for interaction, and through management processes which the parties concerned use to negotiate their roles in any particular context. One of the major potential results of the reforms, as Ball (1993) has suggested, is the 'privatisation of educational values': the relegation to the level of the school of many of those value choices which formerly were determined through democratic political processes at a wider level. For example, it is now the school which will determine the 'market segments' it will seek to serve, how far it will devote additional resources to pupils with particular educational needs, and whether its appointment procedures will embody more than the minimal legal requirements in relation to equal opportunities. The extension of the market, therefore, does not remove the essentially political nature of many managerial decisions in education; it merely relocates them. The openly 'Political' arena of Council and Education Committee is replaced by no less 'political' arenas of the governing body meeting, the senior management team and the staff meeting.

Viewed from this perspective, the 'meta-values' which will underpin the management of the service is a central issue for the future of reform. These key value questions will be explored in the next chapter.

REFERENCES

Bagley, C., Woods, P. and Glatter, R. (1996) 'Barriers to school responsiveness in the education quasi-market', *School Organisation,* Vol. 16, no. 1, pp. 45–58.

Ball, S. (1990) *Politics and Policy Making in Education: explorations in policy sociology,* Routledge, London

Ball, S. (1993) 'The Education Reform Act: market forces and parental choice', in A. Cashdan and J. Harris (eds) *Education in the 1990s,* Sheffield Hallam University PAVIC Publications, Sheffield.

Glatter, R. (1991) 'Boundary management and the new order', *Management in Education,* Vol. 5, no. 4, pp. 27–9.

Hirschman, A. O. (1970) *Exit, Voice and Loyalty: Responses to Decline in Firms, Organizations and States,* Harvard University Press, Boston.

Hughes, M. G. (1985) 'Leadership in professionally staffed organisations', in M. Hughes, P. Ribbins, and H. Thomas (eds) *Managing Education: the System and the Institution,* Holt Education, London.

Kogan, M. (1986) *Education Accountability: an Analytic Overview,* Hutchinson, London.

Kogan, M., Johnson, D., Packwood, T. and Whitaker, T. (1984) *School Governing Bodies,* Heinemann, London.

Kouzes, J. and Mico, P. (1979) 'Domain theory: an introduction to organizational behaviour in human service organizations,' *Journal of Applied Behavioral Science,* Vol. 15, no. 4, pp. 449–69.

Le Grand, J. and Bartlett, W. (eds.) (1993) *Quasi-markets and Social Policy,* Macmillan, London.

Morgan, G. (1986) *Images of Organization,* Sage, London.

Newman, J. and Clarke, J. (1994) 'Going about our business? the managerialization of the public services,' in J. Clarke, A. Cochrane and E. McLaughlin (eds) *Managing Social Policy,* Sage, London.

Pollitt, C. (1993) *Managerialism and the Public Services,* (2nd edn), Blackwell, Oxford.

Ranson, S. (1994) *Towards the Learning Society,* Cassell, London.

Simkins, T. (1994) 'Efficiency, effectiveness and the local management of schools', *Journal of Education Policy,* Vol, 9, no. 1, pp. 15–33.

Winstanley, D., Sorabji, D. and Dawson, S. (1995) 'When the pieces don't fit: a stakeholder power matrix to analyse public sector restructuring', *Public Money and Management*, Vol. 15, no. 2, pp. 19–26.

Woods, P. A., Bagley, C. and Glatter, R. G. (1996) 'Dynamics of competition: the effects of local competitive arenas on schools', in C. Pole and R. Chawla-Duggan, *Reshaping Education in the 1990s: perspectives on secondary schooling*, Falmer Press, London.

1.3

Addressing the Tensions: Culture and Values

BRIAN FIDLER

The culture of an organisation represents an enormously stabilising force for the organisation. It encompasses fundamental assumptions about meaning and purpose and accepted ways of working by organisation members. Thus it has to be taken into account in any thinking about future changes. Choices which are made within the culture will be much easier to accomplish than those which involve changes to an organisation's culture or accepted way of doing things.

This chapter will show the importance of the concept of culture as a unifying force within organisations. It will discuss a number of attempts to capture this elusive concept and explore its relationship to values and management. Finally, it will illustrate the importance of culture in the management of planned change. Leaders need to understand the culture of their organisation before they can adequately manage both the organisation and its culture.

EMERGENCE OF ORGANISATIONAL CULTURE

Until fairly recently school culture was not a widely discussed topic in school management. The Rutter *et al.* (1979) study on school effectiveness referred to the ethos of the school but this was mainly concerned with the way in which pupils experienced the school. In the USA in the 1960s investigations in elementary schools using an organisational climate description questionnaire were carried out but subsequent interest has been intermittent (Owens, 1995).

Unfortunately the terms climate and culture have sometimes been used interchangeably. However, here, in common with recent usage, the terms will be distinguished. Culture represents the distinctive way in which organisation members go about their work and relate to each other in a particular organisation. Climate will be reserved for the reaction of organisation members to their organisation's culture. Climate can be either positive or negative depending upon whether staff are favourably or unfavourably disposed towards the prevailing culture. Thus climate is related to organisational morale. In shorthand culture can be regarded as the organisational equivalent of personality of an individual and climate as the equivalent of job satisfaction of an individual.

Although culture had appeared periodically in the organisational literature, it was Peters and Waterman's (1982) study of successful commercial organisations in the USA which was the major populariser of the concept. This study purported to show that there was a certain way of operating which was likely to lead to long term success. They identified eight features of successful companies in terms of the way in which they carried out their work. However, almost as soon as they were identified a number of these 'excellent' companies began to falter and soon a majority were seen either to be experiencing severe problems or had ceased to be leaders in their field (Pascale, 1991).

Whilst the notion that there was one successful way of operating was seen to be overly simplistic, the importance of the 'taken for granted' assumptions about how an organisation operates was clearly an area worthy of further study. Many commercial organisations have engaged in cultural change programmes (Watson 1994) and a whole literature on cultural change has appeared.

ORGANISATIONAL CULTURE

Culture is seen in the characteristic way in which organisation members go about their work and relate to each other. It encompasses the assumptions which influence thought and behaviour. However, culture is not only descriptive, it is also normative. Whilst it can be used by external observers to describe how an organisation operates, to members of the organisation it represents the accepted way of operating (Willmott, 1993). In this sense it embodies the norms and values of the organisation. It represents what is regarded as 'right' in the organisation.

The simplest description of the concept is that derived by Deal and Kennedy (1988) based on work by Bower (1966) and embodied in the phrase 'the way we do things around here'. This carries with it assumptions about the existence of a characteristic way of doing things within an organisation.

An aspect of culture highlighted by Schein (1992) is that culture embodies assumptions which organisation members share. An important point to note is that these assumptions are rarely made explicit and hence are not questioned. Instead, the way an organisation conducts its business is regarded as natural. Indeed organisation members who have spent a long time in an organisation may be unable to imagine alternative ways of doing things.

Culture can give meaning and purpose to the work of individuals in an organisation. It identifies those aspects of the work of an organisation which are highly valued and those which are disapproved of. Thus an internal 'code' is set up to guide the work of individuals.

There is a trade-off between having an accurate description of a complex phenomenon and having something that is easy to grasp. The attempts to capture and elucidate the idea of culture described below show a range from simple to complex. Each may have value depending on the purpose for which the concept is being used. Each illustrates and highlights some features of the concept whilst together they provide insights into the richness and subtlety of the concept.

APPROACHES TO ORGANISATIONAL CULTURE

Culture is a sophisticated and hard to capture concept. There are a number of ways in which it has been analysed and conceptualised. Each takes a particular aspect as its focal point. These should be seen as alternatives which can be selected depending on the use to which the concept is to be put. The first three accounts presented here are of organisations in general and the final three are specific to schools.

1   General approaches

1A   *Schein's cultural mechanisms*
Edgar Schein (1992) has drawn attention to the deep seated nature of cultural assumptions. He proposes three levels of visibility of culture ranging from norms of behaviour as the most superficial level to basic underlying assumptions about the most fundamental features of human nature at the deepest level. The formulation shown in Figure 1.3.1 based on Hoy and Miskel (1991) illustrates the three levels,

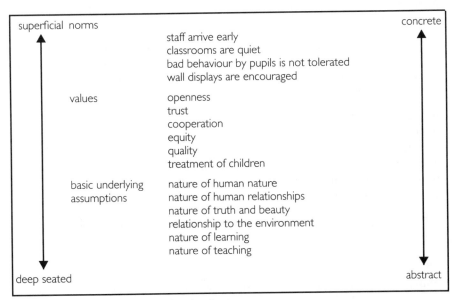

Figure 1.3.1   Schein's three levels of culture

The deepest and most abstract level is that of basic underlying assumptions or beliefs. These are rarely if ever discussed and are thus implicit. However, they are of the most fundamental importance in terms of viewing the world and decision making. Some questions are simply ruled out by one's view of the world. The intermediate level is that of values. These identify what is regarded as important by organisation members. Any explanation of decision making in terms of the principles employed are likely to be in terms of values like these. The final, and most superficial, level is that of norms of behaviour. Often these will not be explicitly stated and newcomers to the organisation will have to make inferences from what existing staff say and do.

Schein has identified mechanisms by which culture can be reinforced or changed. For an organisation with an existing culture there are two sources of change: (1) shared learning experiences of staff as they deal with new situations; and (2) new beliefs and values brought in by new staff and leaders. He identifies primary and secondary transmission mechanisms. He also proposes differences in how these operate depending on how long the organisation has been in existence. They are much more malleable in a recently formed organisation.

Schein (1992, p. 231)) identifies the following primary embedding mechanisms:

- what leaders pay attention to, measure and control on a regular basis;
- how leaders react to critical incidents and organizational crises;
- observed criteria by which leaders allocate scarce resources;
- deliberate role modelling, teaching and coaching;
- observed criteria by which leaders allocate rewards and status;
- observed criteria by which leaders recruit, select, promote, retire and excommunicate organizational members.

Schein (1992) also lists what he terms secondary mechanisms. These do not create the culture but are means to reinforce it. They work only if they are consistent with the primary mechanisms. The secondary articulation and reinforcement mechanisms are:

- organizational design and structure;
- organizational systems and procedures;
- organization rites and rituals;
- design of physical space, facades and buildings;
- stories, legends and myths about people and events;
- formal statements of organizational philosophy, values and creed.

Schein pays particular attention to mechanisms to create a suitable culture in a completely new organisation.

1B Johnson & Scholes' cultural web
Johnson and Scholes (1993) identify a number of contributions to organisational culture which serve to reinforce and sustain it:

routines
rituals
stories
symbols
control systems
power structures
organisational structure

These factors reinforce each other to provide a recipe for solving problems in the organisation or a cultural paradigm. In addition to dealing with routines the recipe provides the ingredients for dealing with new situations. Since the recipe has been found to be successful in the past, it is applied to problems and new situations as they arise.

Some of these factors are within the direct control of the management of an organisation and hence are capable of change as a direct influence on culture. Thus structures, systems and routines can be changed by executive action. Symbols and rituals can be replaced and a positive attempt made to begin new stories which circulate about heroes and heroines.

The value of these factors is that they demonstrate the multifaceted nature of culture and the ways in which it may be influenced but their limitation is that they may give the impression that culture is rather more manipulable in the short term than many believe to be the case.

1C Handy's four 'Gods of Management'

Charles Handy (1985) uses Greek Gods to symbolise four different organisational cultures. He believes that 'the management of organisations is not a precise science but more of a creative and political process, owing much to the prevailing culture and tradition in that place at that time' (p. 9). Thus, to be effective management needs to recognise the dominant culture in an organisation in order to diagnose what actions would be likely to be successful. Each cultural model makes assumptions about 'power and influence, about what motivates people, how they think and learn, how things can be changed' (p. 11). Handy recognises the need for cultural diversity both between and within organisations. He considers that any choice of a culture is contingent on (a) a fit between the predisposition of individuals and the culture, and (b) a fit between the work of an organisation (or part of it) and the culture. This latter fit has two elements – the nature of the particular work and the context within which the organisation sits.

The four cultures are:

club (Zeus)
role (Apollo)
task (Athena)
person or existential (Dionysus)

The symbol of a club culture is of a spider's web. The manager is at the centre of the web and influence decreases as individuals are further from this centre of all action. Little is written down and one powerful individual either makes decisions or others try to second guess decisions which would have been made at the centre. Individuals are valued and trusted if they 'fit' and have the confidence of the leader. The organisation is an extension of the leader with all his or her egocentricities. Its merits are particularly its speed and consistency of decision making.

In contrast to the leader centred club culture, the role culture works by defining functions, jobs and their relationship to each other. The organisation operates by formal rules and rationality. This culture is well suited to predictable and stable external conditions.

The task culture is based upon dealing with problems and achieving results. Groups work in teams created on a short-term basis rather than permanent committees. This culture is good at dealing with one-off problems but is less good at repetitive work.

The person or existential culture is different from the preceding three in that whilst in each of them the individual works for the organisational purpose, in the existential culture the individual and their ends and that of the organisation are one and the same thing. This works best when individuals can work relatively independently and individuals possess particular expertise.

Handy suggests analysing the work to be done in an organisation in three types: maintenance, development, and personal and situational problem solving. He suggests that the choice of an appropriate culture depends on the balance of work to be performed in that part of the organisation and thus there may be a range of cultures in different parts of the same organisation. In any case these are idealised types rather than descriptions of practice and real organisations will have elements of one or more of these cultures in the same section of the organisation.

2 Approaches to culture in schools

2A *Some key dimensions of school culture*

The following six dimensions are the results of a search for the minimum number of independent dimensions to capture the essential assumptions which are the major influences on the life of a school. Schein's (1992) analysis suggests that culture has to deal with the environment in which the organisation finds itself and with the internal mode of working of the organisation. Thus the following factors are proposed with three positions on a continuum for each dimension:

External orientation
a) *attitude to innovation (prospector, defender, reactor)*

Schools' attitudes to innovation range from those schools which positively seek new ideas from outside to those which resist any innovation. In the middle are schools which are selective in their acceptance of new ideas, holding on to some existing and cherished ideas.

b) *aims of school (academic, balanced, social)*
   Some schools have children's academic success as their principal aim, whilst other schools gain their distinction from success at a range of other activities. Schools in the middle seek a balance of academic and non-academic activities.

c) *attitude to parent (customer, partner, mentee)*
   In some schools parents are treated as customers and the schools seek to keep them satisfied. In others, parents are treated as partners in the educational process and are fully involved within and outside the school. In yet others, teachers see themselves as experts with parents in a dependent role.

Internal orientation

d) *leadership style (autocratic, consultative, participative)*
   The leadership styles of headteachers in terms of the influence of others on decisions can vary from the autocratic, through the consultative to the truly participative where corporate decisions are made.

e) *working together (collaborative, cooperative, independent)*
   The way in which staff work together varies from the collaborative where there is substantial mutual influence, through the cooperative where staff plan together, to the independent, where teachers work largely alone.

f) *relationship with children (friendly, business-like, repressive)*
   The way in which children are treated in a school can vary from a friendly, individualised approach, through the business-like where a service is provided in a standardised way, to a regime where education is provided, despite the pupils, in a repressive way.

The scales are intended to be linear and continuous between the three positions which have been described. The value of this formulation is to indicate some key dimensions by which to compare schools and identify differences. Even with only three positions on each scale there are 3^6 or 729 possibilities for the position of an individual school.

2B   Torrington and Weightman's model

Torrington and Weightman (1989), as a result of a study of 24 secondary schools in England in the mid-1980s, proposed a model to demonstrate the tensions of organisation and management. The two dimensions of culture chosen are the degree of individual autonomy for staff (autonomy – tight control) and the degree of shared priorities (consensus – conflict). Three cultures are found to be successful providing they are not located too close to the mid-point of both scales. These are prescription (control over conflict), leadership (consent to control) and collegiality (voluntary agreement). The fourth quadrant which represents individual autonomy in a school with groups and individuals having different priorities is described as anarchy. One of the contributions of this model is to demonstrate more than one successful culture, although it should be recognised that only certain aspects of culture are considered in the model.

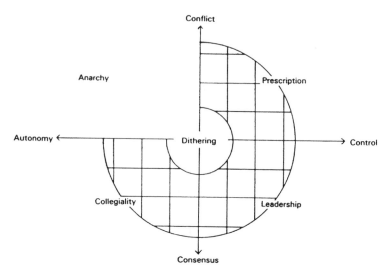

Figure 1.3.2   Torrington and Weightman's model of culture

2C   Hargreaves' school model

As part of a programme which was intended to identify the preconditions for change in schools Hargreaves and colleagues (Hargreaves 1995; Ainscow *et al.*, 1994) drew up a model of school culture which connected staff and pupil experiences of culture. In this case the components represent staff attitudes towards children. In the terms defined here, this is a model of the interaction between ethos and culture.

A square grid has four corners each of which contains a point high on one dimension and low on the other. The two dimensions are instrumental/social control – the degree to which there is a concern for results – and expressive/social cohesion – the degree to which there is a concern for social relationships. The four corners represent:

> *custodial* (high instrumental: low expressive)
> *hothouse* (high instrumental: high expressive)
> *welfarist* (high expressive: low instrumental)
> *survivalist* (low expressive: low instrumental)

Intermediate positions between these extremes allow a gradation of instrumentality and expressivity.

The value of this typology is its simplicity, its diagrammatic representation and the fact that it deals with staff–pupil interaction.

SOME EMERGING ISSUES

From the previous elaborations of culture some general points for discussion emerge.

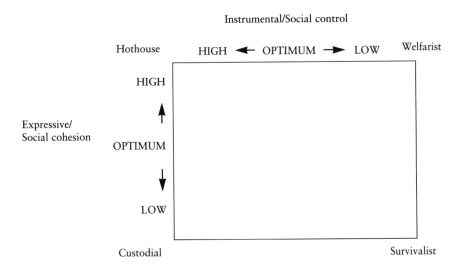

Figure 1.3.3 Hargreaves' model of school culture

Reification

To talk of the culture of an organisation is to imbue it with a reality which is illusory. Organisations are made up of individuals each of whom has their own understanding of how they should act and their own set of values. Whilst this is true, it is argued in this chapter that the abstraction of culture is a helpful one. Reification tends to obscure the question of whose values are incorporated in the culture. In this respect the leader is likely to be very influential. Deal and Kennedy (1988) argue that a culture should be promulgated which will make the organisation successful so that although the leader may have value preferences these should be subordinate to judgements about what values are likely to lead to long term success of the organisation. Values, however, are not handed down. They are shared because culture is experienced, acquired and transmitted by organisation members learning together and sharing common experiences. There is, to a large extent, a common understanding of how to act in the organisation and a shared understanding of its purpose.

Managed or influenced?

In the literature on culture there are debates about whether culture can be managed in a predictable way or whether it can only be influenced. The multi-faceted and deep seated nature of the underlying assumptions of culture suggest that it is not easily changed (Wilkins and Patterson, 1985; Schein, 1992).

There may be a situation of crisis when organisation members are more recep-
tive to a need for change but in the main it appears that culture is very difficult
to change. There is evidence that where attempts to change culture which do
not command confidence are attempted then organisation members adopt an
unofficial culture which is resistant to the proposed change (Watson, 1994).
Whilst outward signs may change, the inner beliefs of actors may be much
more resistant. It may be that culture acts rather like the stability provided by a
scientific theory. Despite experimental refutations scientists still continue to
think in terms of a discredited theory until a better theory comes along.
Similarly only another new and convincing cultural paradigm can begin to
replace an existing paradigm rather than attempts to eliminate the old. This
may help explain the failure of many cultural change programmes which were
instituted after the Peters and Waterman research had appeared to provide a
route to organisational success.

Pupils or staff?

Schools like hospitals and prisons are unusual in having a large number of
people within them who are not employees. Thus there may be one culture for
patients, inmates or pupils and another for staff. The two cultures must interact in some way but they are unlikely to be the same. Conventionally, in school
the culture for pupils is called the school ethos whilst the term culture has been
reserved for the shared assumptions of staff.

How a school ethos is changed is an interesting question. The headteacher
and staff may attempt to create a new ethos. If this does not take into account
the nature of the pupils and the prevailing ethos then it is unlikely to be
willingly adopted by pupils. In such a case there may be one ethos which is
espoused by the school (in its public and official expectations) but a different
ethos-in-use by pupils or at least by influential sub-groups of pupils. This
illustrates a fundamental constraint. Ethos and culture cannot be selected *ab
initio* as if out of a catalogue; they have to be appropriate for the context. Any
choice has to be contingent on analysis of the present and a realistic vision of a
possible future (see Chapter 2.2 on strategy).

The nature of the relationship between ethos and staff culture is an interesting one. The principles and values shared by staff about the education of pupils
can be expected to be determining factors in the espoused ethos of the school.
The staff culture and the pupil ethos will interpenetrate since the staff culture
has to embrace external success and internal working practices which involve
pupils. The performance and behaviour of pupils will figure large in both ethos
and culture.

One culture or many?

Those who speak of a strong culture have in mind a shared, consistent culture
with some clear signals about what the organisation stands for. It is clear that

large organisations, and those composed of staff affected differentially by external pressures, can be expected to show some differences in culture within an organisation. Professionals are known to have a loyalty to their profession and also to their organisation. Professional socialisation during training may lead to differences such as the values of teachers in primary schools differing from those in secondary schools. So there are likely to be cultural differences between schools in one phase of education compared to another. In addition teachers are likely to be qualified in a particular academic discipline which has distinctive values and so it is to be expected that schools will show differences in culture in different sections.

Peters and Waterman's (1982) assumption was that there is one successful culture which should be shared by all organisation members. The phrase a 'strong culture' has this implication. However, it has been recognised that some variation in culture within an organisation is an advantage when contemplating change (Stacey, 1995). A strong culture has dangers particularly in 'groupthink' (Pascale, 1991). Some differences of value within a largely shared culture has distinct advantages.

Control or autonomy?

A strong organisational culture has been suggested as a more subtle form of control mechanism for organisation members than traditional pseudo-bureaucratic forms of structure. If there are largely shared assumptions then there is less need for explicit control since organisation members are operating as their managers would anyway. The morality of this can be questioned particularly where a strong culture is imposed by management and where there is an attempt to control under a guise of liberation (Willmott, 1993).

CULTURE, PURPOSE AND VALUES

Organisational purpose and organisational culture are intimately related. The significance of purpose and the values which support it need to be embedded in the culture. In this way organisation members come to understand what the organisation is trying to achieve, to be supported in their work by the values which are espoused by the organisation and to be convinced of the worth of organisational ends. Some organisations are more successful at this than others as Deal (1990) points out: 'Some McDonald's franchises show more enthusiasm for hamburger buns than educators demonstrate in working with young people' (p. vii)

How is this to be brought about? A key ingredient is leadership. It is the task of the leader to articulate a vision of a successful organisation and to make this seem worthwhile. There are choices to be made about the process of deciding on organisational purpose and the involvement of organisation members.

Although the above is the case in all organisations it is clear that the leaders of educational institutions are in a different position from, for example, managers of factories. Such managers will have a responsibility to the staff of the organisation and would have a general moral duty not to produce products which are harmful. However, the leader of a school has to make moral and value choices about the process of managing, about the process of education and about the ends of the process of education. Writers have drawn attention to the particular position of schools as training grounds for the education of children in morals and values. This raises the issue of whether practices within schools are intended to be models to emulate or whether what the young should practice is different from what staff of the institution practice. Is it do as I do or do as I say? It has been said that schools should be moral organisations and that one of the tasks of a school leader is to give moral leadership (Sergiovanni, 1991).

Some have suggested that the management of a school should emulate the principles of a democratic society for which the young are being prepared (Bottery, 1992). Thus staff should be involved in decision making. In this case involvement in decision making would not be to improve the quality of the decision, or for any of the rational technical reasons which might be adduced for involvement, but as a matter of principle.

Others have pointed to the moral trust placed in those in leadership positions to articulate a vision and inspire others to follow (Sergiovanni, 1991). The relationship between the principal and staff is an unequal one and therefore is a moral relationship. It is the duty of the leader to lead and to influence the organisational culture to support the mission of the organisation.

Although some functions of schools are prescribed, for example, to teach the National Curriculum, there is a substantial measure of freedom for schools to identify other purposes and to prioritise amongst them. The intended outcomes of schooling represent value choices. The constraints on these choices will be examined a little later.

A particular case where such considerations are particularly apposite is the case of a new school. Since there are rather few completely new schools created at the present time it is easy to overlook the importance of creating a school culture rather than merely allowing one to develop in a *laissez-faire* manner. When assumptions are not present about how things are done, misunderstandings and conflicts can easily arise and things can quickly become chaotic. There are similar but different problems which arise when two schools merge. Generally they have different traditions and decisions have to be made about whether one school is in effect taking over the other and hence where the prevailing assumptions arise or whether a genuine merger is taking place and a new culture, different to either predecessor is to be created. In this case the symbolic aspects of culture and its reinforcement may be particularly strong. Actions may be analysed for their cultural significance and this identified whether it was intended to be present or not.

MANAGING WITH PRINCIPLES AND VALUES

The purpose of this short section is to raise some fundamental issues concerning moral principles and value positions. The aims of doing this are to place such considerations on the agenda for education managers, for such issues have not generally been explicit in the past, and to warn that not only are there no easy solutions, but also that finding means of making progress in this area is difficult.

In their educative theory of leadership Duignan and Macpherson (1992), add a realm of ideas or 'valuing' to the more conventional functions of management from the business world. Thoughts about the moral and value education of the young come from this realm of ideas. The morality and values of management are also concerns of this realm of ideas.

Sergiovanni (1991) believes that a key to understanding the moral dimension of leadership is an appreciation of the difference between normative rationality (rationality based on what we believe to be right and good) and technical rationality (rationality based on what is effective and efficient). He claims that the former has been neglected because prominence has been given to the latter. Increasingly management and decision making have been treated as technical issues rather than being intimately connected with values.

Words like efficient, economy and effective have come to greater prominence. These appear to have a value neutrality. However, efficiency and economy are values themselves. Both are economic values which, in the abstract, few would wish to oppose. In their operation, on the other hand, their application can pose dilemmas when they conflict with other values.

The term effective management hides the moral and value dimension of the process. A dilemma is created where effective actions (in terms of outcomes) are not wholly moral. Good (effective) management may not be good (moral) management and good (moral) management may not be good (effective) management. The tension is likely to be most apparent where moral actions have led to a less than effective result and less moral actions would have been likely to lead to an effective result.

Beck and Murphy (1994) after examining the treatment of ethics in courses of preparation for educational administrators in the USA attest to the difficulties involved in considering ethics. They cite three typical reactions: agreement in principle on ethical principles but disparate practice; proponents of a particular course of action impugning the moral integrity of those who hold opposing views; and, an acceptance of moral relativism, by which any moral code which is not self-contradictory is regarded as being as good as any other.

The discussion here will necessarily be selective and partial. This is an area where both methodologies and outcomes are highly contested. The stance taken here will be to raise issues and offer suggestions knowing that some writers will have differing stances.

The first necessary discussion is to try to differentiate between moral principles and value positions. Hodgkinson (1991) proposes an ethical hierarchy.

This has a value system which ranges from the 'good' to the 'right' or, in other words, the desirable to the obligatory. This poses a requirement to be able to recognise different positions on this hierarchy.

Strike *et al.* (1988) suggest that moral and ethical judgements which involve principles which are generally accepted in society should be distinguished from the more organisational based values which can vary from organisation to organisation. Moral statements apply to other people and ourselves. Value judgements and personal preferences only apply to ourselves (or are exercised on behalf of others). A further difference is in the morality of coercion. It may be moral to coerce people who do not follow moral principles but not personal value positions. It is contended that there are some moral precepts which would be shared by most people in society and many that are backed by law. It is argued that all schools should manage using essentially these same moral principles. Values, on the other hand, represent choices and so may be different in different schools and also may be subject to change. Thus there are some principles which are unchanging (or only very slowly changing in some cases) and values which a school can choose and which may need to change. This leads to a distinction between moral imperatives and value choices. Moral principles could include such codes as honesty, equal respect for persons, due process, individual responsibility, and personal liberty.

If moral principles and values are to influence decision making explicitly, the first stage is to recognise that there should be a moral and value dimension in managerial decision making. The second stage is to recognise the moral principles and values involved in any particular decision and, finally, some systematic way of considering the implications of these moral principles and values is needed (Strike *et al.*, 1988).

Moral and value judgements are rarely straightforward. In many problems there are conflicting moral principles and value positions and hence no 'right' answers. An example of this is where parents use their personal right to express a preference for the education of their child and this clashes with the principle of equality of opportunity for all children.

CULTURAL CHOICES IN MANAGING: STYLE AND SUBSTANCE

There are two distinct sets of cultural choices. One set concerns the extent to which principles and values will be used to guide the process of managing – both ends and means. The other set concerns style or the extent to which organisational values are high profile both within and outside the organisation. It is this second aspect of choice which will primarily be considered here.

Leaders need to be clear about where they and their organisation stand on ends and means. Do ends justify means? There is almost no simple answer to this question but a general stance is needed that either means are as important as ends or that the end justifying the means can mitigate censure from using dubious means. This is a particularly important issue for managers. Is management a morally neutral process for achieving any ends by any means? Should it only be used to achieve moral ends? Should only moral means be used to achieve moral ends? It should be recognised before taking an openly moral and value stance that this commits the school and its leaders for the foreseeable future to act in this way. Such pledges cannot be suspended temporarily with any credibility.

The symbolic significance of actions should not be underestimated. If a school has espoused and widely known values, staff and others will analyse actions to see whether these values are followed in practice, perhaps the degree of analysis may be related to their own personal preferences. Actions which appear to, let alone do, depart from espoused values can be expected to be stored in people's memories along with other evidence to be interpreted. Evidence of this kind can be expected to sow the seeds of increasing cynicism and disillusionment. It follows from this that a clear explanation about why actions are taken is necessary especially when there is a possibility that they will be seen to be at variance with espoused values.

At the deeper levels an organisational culture represents the values which prevail in the organisation. The culture not only represents the way we do things here but also the way we think it is right to do things here. Since there are a number of components of culture it does not follow that they are all consistent. It is possible that certain values are espoused in rhetoric and symbolic actions and different values underlie practice.

This state of affairs represents a rather unstable situation. If it persists there is likely to be a great deal of cynicism about real values compared to rhetorical values. There are many examples where the contrast has not been explicit until some seminal event occurred when practice was shown to be at variance with the espoused values of the organisation. This can lead to instability and change. Indeed this can be one aspect of an attempt to change culture by demonstrating the inconsistencies in current practice.

Pascale (1991) suggests keeping large issues which involve value positions under review rather than making a definitive and binding decision on them. This is not to suggest that such principles as honesty might only be regarded as provisional but such large issues as cooperation and competition should be recognised as value positions which should not be decided once and for all but may be subject to changing trends. For schools, issues of selection and pupil grouping may provide such issues. There are competing moral principles which can be used to justify either of these courses of action and there are corresponding negative features in practice. A continuing debate which includes the principles and any empirical findings from practice has the power to attempt to mitigate the negative features of prevailing practice. A dialogue of the deaf leads only to a power contest with a winner-takes-all mentality and periodic change but no progress.

Turning to choices about purpose and values, there are constraints on choices. These include the prevailing values in the organisation, needs indicated by the external environment and the current preferences of those in senior positions. All of these would need to be weighed in any decision to change. As has previously been remarked the strength of the present culture is an important stabilising factor which will make radical change difficult.

Espoused values of an organisation may need to change. A school which has embraced cooperation and eschewed competition may find itself increasingly out of step with a society that accepts and rewards competition. Unless the school is meeting the aspirations of its clientele it may need to change its values. This will be difficult and deeply distressing to those committed to the previous values.

CHANGING CULTURE

Changing culture brings together a number of the issues in this chapter and thus provides an appropriate conclusion to the chapter. A number of proponents of the head's need to manage culture base their advice on Schein's (1992) remark about the role of the leader being to create the organisational culture but they do not note the context of Schein's statement. He makes it clear that in a new organisation it is the task of the leader to create a culture where none exists. Thereafter new leaders may attempt to change the culture but as he recognises leaders are only one of a number of influences on culture (p. 5).

Leaders have a choice about whether to influence culture with the hope of changing it or whether to accept the existing culture. According to Schein (1992) this is one of the differences between leaders (who seek to change) and managers (who don't). There are a number of possibilities here. A new leader may wish to change because the values inherent in the culture do not accord with his or her own personal preferences. Alternatively a leader may wish to change the culture because he or she identifies it as dysfunctional – either internally or externally. There may be important and different moral implications of change in these two cases.

There are further decisions about the means used to bring about the change. It could be done by a combination of symbolic acts and administrative measures but without open discussion about the reasons for change. Indeed the honest reasons in this case might appear somewhat egotistical. Alternatively, the change might be brought about by a long period of unfreezing (see Chapter 1.4) followed by intense discussion and persuasion and general acceptance. Changing culture is discussed more fully in Fidler *et al.* (1996).

Whereas moral principles may be fixed, values can be chosen. There are choices of which values to espouse as well as how to reconcile and prioritise them when they are in conflict in any particular situation. The fundamental and vital point is that values are chosen. Whilst this may not seem a free and open choice, it is nevertheless a choice and an important choice. Changes of values and the part played by culture underpin many of the choices discussed in this book.

The starting point for change is for a leader to understand an organisation's culture. This is easier for a new leader to appreciate than an existing leader who is steeped in unspoken and unrecognised assumptions. Having recognised a need for change the difficulties of change need to be assessed. Deal and Kennedy (1988) identify three factors which may affect the difficulty of changing an organisational culture:

a) *evident crisis*: where an organisation is evidently in trouble or heading for trouble, there is a greater willingness to consider deep-seated change;
b) *attractiveness of change*: the proposed change needs to have all its highly desirable features emphasised;
c) *strength of present culture*: the stronger the present culture the more difficult it is to change.

Finally, the difficulties of attempting to change an organisation's culture should not be underestimated. In the words of the title of an article by Wilkins and Patterson (1985) 'You can't get there from here'. Without the appropriate conditions some changes may just be too large to make in one move. Large scale change may need to be accomplished in stages over a number of years and as circumstances permit. This is the role of strategy as outlined in Chapter 2.2.

REFERENCES

Ainscow, M., Hargreaves, D. H., Hopkins, D., Balshaw, M. and Black-Hawkins, K. (1994) *Mapping Change in Schools: The Cambridge Manual of Research Techniques*, Cambridge Institute of Education, Cambridge.

Beck L. G. and Murphy, J. (1994) *Ethics in Educational Leadership Programs: An Expanding Role*, Sage, Thousand Oaks, CA.

Bottery, M. (1992) *The Ethics of Educational Management*, Cassell, London.

Bower, M. (1966) *The Will to Manage*, McGraw-Hill, London.

Deal, T. E. (1990) Foreword in Sergiovanni, T. J., *Value-Added Leadership: How to Get Extraordinary Performance in Schools*, Harcourt Brace Jovanovich, San Diego, CA.

Deal, T. E. and Kennedy, A. A. (1988) *Corporate Cultures: The Rites and Rituals of Corporate Life*, Penguin, London.

Duignan, P. A. and Macpherson, R. J. S. (eds) (1992) *Educative Leadership: Practical Theory for New Administrators and Managers*, Falmer, London.

Fidler, B. with Edwards, M., Evans, B., Mann, P. and Thomas, P. (1996) *Strategic Planning for School Improvement*, Pitman, London.

Handy, C. (1985) *Gods of Management: The Changing Work of Organisations*, Pan Books, London.

Hargreaves, D. H. (1995) School culture, school effectiveness and school improvement, *School Effectiveness and School Improvement*, Vol. 6 no. 1, 23–46.

Hodgkinson, C. (1991) *Educational Leadership: The moral art*, SUNY, New York.

Hoy, W. K. and Miskel, C. G. (1991) *Educational Administration: Theory, Research and Practice* (4th edn), McGraw-Hill, New York.

Johnson, G. and Scholes, K. (1993) *Exploring Corporate Strategy* (3rd edn), Prentice Hall, Hemel Hempstead, Herts.

Owens, R. G. (1995) *Organizational Behavior in Education* (5th edn), Allyn & Bacon, Needham Heights, MA.

Pascale, R., (1991) *Managing on the Edge: How Successful Companies use Conflict to Stay Ahead*, Penguin, London.

Peters, T. J. and Waterman, R. H. (1982) *In Search of Excellence: Lessons from America's Best-Run Companies*, Harper & Row, New York.

Rutter, M., Maughan, B., Mortimore, P. and Ouston, J. (1979) *Fifteen thousand hours: Secondary schools and their effects on children*, Paul Chapman, London.

Sergiovanni, T. J. (1991) *The Principalship: A reflective practice perspective* (2nd edn), Allyn & Bacon, Needham Heights, MA.

Schein, E. H. (1992) *Organizational Culture and Leadership* (2nd edn), Jossey-Bass, San Francisco, CA.

Stacey, R. D. (1995) *Strategic Management and Organisational Dynamics*, Pitman, London.

Strike, K. A., Haller, E. J. and Soltis, J. F. (1988) *The Ethics of School Administration*, Teachers College Press, New York.

Torrington, D. and Weightman, J. (1989) *The Reality of School Management*, Blackwell Educational, Oxford.

Watson, T. (1994) *In Search of Management*, Routledge, London.

Wilkins, A. L. and Patterson, K. J. (1985), You Can't Get There From Here: What Will Make Culture-Change Projects Fail, in Kilmann, R. H., Saxton, M. J., Serpa, R. and Associates, *Gaining Control of the Corporate Culture*, Jossey-Bass, San Francisco, CA.

Willmott, H. (1993) Strength is ignorance; slavery is freedom: managing culture in modern organizations, *Journal of Management Studies*, Vol. 30 no. 4, 515–52.

1.4

The School as a Whole: School Improvement and Planned Change

BRIAN FIDLER

The purpose of this chapter is threefold:
(1) to examine influences urging schools to improve and to assess their implications;
(2) to discover what is known about how schools change and improve;
(3) to identify a range of techniques and approaches from which senior managers in schools may choose in planning improvement.

PRESSURE TO IMPROVE

This book is being written some twenty years after the famous Ruskin College Speech of the then prime minister James Callaghan. In 1976 he identified what he saw as a number of failings in primary and secondary schools. A Great Debate was inaugurated to open up to public discussion what had previously been the preserve of educationalists. Schools have been under pressure ever since.

In the intervening 20 years a good deal more information has been forthcoming about the operation of the educational system and the performance of individual schools. After years of investigation, pressure and piecemeal change, large scale structural change was accomplished in the 1988 Education Reform Act. Its principal features were the imposition of a standardised National Curriculum and systematic pupil testing, financial delegation and the harnessing of parental choice to engender competition between schools. New types of school were created – City Technology Colleges and Grant Maintained Schools – to act as beacons for other schools to follow.

These structural changes now provide the framework within which schools operate. Various forms of pressure have resulted and yet more types of influence and support are being applied in an effort to make improvement a reality at school level. The assumption has been made that the external structural conditions for school improvement are now in place and that a final element is required – a response at individual institutional level.

WHAT IS SCHOOL IMPROVEMENT?

What counts as school improvement is a highly contested issue. Various writers have adopted complex and value based definitions whilst the government has sought to focus on particular outcomes of schooling.

The definition given in the International School Improvement Programme (Miles and Ekholm, 1985, p. 48), gives a quite neutral view: 'a systematic, sustained effort aimed at change in learning conditions and other related internal conditions in one or more schools, with the ultimate aim of accomplishing educational goals more effectively.' This definition focuses ultimately on educational goals but covers any intermediate process necessary to achieve those goals. This leaves the choice of what to improve quite open. This is the approach adopted by this chapter.

There are in fact three separate but related issues:

1   whether to improve;
2   what to improve;
3   how to improve.

As will become apparent there are quite a number of external pressures on schools which seek to influence the agenda of any discussion of what to improve. These range from general trends at the national level through to specific demands at the local level. These pressures are also exerted in different ways. Some take the form of providing information so as to influence the likely input into any discussion whilst others require a specific response from schools. This is a process in which all can take part – laypeople and educational professionals.

How to improve, on the other hand, has generally been left to educationalists although there has been some attempt by central government to stimulate processes, such as school development planning, and to recommend some techniques. A later section of this chapter will attempt to bring together the array of choices from which senior managers in schools can choose.

Perhaps the single most unremarked feature of current attempts at school improvement in England compared to what has happened elsewhere is that decision making at school level is recognised as the focal point for school improvement. Partly this is an inevitable result of decentralising the management of schools – there are no other agencies – but it also reflects the negative experiences of many external attempts to improve schools both here and elsewhere. The dilemmas involved in this approach to school improvement will be discussed later in this chapter.

INFLUENCES ON 'WHETHER AND WHAT'

School leaders are subjected to a number of pressures and influences which attempt to steer their thinking about whether anything in their school needs improving and, if so, what. Some parameters for attempting to classify these forces are – who is applying the pressures and how are they being applied? These issues are inevitably related since central government is a major player and seeks to influence both agendas. This also has an indirect effect since other sources of influence, such as parents, are, in their turn, influenced by such official pronouncements.

The significant players in attempting to affect schools' thinking are – central government and its agencies, local government (to a limited degree), the clients of schools and educational professionals inside and outside schools. The DFEE set up a School Effectiveness Unit in 1993 and launched a school improvement programme in 1995. LEAs and to a lesser extent universities and TECs have also recently been active.

In addition to a flow of press releases, leaflets and speeches which have been taken up by the media, more formal means by which power and influence have been used include:

- school inspections and reporting;
- salary payments for headteachers and deputy heads;
- formal target setting;
- parental reporting;
- publication of 'league tables';
- advice and support;
- additional funding.

Thus schools are under considerable, sustained and multiple-voiced pressure to consider improvement and to focus on particular kinds of activity. The discussion of the 'who' and 'how' will be conducted under five headings – (1) OFSTED inspections, (2) climate setting, (3) school effectiveness findings, (4) clients' views and (5) assisted self-evaluation. The order of discussion is not intended to give an order of importance. The order has been chosen because a number of these measures are inter-related and a measure needs to be introduced before the ways in which other agencies are building on the same measures can be appreciated.

(1) OFSTED inspections

Arguably the most potent pressure for school improvement has been the introduction of a compulsory system of regular inspections for all state schools in England and Wales. In addition to its evaluatory role, there is research evidence from inspected secondary schools that heads find the process developmental (Ouston *et al.*, 1996).

The Education (Schools) Act 1992 instituted a regime of systematic inspections of all state schools on a regular cycle. Inspections were to be carried out according to a framework produced by a newly formed Office for Standards in Education (OFSTED). Independent inspectors were required to pass a registration assessment and were contracted to carry out inspections after having a tender accepted by OFSTED. OFSTED school inspections are important at a number of levels. They provide a database for national statements about the generality of schools. At the individual school level, the inspection report on the school is made public and the school is required to produce an action plan following its inspection report. Perhaps the most noteworthy feature is that the process affects all state schools and thus its influence is universal.

The Office for Standards in Education organises the inspection of each state school according to a framework which covers the four areas (OFSTED, 1995a):

(a) the quality of education provided by the school;
(b) the educational standards achieved by pupils;
(c) the efficiency with which resources are managed;
(d) the spiritual, moral, social and cultural development of schools.

A summary of the resulting report is sent to each parent and the full report is available from the school and also on the Internet. It is possible to search inspection reports on the internet (http://www.open.gov.uk/OFSTED) to find good practice on any of the areas of a school's work which are inspected. There are two possible effects from inspections:

i)   any effect on parental choice as a result of the findings of the inspection and any attendant publicity;
ii) an action plan has to be formulated and sent to OFSTED (and the main-taining body for the school) which responds to a prioritised list of issues compiled by the inspection team.

(OFSTED, 1994, 1995b)

The first effect is outside the control of an individual school although it may attempt to manage the publicity following a report by providing press releases and by commenting on the inspection findings when sending them to parents. An element of injustice for a particular school, irrespective of the quality of the inspection, may follow publication of the inspection report. Firstly, the media or the general public may make comparisons with other local schools which may have quite different 'catchment areas' and, secondly, on the order in which local schools are inspected and the attendant publicity. Whilst the first injustice was foreseeable and, perhaps, inevitable, the second effect was less apparent. The first schools inspected received generally more interest from the media than later schools. This either had a positive or negative effect on the school depending on the nature of the report itself and the way in which the media perceived it. The point is that the inspected school received comment in a way in which similar schools which had not been inspected did not.

The second effect of inspections is more uniform in that all schools must respond to action points in their inspection report. The nature of the individual school response, however, will vary enormously. Nevertheless, the action points arise from an agenda set by the inspection framework. In inspections taking place since April 1996 any points for action arising from the report should take account of the school's own pre-existing developmental priorities but be based on issues identified by inspection evidence. A sanction has been imposed on schools which fail to submit an action plan: they will not receive specific funding to help implement the action plan (DFEE, 1996d).

The inspection regime which has been introduced has, for the first time, included a systematic procedure for dealing with schools which are deemed, as a result of inspection, to be failing their pupils. The number of such schools appears to be around 2 per cent of schools inspected (DFEE, 1995b) and thus such schools can be viewed as pathological but a great deal of media and researcher interest has been devoted to these relatively few schools. By late 1996 only one school had been closed following the failure of remedial measures after a damaging inspection report but a small number of others may have been merged or closed in anticipation of such a report. The majority of failing schools are reported to be improving and a number have been released from special measures as a result of their improved performance (DFEE, 1995b).

(2)   Climate setting

There has been prolonged discussion since the Great Debate (and before that) on the inadequacies of schools in general and some schools in particular. International comparisons of student achievement show English children doing less well than selected overseas nations and this is assumed to be related to industrial competitiveness which also shows the UK slipping down world league tables. Criticisms have come from government and also been taken up and orchestrated by government when they originated elsewhere. This has been with us for some time but some particular themes have emerged and some new measures have been introduced.

The publication since 1993 of examination results for leaving students for secondary schools has focussed discussion both nationally and locally on certain parameters. The tables contain a small number of statistics and some background information on each school. Although they contain a number of different statistics expressing examination performance, the publication of the tables has targeted comment on the percentage of children in a year group leaving with 5 or more A* to C grades at GCSE and an A level points score. This is somewhat unfortunate since children who are unlikely to achieve this level do not contribute to a school's statistic. It does not provide an incentive for a school to achieve the highest examination performance from the less able. A total GCSE point score would have included a contribution from all children achieving any grade. There is also increasing attention directed at the proportion of higher grades at both GCSE and A level. Other statistics for schools such as attendance and exclusion rates are also published but appear to be less discussed.

The national publication of these comparable statistics is the latest in a series of measures to provide parents with factual data to inform their choice of school. Although there has been much media interest in these results when they were published it is not clear how far they affect parental choice of school. Informed wisdom suggest that the effect is indirect. The local 'grapevine' may pick up casual comments about the results from local schools, which parents then hear, rather than each parent consulting the tables and making their own analysis. There is some evidence that many parents have difficulty interpreting the tables. Trends may vary by social class, with more middle-class parents engaging in their own perusal and conclusions.

The publication of leaving examination results is now commonplace for secondary schools and the process is to be widened to cover other results of national curriculum testing in both primary and secondary schools. Individual schools are required to make additional information known to parents at the Annual Meeting of Parents such as the destination of school leavers.

Specific measures are beginning to follow the provision of information. Such measures have in the past provided incentives to improve but more recently they are also encompassing a degree of coercion. Since 1994 school effectiveness has featured as one of the areas to which central government has made finance available to LEAs and GM schools for in-service training through GEST funding and its equivalents. In 1996 such funding has been partially targeted at schools producing an action plan following an inspection report. Some funding has been made available to LEAs to assist schools which were deemed 'failing' when inspected and extra funding was offered on a competitive basis for general school improvement in 1996. Under this scheme 81 LEAs applied and 23 were successful, each receiving £100,000 of extra funding.

Some measures which indicate increasing coercion include the following. Governing bodies are required to report to parents what action they intend to take in response to an inspection report's points for action. The governors are also required to report yearly at the annual meeting of parents on progress on the action plan which they have devised in their response.

As a measure to improve the performance of teachers the School Teacher Review Body has given increasing freedom and encouraged governing bodies to reward teaching staff according to their performance. Take up has been low and a pilot scheme of 10 schools, which investigated performance related pay, has never reported. However, in 1996 governing bodies were required to set targets for their headteachers and deputy headteachers. Progress against these targets is to be assessed in 1997 as part of the annual salary review. Conversely, after 1997 extra payments, excluding functional factors such as increasing size of school or additional duties, may not be made to heads and deputies unless targets have previously been set. This target setting approach to performance related pay follows generally researched principles in the public sector (Fidler, 1992). The particular areas suggested for targets (DFEE, 1996a) are:

(a) examination/test results;
(b) pupil attendance;
(c) financial management;

(d) where there has been an OFSTED or OHMCI inspection, progress in implementing the resulting action plan.

A further requirement which is to be imposed on governing bodies is a requirement to set targets for improving their pupils' performance and to publish these in annual reports (DFEE, 1996b, 1996c). Finally, a new National Professional Qualification for Headship is being set up by the Teacher Training Agency (1996) for aspiring headteachers. This claims that the one of the key principles is that the qualification 'is rooted in school improvement'.

(3)   School effectiveness research findings

An influence of somewhat unknown magnitude derives from research on effective schools. This research has attempted to investigate the factors which are displayed in schools which are found to be 'effective'. The neutral word 'effective' conceals the value-based outcome measure which determines effectiveness in most studies – pupils' test scores on basic skills which are greater than would be expected in view of their prior attainment or other background variables.

OFSTED commissioned a report to synthesize the findings from this work (Sammons *et al.*, 1995). A summary of this has been widely distributed, with funding from the Banking Information Service, and a copy was sent to every governing body of a state school. The 11 factors associated with an effective school which the leaflet included (DFE/OFSTED/BIS, 1995) are:

1   professional leadership
2   shared vision and goals
3   a learning environment
4   concentration on teaching and learning
5   explicit high expectations
6   positive reinforcement
7   monitoring progress
8   pupil rights and responsibilities
9   purposeful teaching
10 a learning organisation
11 home–school partnership

Lists like this have appeared both in academic books and articles and also in more popular sources for those in schools and there is some general notion of an effective school which is seen to legitimate a number of prescriptions. This is not the place to engage in a critical appraisal of this work but equally it would be anti-educational merely to relay such a list without issuing a health warning and providing the interested reader with further references to follow up.

Since most of the research has been carried out on elementary schools in the USA, it is perhaps not surprising that there has been an extensive literature critically appraising this work and its results in the USA (Purkey and Smith,

1983; Good and Brophy, 1986; Bliss, Firestone and Richards, 1991). The methodology and findings have been highly contested. There has been rather less critical discussion in the UK until fairly recently (Ouston, 1996; Fidler *et al.*, 1996; Elliott, 1996). Reynolds (1992) has been one writer in the UK who has consistently drawn attention to a number of limitations of this work, in particular whether:

(a) the factors would be the same for a school with more diverse aims than results in tests of basic skills;
(b) an effective school remains so year after year;
(c) effective schools have the same effects on all pupils.

In the USA effective schooling programmes began in the 1980s with Federal funding to implement school effectiveness factors. Perhaps the most worrying aspect of this search for factors is the attitude of mind which lies behind the search. Whilst an attitude of mind which welcomes simple, certain answers to complex questions is understandable, such trust is deeply worrying. If it were possible to find a single model to replicate, managing schools and teaching in them would be reduced to a technical activity. It should be remembered that a service is provided to human beings by human beings with all their variability and complexity. The search for school effectiveness factors implies a theory of human behaviour which is highly deterministic. Views of human behaviour extend along a continuum which runs from, at one end, a belief that there are inalienable rules of human behaviour to, at the other, the belief that each person has their own subjective understanding of the world and that this informs their personal actions.

A few moments' reflection on the prospect of there being a universal set of factors which, if not responsible for an effective school, are nevertheless associated with an effective school should give rise to a consideration of the effects of context on good schooling. The word good has been chosen to reinstate the clear value base for the judgement of the outcomes of schooling. Context has two implications, firstly, that the concept of good might be different in particular schools, and secondly, that what processes are associated with any particular good school are likely to be contingent. In other words, the factors and their magnitude are highly likely to be dependent on the prior history of the school and its current circumstances. Circumstances will include the nature of the staff and headteacher, the nature of the pupils and the nature of the parent body. The implication of such a view is that the job of the headteacher and senior staff is to make judgements about context and propose action based on this assessment rather than following any recipe. Thus context has implications for both the 'what' and the 'how' of school improvement.

Finally, it should be made clear that writers, whatever their views on the validity of the school effectiveness correlates, are agreed that such lists are of little direct help in turning an ineffective school into an effective one. How to improve schools is the subject of a later section of this chapter.

Value-added research

There are two discrete strands to research on school effectiveness. The first is that previously described which has been mainly carried out overseas and has been by far the most prominent internationally. In the UK there has been rather more emphasis on trying to discover the size of differences between schools or the 'school effect factor' and trying to distinguish 'effective' from 'ineffective' schools. This has mainly used secondary school leaving exams – GCSE and A level – as the indicators of achievement and some prior measure of ability or attainment in order to examine the progress of children within the school (Willms, 1992).

This type of research has contributed a methodology to aid the study of pupil progress. These ideas have acquired a more general interest following the publication of examination results of all schools. It is fairly clear that outcome results which take no account of the abilities of children when they entered the school provide little information about how well the school is performing (Glogg and Fidler, 1990). However, there was some initial reluctance to examine other ways of presenting comparative results.

Partly this was because there was some suspicion of the original practice of adjusting for pupils' prior attainment by using measures of social background. The more recent method, which requires more calculation and more data, compares the attainment of each pupil on entering the school with his or her performance on leaving the school. This more sophisticated analysis has been extended by the use of multilevel modelling to try to analyse the contribution of different levels of aggregation – classroom, school, LEA – but this brings its own attendant problems (Fitz-Gibbon, 1991).

When attempts are made to account for the variance in the performance of individual pupils, the contribution of prior attainment typically accounts for about 40–50 per cent of the variance in pupil outcome scores (this means that 50–60 per cent is explained by other factors or error). Estimates of the school's contribution are typically 10 per cent. Whilst this might seem a small proportion of the total variance it should be viewed as quite large when the pupil's own measured ability only accounts for less than half of the variance. Despite attempt to add further factors such as gender and measures of family background there is a relatively large amount of unexplained variance (including error). Thus this is a far from ideal comparator for the performance of individual schools (Willms, 1992). It may be an improvement on raw scores but it still has the potential to be quite unfair to individual schools. In addition to the technical difficulties of calculating valid measures of value-added, there are huge problems of communicating them to teachers and to parents (Fidler, 1993; SCAA, 1994).

Individual schools can adapt the method to compare the progress of one intake of children with the progress of children in the next intake but this gives no indication of how well children are progressing compared to similar children in other schools. For progress between GCSE and GCE A level there are statistics from previous years with which to compare all schools (DFE, 1995a, 1995b). It is the lack of a common measure of attainment on entry to secondary schools which prevents such comparisons with all schools for previous years for mainstream secondary schooling. Only if groups of school use a common test for the attainment of children on entry to secondary school and these are used five years later to chart progress to GCSE in these same schools can valid comparisons be made between schools. Surprisingly as originally envisaged the Key Stage 2 National Curriculum tests results did not lend themselves to this (William, 1992) as the Dearing report noted (Dearing, 1993).

Internal comparisons within a school can be made of the performance of individual departments. The method compares the average performance of each child with its performance in a particular subject. Whilst this does not give any indication of progress compared to other school, its use within an individual school provides a reasonably valid means of comparing departmental performance. Using this in combination with a comparison of pupils' actual performance with teachers' estimates (Beckett, 1982) it is possible to use the information in a prospective way to set targets for improving performance rather than solely for analysing previous performance (DFEE, 1996b).

(4) Clients' views

In view of the power given to clients by the 1988 Education Reform Act as regards their choice of school, it might be expected that the views of clients would be decisive in exerting influence on what aspects of schools needed improvement. However, there have been contradictory trends. Whilst the Act increased parental choice it also gave less freedom to schools to respond by prescribing many details of school work especially curriculum and testing. This contradictory trend has typified the schism in the policies of the new right between liberal marketeers and neo-conservatives (Lawton, 1992). The net effect has been that the choices offered to clients have been fairly limited. This is not to say that in certain areas parental perceptions have not had a large influence on some schools.

Client influence can be felt in two ways. Firstly, there are the wishes of potential clients. That is those clients who are yet to make their choice of school. If there is a strongly articulated desire for certain school attributes then this will influence schools which are anxious about their pupil recruitment. Secondly, there are the wishes of current clients.

One needs to recognise that the client of a school is a multiple entity. The two principal ones which will be considered here are the parent and the child, although there are others, for example, the local community and the taxpayer. When it comes to choice of school there is evidence that in many cases both parents and children play a part in the decision. Thus for recruitment purposes both aspects of the client have influence.

How far a school seeks to investigate the satisfaction of its present clients is a choice which is currently left to the school. Those schools which wish to adopt a responsive stance (Kotler and Andreasen, 1987) will not wish to await complaints but will wish to solicit client views both of their current satisfaction and their future needs. Some schools currently conduct parental satisfaction surveys but rather fewer appear to consult pupils for their views (Rudduck *et al.*, 1995).

It should be recognised that client views at least in part will in their turn be influenced by the climate created by the media and central government. In many ways it is parents who are being relied upon to ensure that messages from the centre are acted upon locally.

(5)   Assisted school self-evaluation

Finally, there will be the voice of teachers who as part of their professional practice identify areas of the school's work for improvement. School self-evaluation began in the 1970s but evidence showed that teachers were rather better at identifying areas for improvement than in bringing about improvement. Since then GRIDS (McMahon *et al.*, 1984) and school development planning (Hargreaves and Hopkins, 1991, 1994) have been developed as means for planning improvements when suitable areas have been identified.

A recent addition to assist self-evaluation is the process of benchmarking (LGMB, 1994; DFEE, 1995a). For many school processes senior managers have little comparative information about how other schools perform on similar processes. The examination league tables provide comparative information on some pupil outcomes but much more can be provided to schools such as comparisons of spending patterns, pupil progress, etc. Schools need to provide information to some organisation which can process the information and feed it back in a form to allow schools to make meaningful comparisons. LEAs are in a good position to carry out such a function (Fidler and Morris, 1996).

'HOW' TO IMPROVE

In searching the literature to collect research findings on school improvement, it is not easy to set boundaries to determine what qualifies as 'school improvement' especially given the broad definition used earlier. Findings from previous projects on curriculum innovation are relevant despite their not being described as improvement projects at the time.

It is useful to distinguish externally-initiated attempts to change schools from those which are school-initiated particularly since much of the evidence on school change comes from the former, especially in the USA. The distinction is important since the processes are different in the two cases. Experience in one will need some translation before it is of value to the other. The characteristics of the two cases are as follows:

School-initiated change: This change fundamentally begins with a problem or an internally generated need for change. Characteristics of such projects are shown in Table 1.4.1.

Externally-initiated change: This change fundamentally begins with an

Table 1.4.1 School change

School-initiated	Externally-initiated
• Internal problem leads to a solution	• General external solution to an unknown problem in a particular school
• Recognition and prioritisation of the problem and its solution is a school responsibility: the school is the centre of action	• External curriculum initiative or other innovation on offer
• Agenda for improvement is influenced from outside but not mandated	• School is selected to join in or 'volunteers'
• External support is available but at the school's control and expense	• The project is directed from outside the school
• Limited resource and training support	• The package usually includes some process advice on how to implement the innovation
• Builds on previous school-based development processes and experience	• The package usually includes some training

external solution to a general problem in schools. Characteristics of such projects are also shown in Table 1.4.1.

The crucial distinction concerns the locus of decision-making. In a school-initiated change the sole responsibility lies at school level. This includes the requirement to recognise a need for process advice, training and consultancy help as well as the need to plan the introduction of the change.

There has been extensive use of the findings from curriculum innovations introduced in the 1970s and early 1980s in the USA to augment the literature on change and school improvement. It should be remembered that these were generally single innovations introduced from outside the school. Hall and Hord (1987) identify the following findings:

1   Change is a process not a single event.
2   More is required than just identifying the appropriate innovation and assuming that it will work. In addition to the innovation and its attributes and requirements, there is a change process which needs to be separately considered.
3   The support and encouragement of the headteacher or principal is essential.
4   It is possible to anticipate much that will occur during the change process.
5   There are three stages to the change process: initiation; implementation – mutual adaptation of the innovation and the school; institutionalisation.
6   A change facilitator is needed, either within the school or outside, to diagnose attitudes to the change and skills needed to implement the change and respond accordingly.
7   Understanding the change from the point of view of *participants* is critical.
8   More than one person in the school needs to be committed and a driver of the change. Hall and Hord (1987) refer to complementary styles and roles in the main change facilitator and a second change facilitator or consigliere.

Many of these findings have been endorsed by Fullan (1993) who in addition has drawn attention to some further insights:

9   Ready-fire-aim is a more apt description of progress on complex innovations rather than the more rational ready-aim-fire. This recognises the difficulties of planning very complex innovations and acknowledges that often participants become clearer about the deeper implications of a change as they proceed with it.

Finally, Joyce and Showers (1988) and others have drawn attention to the timing and follow-up of training to ensure that participants have skills and confidence to change their practice.

10 Familiarisation, training and coaching (and other forms of support) need to be sequenced throughout the project rather than being concentrated at the start. People recognise new needs for training and development as they

appreciate the requirements on themselves more clearly through experience of trying to implement the innovation.

PRESSURE AND SUPPORT

Perhaps the most helpful conceptualisation of a general condition for successful innovation is the identification of a simultaneous need for pressure and support. This need is present at all levels. The institution needs pressure and support from outside just as individuals and groups internally also need pressure and support. The pressure is to legitimate and demand, when progress is in peril, whilst the support is to encourage and make possible.

Two main constraints on change are likely to be:

(a) the reluctance of many staff to change their practices and acquire new skills;
(b) how to find ways of working together on change whilst also maintaining most current activities.

Ideas for dealing with the first, perfectly natural, reaction to change are given in the next section on planned change. There are two aspects to the second issue.

Firstly, efforts on change have to be prioritised against efforts on maintaining the present pattern of work for all those aspects of practice which are not to be changed. At the institutional level this requires a development plan which has an appropriately small number of areas for development and connects this with an appropriately small set of development targets for individuals through the appraisal process (Fidler and Cooper, 1992).

Secondly, how to work together? Detailed issues of involvement are not straightforward (Fidler *et al.*, 1991) and yet a general expectation of working together harmoniously is the foundation of any cooperative change. Few changes will involve teachers making personal changes in their teaching without reference to other staff (and even in this case mutual support would aid implementation). A project at the Cambridge Institute of Education has recently examined the preconditions for change and devised a short questionnaire to identify ways of working in the school and whether individuals wish these to be changed (Ainscow *et al.*, 1994). These ideas are linked to organisational culture discussed in Chapter 1.3 and strategy in Chapter 2.2.

MANAGEMENT OF PLANNED CHANGE

Institutionally initiated change has been the norm in the organisational literature (Beckhard and Harris, 1987) which has provided the source for many school management approaches (Everard and Morris, 1996). This approach assumes that a manager plans change. It should be emphasised that this does not imply that decisions to change will be made autocratically. Many of the techniques provide information on the need for a change and the problems which will have to be surmounted to implement the change. These need to be considered before a decision to change is made. Such a decision can be made corporately. There are a number of ideas from which to choose.

Chin and Benne (1976) have identified three approaches to change. The first is the power–coercive. In this approach organisation members are compelled or put under great psychological or other pressure to change. The second is the rational–empirical approach where the logical advantages of the proposed change are set out. Finally, the normative–re-educative approach uses more emotional and interpersonal means to persuade people to accept the change. These are not necessarily alternatives but rather should be seen as an armoury of approaches from which to select or use in combination at appropriate points in the change process.

Kurt Lewin's work (1951) has been very influential in conceptualising and planning change. A range of very valuable devices owe their origin to him. He conceptualised the change process in three stages which are graphic in their illustration of what is required. These are

unfreezing
moving
refreezing

This draws attention to the importance of the beginnings of planning the change and the importance of assimilating the change into the normal work of the school at the end of the implementation. In particular the term 'unfreezing' is helpful in terms of diagnosing readiness for change. In his terms unless the present state is sufficiently unfrozen, change will not take place successfully. This means that people have to begin to feel uncomfortable with the present state before they will readily contemplate moving. Schein (1992) has elaborated three steps within the unfreezing process:

1   presence of evidence of a problem;
2   connection of this problem with the organisation's purpose causing anxiety and/or guilt;
3   a possible solution which is not so unsettling as to cause a denial of the problem.

If all three steps have been completed to some degree, the unfreezing has taken place so the change can be planned.

Lewin's basic assumption is that an organisation is at equilibrium with its surroundings when forces for change balance forces resisting change. His force field analysis diagram allows the relevant forces to be identified (Fidler *et al.*, 1991). By decreasing the resisting forces and increasing the driving forces change can be accomplished. The analysis helps choose the appropriate forces to work on.

Beckhard and Harris (1987) have suggested the use of readiness and capability charts to examine whether key organisation members are ready for the change and also, and quite separately, whether they have the skills and attitudes to deal with the change. Action to unfreeze and/or develop skills and provide support can be planned. They have also designed a simple commitment chart to analyse the present and desired positions of key people concerned with the change. This can be adapted for use in schools (Everard and Morris, 1996).

CONCLUSION

Change and improvement are likely to be major features in the management of schools for the foreseeable future. The purpose of this chapter has been to provide some information to make informed choices about what and how to improve. It has tried to identify some forces and sources of pressure urging change.

These pressures will come from both outside and inside a school. The challenge for senior managers is to lead an informed debate about a need for improvement which balances, on the one hand, the urgent and the long-term and, on the other hand, the demands of laypeople and professionals. An informed debate means that no external (or internal) pressure should be accepted as inevitable but the implications and consequences of failing to respond should also be considered. Hard choices will be required to prioritise competing demands but these can only validly be made when needs for improvement and the feasibility and success of change are adequately assessed.

REFERENCES

Ainscow, M., Hargreaves, D. H., Hopkins, D., Balshaw, M. and Black-Hawkins, K. (1994) *Mapping Change in Schools: The Cambridge Manual of Research Techniques*, Cambridge Institute of Education, Cambridge.

Beckett, J. T. (1982) Assessment of departmental performance in examinations, *Educational Management and Administration*, Vol. 10 no. 3, 233–6.

Beckhard, R. and Harris, R. T. (1987) *Organizational Transitions: Managing Complex Change* (2nd edn), Addison-Wesley, Reading, MA.

Bliss, J. R., Firestone, W. A. and Richards, C. E. (eds) (1991) *Rethinking Effective Schools Research and Practice*, Prentice Hall, Englewood Cliffs, NJ.

Chin, R. and Benne, K. D. (1976) General Strategies for Effecting Changes in Human Systems in Bennis, W. G., Benne, K. D., Chin, R., and Corey, E. (eds) *The Planning of Change*, Holt, Rinehart & Winston, New York.

Dearing (1993) *The National Curriculum and its Assessment: Final Report* (Chairman Sir Ron Dearing), SCAA, London.

DFE (1995a) *Value Added in Education: A Briefing Paper from the Department for Education*, DFE, London.

DFE (1995b) *GCSE to GCE A/AS Value Added: Briefing for Schools and Colleges*, DFE, London.

DFE/OFSTED/BIS (1995) *Governing Bodies and Effective Schools*, DFE, London.

DFEE (1995a) *Benchmarking School Budgets: sharing good practice*, DFEE, London.

DFEE (1995b) *The Improvement of Failing Schools: UK Policy and Practice 1993–1995* (OECD UK Seminar November 1995), DFEE/OFSTED, London.

DFEE (1996a) *School Teachers' Pay and Conditions of Employment 1996* (Circular 4/96), DFEE, London.

DFEE (1996b) *Setting Targets to Raise Standards: A Survey of Good Practice*, DFEE/OFSTED, London.

DFEE (1996c) *Shephard to legislate to raise school standards* (Press release 309/96), DFEE, London.

DFEE (1996d) *Grants for Educational Support and Training* (Circular 13/96), DFEE, London.

Earley, P., Fidler B. and Ouston, J. (eds) (1996) *Improvement through Inspection? Complementary Approaches to School Development*, David Fulton, London.

Elliott J (1996) School effectiveness research and its critics: alternative visions of schooling, *Cambridge Journal of Education*, Vol. 26 no. 2, 199–224

Everard, K. B. and Morris, G (1996) *Effective School Management* (3rd edn), Paul Chapman Publishing, London.

Fidler B (1992) Performance related pay in local government and public sector organisations: lessons for schools and colleges in Fidler, B. and Cooper, R. (eds) *Staff Appraisal and Staff Management in Schools and Colleges: A Guide to Implementation*, Longman, Harlow.

Fidler, B. (1993) How to Measure Value-added in Schools? Paper presented at the BEMAS Annual Conference, Heriot-Watt University, Edinburgh, September 1993.

Fidler, B. and Bowles, G. with Hart, J. (1991) *Planning Your School's Strategy: ELMS Workbook*, Longman, Harlow.

Fidler, B. and Cooper, R. (eds) (1992) *Staff Appraisal and Staff Management in Schools and Colleges: A Guide to Implementation*, Longman, Harlow.

Fidler, B. with Edwards, M., Evans, B., Mann, P. and Thomas, P. (1996) *Strategic Planning for School Improvement*, Pitman, London.

Fidler, B. and Morris, R. (1996) The LEA contribution to school improvement. Paper presented to the BEMAS Annual Conference, Coventry, September 1996.

Fitz-Gibbon, C. T. (1991) Multilevel Modelling in an Indicator System in Raudenbusch, S. and Willms, J. D. (eds) *Schools, Classrooms and Pupils: International Studies of Schooling from a Multilevel Perspective*, Academic Press, San Diego, CA.

Fullan, M. (1993) *Change Forces: Probing the depths of educational reform*, Falmer, London.

Glogg, M. and Fidler, B. (1990) Using Examination Results as Performance Indicators, *Education Management and Administration*, Vol. 18 no. 4, 38–48.

Good, T. L. and Brophy, J. E. (1986) School Effects in Wittrock M. C. (ed.) *Handbook of Research on Teaching*, Third Edition, Macmillan, New York.

Hall, G. E. and Hord, S. M. (1987) *Change in Schools: Facilitating the process*, State University of New York Press, New York.

Hargreaves, D. H. and Hopkins, D. (1991) *The Empowered School: The Management and Practice of Development Planning*, Cassell, London.

Hargreaves, D. and Hopkins, D. (eds) (1994) *Development Planning for School Improvement*, Cassell, London.

Joyce, B. and Showers, B. (1988) *Student Achievement through Staff Development*, Longman, New York.

Kotler, P. and Andreasen, A. R. (1987) *Strategic Marketing for Nonprofit Organizations* (3rd edn), Prentice-Hall, Englewood Cliffs, NJ.

Lawton, D. (1992) *Education and Politics in the 1990s: Conflict or Consensus?*, Falmer Press, Lewes.

Lewin, K. (1951) *Field Theory in Social Science*, Harper & Row, New York.

LGMB (1994) Performance Benchmarking for Schools: Commentary by the National Employers' Organisation for School Teachers, Local Government Management Board, London.

McMahon, A., Bolam, R., Abbott, R. and Holly, P. (1984) *Guidelines for Review and Internal Development in Schools (GRIDS): Primary and Secondary Handbooks*, Longman for Schools Council, York.

Miles, M. B. and Ekholm, M. (1985) What is School Improvement? in Van Velzen, W. G., Miles, M. B., Ekholm, M., Hameyer, U. and Robin, D. (eds) *Making School Improvement Work: A Conceptual Guide to Practice*, ACCO, Leuven, Belgium.

OFSTED (1994) *Improving Schools*, HMSO, London.

OFSTED (1995a) *The OFSTED Framework: Framework for the Inspections of Nursery, Primary, Secondary and Special Schools*, HMSO, London.

OFSTED (1995b) *Planning Improvement: Schools' post-inspection action plans*, HMSO, London.

Ouston, J. (1996) School effectiveness, school improvement and good schools in Earley, P., Fidler, B. and Ouston, J. (eds) *Improvement through inspection: complementary approaches to school development*, David Fulton, London.

Ouston, J., Earley, P. and Fidler, B. (1996) Secondary schools responses to OFSTED: Improvement through inspection? in Ouston, J., Earley, P. and Fidler, B. (eds) *OFSTED Inspections: The Early Experience*, David Fulton, London.

Purkey, S. C. and Smith, M. S. (1983) Effective schools: a review, *Elementary School Journal*, Vol. 83 no. 4, 427–52.

Reynolds, D. (1992) School Effectiveness and School Improvement: An Updated Review of the British Literature in Reynolds, D. and Cuttance, P. (eds) *School Effectiveness: Research, policy and practice*, Cassell, London.

Rudduck, J., Chaplain, R. and Wallace, G. (1995) *School Improvement: What can pupils tell us?*, David Fulton, London.

Sammons, P., Hillman, J. and Mortimore, P. (1995) *Key Characteristics of Effective Schools: A review of school effectiveness research*, OFSTED, London.

SCAA (1994) *Value-Added Performance Indicators for Schools*, Schools Curriculum and Assessment Authority, London.

Schein, E. H. (1992) *Organizational Culture and Leadership* (2nd edn), Jossey-Bass., San Francisco, CA.

TTA (1996) *The National Professional Qualification for Headship: Key Principles and Draft National Standards for New Headteachers*, Teacher Training Agency, London.

William, D. (1992) Value-added attacks: technical issues in reporting national curriculum assessments, *British Educational Research Journal*, Vol. 18 no. 4, 329–41.

Willms, J. D. (1992) *Monitoring School Performance: A Guide for Educators*, Falmer Press, Lewes.

PART 2

THE COMPONENTS OF MANAGEMENT

2.1

Managing with Governors

KATHRYN RILEY WITH DAVID ROWLES

Governor power in the 1990s has been described recently as, 'a mixed blessing'[1] (Thornton, 1993) and 'a brave experiment in local democracy'[2] (Millett, 1993). Yet, although governor powers have increased considerably over recent years, the school governing body is not a new invention. School managers of state schools – precursors of school governors – have been with us for over a century. The purpose of this chapter is to explore the changing role of the school governing body and the impact of its new powers and to ask the question: is the governing body 'experiment' of today working?

With the post-war establishment of secondary education, local education authorities (LEAs) were obliged under the terms of the 1944 Education Act to appoint school managers. However, there was no requirement to appoint managers for individual schools and by the mid-sixties only 21 out of 78 county boroughs had set up governing bodies for each school (Tomlinson, 1993).

For the two decades following the 1944 Act, the role of school managers was somewhat ill-defined. Governors were expected to provide 'oversight' of what was happening in schools and generally to be supportive. According to Gerald Grace (1995), during this period English schools acquired a relatively large degree of pedagogical and cultural autonomy from which headteachers, rather than school managers, benefited. The content of the curriculum, modes of assessment, teaching and learning became *de facto* the responsibility of teachers, and in particular of headteachers. Although some formal power was vested with the school managers, it was only in extreme circumstances that this was put to the test and questions about the autonomy of heads, or the authority of governors raised. William Tyndale Junior School in Islington, London, came to typify this power struggle (ILEA, 1976; Ellis, *et al.*, 1976).

The events at William Tyndale brought into sharp relief questions about the balance of power between local authorities, schools and school governors and created demands for a clearer settlement. The Taylor Committee of 1979 tried to reconcile those differences and create a clearer framework which Joan Sallis described as an equal partnership between parents, staff, teachers, the local authority and the local community designed to share decisions and promote good relationships (Sallis, 1988). However, findings from research conducted five years after Taylor suggested that school governing bodies had not achieved that partnership role and were uncertain of their purposes (Kogan, *et al.*, 1984).

> Many are diffident about their their ability to substitute their lay knowledge for that of professionals. While some governors think that they should ensure that the teachers account to a wider public than their own staff room, the terms of reference are shaped by the local political, community and school culture and the conventions established by key figures in and around the school

(Kogan, 1986, p. 68)

Over the last decade, the accretion of powers to governors in both local authority and grant-maintained schools in England and Wales has been considerable. With the introduction of local management of schools, the governing bodies of LEA schools have been given responsibility for school budgets, for the appointment of staff, for school action plans following an OFSTED inspection, and for the implementation of the National Curriculum and a range of policy initiatives. Governors of GM schools have been given even greater responsibilities and autonomy. These changes have taken place within a climate in which central government has sought to challenge professional control of education and move the locus of decision-making away from the producer to the consumer and from local authorities to schools within a quasi-market framework which emphasises individual rights and parental choice. The Thatcher revolution has served to move governing bodies into the front line of education reform and, ultimately, political debate. In relation to staffing alone (including appointments and dismissals), seven different Acts of Parliament (and a further seven sets of Regulations) now determine the legal parameters of what governors may do and how they may do it (Mahony, 1995).

As the expectations and demands on governors grow, so inevitably do the demands on their time. The plethora of legislative changes has resulted in a proliferation of sub-committees and meetings for governors. Governors are also struggling with increased financial pressures as budgets continue to shrink. The governing body of today has to have detailed policies on pay and conditions, and clear guidelines on sex abuse, drug abuse and child abuse. They must follow complex procedures on admissions and exclusions, although many rely on support and guidance from local education authorities to deal with these matters, and others such as personnel issues and appointments.

Unsurprisingly, the evidence is that school governorships are becoming harder to fill and where places are taken up, new governors are increasingly likely to be retired, or not in paid employment (Riley, Johnson and Rowles, 1995). A national survey of some 500 schools in England and Wales carried out in 1993–94 found that one-third of governing bodies had one or more vacancies and that recruitment difficulties were more likely to be found in inner city schools and those with a high percentage of pupils entitled to free school meals (Earley, 1994).

SEARCHING FOR A ROLE

For those governors who remain in post, there are difficulties and confusions about the nature of the role. In the wake of the Taylor Committee in 1979, as was suggested earlier, governors were uncertain about their role or legitimacy. A prescient research study on governors carried out in the mid 1980s proposed four ideal types of governing bodies:

- an accountable governing body which ensured that the school was operating within 'prescribed policies';
- an advisory governing body which aimed to legitimate the work of the professionals;
- a supportive governing body which promoted the interests of the school in the locality;
- and a mediating governing body which aimed to bring together different interests. ·

(Kogan, *et al.*, 1984)

In the late 1990s, whilst governors are largely clear about their legal functions, they are still struggling to find an appropriate role in school governance. The 'supporters' club model of the 1980s remains a favourite but governors increasingly find themselves caught between competing forces and struggling with issues of accountability and teacher professionalism. For example, a bitter dispute erupted in 1996, at Manton Junior School Nottinghamshire, when a governors' panel decided to reinstate a boy who had been suspended for alleged bullying. Staff vigorously opposed this decision and threatened industrial action. Governors responded by setting up individual tuition for the boy, a decision which in its turn upset a number of parents who then picketed the school in protest.

In examining the complexities of school governance, Peter Newsam (1994), at one time the Education Officer of the Inner London Education Authority has suggested that the roles of governors revolve around issues of management, support and accountability. Firstly, governors are directly a part of the school helping its management in particular ways such as through their responsibilities for finance. Secondly, they are semi-detached from the school, supporting it and its parents when this is required. Thirdly, they are the body to which the school is accountable. Whilst each of the three roles is consistent in its own right, it is in reconciling them that tensions emerge.

Looking at the first role, helping the school with its management, some governors have interpreted this role as being comparable to that of a Board of Directors: setting clear financial targets and parameters for the performance of the headteacher who acts as the chief executive of the organisation, a view endorsed by Rosemary Deem (1993). Others have chosen to take a less market-orientated approach, reinterpreting Government directives to fit in with the school's own ethos. In the example of 'St Catherine's' (see Case Study 1), the governors chose to broaden the policy on performance related pay for heads and deputies and to develop a model which recognised the contribution of a wider group of staff to the development of the school. The policy was designed specifically to minimise divisions within the school and to maximise collegiality within the management team.

In their second role as semi-detached supporters of the school and its parents, according to Newsam, governors are potentially a powerful group. 'When they act collectively, they can be an increasingly powerful and well-

---

Case Study 1: Performance Related Pay: The solution from St Catherine's School

Following the 1996/97 pay award to teachers, the Pay and Conditions Document made it clear that governing bodies of schools are obliged to review the salary levels of heads and deputies on a formal annual basis, taking into account as one factor their performance in post. In response to this, the governing body of St Catherine's, a large secondary school, decided to apply this annual performance related review not only to headteachers and deputies but to all members of the senior management team, using the 'excellence' points. In 1996/97, the governors made available some £7,000. The governors made the decision to extend the performance related pay principle to the whole senior management team because they were concerned that the system as constructed was divisive and that the leadership task of school improvement was one shared by the whole management team.

The governors were keen to make the whole process as transparent as possible and to tie it to the school's priorities. Governors therefore identified priority areas within the school development plan and drew up criteria for selection. Interested teachers were asked to submit written applications highlighting objectives, time scale and success criteria. Successful applicants would receive a short term enhancement of their salary (equivalent to a half or a full point) for the delivery of specific aspects of work. Applicants were interviewed and selected by the governors and the headteacher. The system is subject to regular monitoring and annual review.

The tasks taken on by successful applicants included:
☐ the development of strategies to target the underachievement of pupils;
☐ the development and administration of a Student Progress spreadsheet which would enable comprehensive tracking of individual pupil progress;
☐ improvement in the public display and information boards throughout the school;
☐ improvement in the efficiency of teaching, learning, pupil support and guidance for pupils who are bilingual or are speakers of English as another language;
☐ improved continuity and progression between Key Stages 2 and 3.

informed influence in support of the public education system' (Newsam, 1994, p i). There have been several instances when this potentiality has become a reality. In 1993, governors supported teacher opposition to national tests because of their sympathy with teachers and concerns about the excessive demands of the national curriculum. Hostility was fuelled by the perceived overbearing attitude of the then Secretary of State, John Patten. More recently, governors have been involved in national protests about the funding of education and local protests about LEA decisions on a number of issues, such as school reorganisation. Some governors, such as Frank Allen chair of governors of a Cambridge school, have argued that Government policies to push through contentious policies, whilst at the same time attempting to eliminate local accountability through LEAs, have in fact served to create a new local consensus and political force (Allen, 1995).

The third suggested role of the governors, the body to which the school is accountable, presents the greatest difficulties. If the governing body is engaged in managing and supporting schools, then tensions emerge about accountability: who is accountable to whom, and for what? Are staff accountable to the governing body for school performance, or is the governing body itself accountable to a wider community? If so, governors will need to find ways of enabling parents to engage in what is going on within the school and to locate the school within the broader community framework.

The issue of accountability becomes particularly complex in looking at curriculum issues. Governors are responsible in law for ensuring that the national curriculum is taught, although they have no say in the content, except for particular areas such as sex education. They are required to take a proactive role in the inspection process and in curriculum matters, no matter how successful the school is in delivering the curriculum. This irony was brought home in an OFSTED inspection report of a London secondary school which described the school in the following terms:

> This is a very good school; pupils achieve high standards of attainment in relation to their prior attainment. Its most significant strengths are its concerns for all aspects of its pupils development. There are no major weaknesses . . . Leadership is collegial . . . everyone feels appreciated and valued and therefore wants to do their best for the school . . . The finances are carefully managed and administered. The school achieves good value for money.

Despite this affirmation of the school's work, the report concluded by stating that the governors were insufficiently involved with the curriculum and the school was exhorted to ensure through its action plan that 'Governors fulfil their responsibilities in relation to the curriculum'.

This example illustrates some of the current difficulties and tensions. Are governors only fulfilling their responsibility if they are directly involved in the curriculum? If so, to what extent should governors be so 'involved', particularly given the other demands on their time? What does 'involvement' mean in reality? How and to what extent is their involvement different from that of the headteacher, or the local LEA adviser? What is the governors' role in the management of the school? What does 'oversight' mean in practice?

The tension here is that headteachers are responsible for the educational leadership, management and organisation of schools but governors can be called to account not only for any financial mismanagement in the school but for any failure of educational leadership. Giving headteachers and governors dual responsibility for the management of the school assumes high degrees of consensus on both policy and practice (Ribbins, 1989). Yet, according to a national study of some 1,200 schools in England and Wales carried out in 1996, only one in three headteachers believed that the increase in the powers of school governors had improved management and four out of five were of the view that the role of governors had to be more clearly defined (TES, 1996a).

The appointment of staff, and of headteachers in particular, has become one of the main levers that governors can use to influence the character and management style of a school. There is some evidence that governors' expectations of the personal and professional qualities necessary for headship are increasingly shaped by the belief that, since running a school is comparable to running a business enterprise, then what is required is 'hard-headed management' of the kind to which men are judged best suited (Riley, 1994a). There is also some evidence that governing bodies are tending to appoint long-serving internal applicants for the post of head over external candidates of a higher calibre (Mahony and Riley, 1995).

In general terms, however, recent delegation of local authority powers and responsibilities to school governors has strengthened the role and influence of headteachers rather than governors. The headteacher of the 1990s still remains the organisational leader of the school, as was his or her counterpart of the 1950s, 1960s and 1970s. However, the issues are complex and it is clear that headteacher authority is now tempered by governing bodies and there is much still to be negotiated in the relationship between heads and governors. The problems and tensions of those involved in the new relationship have been described in the following terms:

A *Governor's view*: 'We are a group of amateurs often faced with very tricky situations.'

An *LEA officer's view*: 'Most governors have neither the skills, the time, nor the willingness to carry out their intended role. Their interpretation of what makes a good school is superficial and not based on real knowledge.'

A *headteacher's view*: 'The role of the governor isn't clear cut. The governors, particularly the parent governors, tend to see quality in terms of individual teacher quality.'

A *councillor's view*: 'Governors are placed in an unfair situation in that they simply do not know enough to challenge management activities in schools.'

(Riley, Johnson and Rowles, 1995, p. 11)

Given the relative newness of governing bodies in their current form, it is unsurprising that school governance remains complex and fluid. Initial findings from a research study on school leadership suggest that headteachers give a high priority to developing effective working relationships with individual governors and with the governing body and that governors are very committed to their work. Some headteachers characterise this as taking a lead in enabling the governing body to carry out their responsibilities, through the provision of information and through shaping their role. Where governors are supportive, the head's leadership role is enhanced. However, the accountability relationship is complex and tensions emerge where governors and headteachers have conflicting views on value issues such as equal opportunities (Mahony and Riley, 1995).

Problems obviously exist on both sides – despite much evident goodwill. Ten of the nineteen headteachers in Gerald Grace's study on school leadership identified emergent or potential difficulties in the headteacher–governor relationship, particularly around the issue of management, as is typified by the following account:

> 'One of the problems that we faced was an initial, acute enthusiasm for power . . . [In reporting to the Governing Body] I used the expression "senior management think" i.e., the Head and the Deputies, and he [the chair of the governors] stopped me immediately and said, "We are the senior management now" '
>
> (Grace, 1995, pp. 81–82)

One governor's legitimate interest in a school's well-being and performance may be defined by the headteacher as an example of governor interference, or vice-versa. It is therefore unsurprising that LEAs have increasingly found themselves in the middle of some difficult struggles, with governors asking for support to help them deal with headteachers who are 'underperforming' (in their terms and possibly also those of OFSTED and the LEA) and headteachers complaining of the excessive demands of governors (Riley, Johnson and Rowles, 1995). Grant-maintained schools have faced another set of difficulties and in response to concerns that GM school governors have too much power, GM governing bodies will be required to appoint an independent member to appeals panels where headteachers face the threat of dismissal (TES, 1996b).

The role of the governors in quality has become one of the most sensitive areas for negotiation. Research evidence suggests that there is a reluctance for governors to visit classrooms or make judgements, although many are happy to act as classroom helpers (Riley, 1994b). In practice, many governors do not feel that they have the knowledge or confidence to probe about quality and standards, or to question recommendations from the senior team. How this quality issue is played out will vary from school to school. One chair of governors interviewed in a study of the role of the LEA in quality explained that she had become the chair because the previous incumbent had thought that governors should not have a say in quality. In her view, governors brought a useful external perception to what was happening in schools but it was difficult for governors to solidify their concerns without appearing critical. 'We fear to tread and don't ask searching questions since this could be taken as criticism of the professionals.' In her view, the backup of the LEA was absolutely critical if governors were to be effective. The local education authority could legitimate the role of the governors in quality.

At Firbank school (see Case Study 2), the governors decided that if they were to play a role in understanding quality in the school, they would need to make focused and systematic visits which were linked to the school's development plan. Governors and staff therefore worked together to see how this could be achieved but in doing this, they were keen to define their role. 'It is understood that the Governors are not appointed to check up on the professional work of the school, but to keep under review the way in which the school is working and developing.'

Case Study 2:   School Visits by Governors at Firbank School

The governors of Firbank primary school were concerned that school visits by governors were productive. Governors themselves lacked confidence in making the visits and teachers often felt threatened. It was important therefore that governors were clear what they were looking for when they made a visit and that the visits did not exist in a vacuum but were part of a planned programme that was linked to the development of the school overall.

Before the programme of visits took place, the governors and staff met for an evening to discuss how the visits would be structured and what would be the outcomes. The final school visits policy (which was agreed by staff and governors) included a procedure for the pre-visit, ways of formulating questions during the visits, recording and evaluating the visit, and the formal process of reporting back to the full governing body. It was also decided that the visits would be carried out as paired activities, once per term. Once the policy had been agreed, two governors agreed to pilot the policy and, following this, amendments were made to the policy statement which is as follows:

POLICY STATEMENT

Staff and Governors are agreed that the best way for Governors to get to know the school, staff and pupils, is by visiting. It is understood that the Governors are not appointed to check up on the professional work of the school, but to keep under review the way in which the school is working and developing.

An informal visit, or occasional invitations to social events, provide good opportunities to come into the school. However, there should be regular arrangements made for Governors to take part in a planned school visit where all concerned know the purpose and format of the visit. Therefore this policy will guide and inform visiting Governors and will be reviewed after each visit.

Guidelines

I The focus of the visit
The focus of the school visit will be decided at the governing body meeting. In almost all instances the focus of the visit will be linked to the School Development Plan. This gives Governors an opportunity to review an area of the curriculum that is a priority at the time.

2 Before the visit
The governors are appointed at the governors' meeting. Governors who are also members of staff also carry out the formal governors' visit. Two visiting governors are appointed to offer each other support and to reach a consensus for the report back to the full governing body meeting.

There is a formal Governors' visit each term which will last for a minimum of half a day.

The importance of releasing the Curriculum Coordinator to accompany the visiting Governors is acknowledged. Supply cover is offered for the coordinator on the morning or afternoon of the visit. This offers the Governors access to the coordinator's expertise to inform their visit and to answer any questions that arise related to the focus area during the visit. Also it enables the teaching staff to get on with teaching while Governors are in their classes.

If the coordinator has a class he/she will be observed in the teaching role as well, but will then be released to go to other classes with the visiting Governors.

If governors are to have some oversight of quality, they will need to be able to answer the question: 'How do you know if this is a good school?' and have an answer other than: 'The head tells us it is good,' 'We have a large waiting list for school places', or 'The teachers work hard.' As well as having some sense of the school on a day-to-day basis, governors will need clear and accessible information about the school's performance over time, and in relation to that of similar schools. Such factual information about examination performance and school attendance is, of course only a small part of the story and needs to be supplemented by other information which will give important messages about the school: What is it really like for pupils and teachers? Are the parents well informed and satisfied?

A number of examples exist of how such work can be undertaken. One of the most comprehensive approaches has been adopted by the Scottish Office Education Department, in partnership with Jordanhill College. Drawing on work on school effectiveness, the researchers identified twelve broad areas which provide indicators of the ethos of a school – the atmosphere, climate or tone that exists in a school. The twelve indicators were:

Pupil morale
Teacher morale
Teachers' job satisfaction
The physical environment
The learning context
Teacher–pupil relationships
Discipline
Equality and justice
Extra-curricular activities
School leadership
Information to parents
Parent–teacher consultation

Surveys were conducted with staff, pupils and parents to find out exactly what they thought about the school. That information was used to move the school forward. It provided governors with measures of the parental and community view of the school: a fundamental part of the quality role of the governing body (Scottish Office Education Department, 1994).

Whilst governors need to have a handle on quality, they can be overwhelmed by the enormity of the task. A 1996 broad sheet from the School Curriculum and Assessment Authority and the Centre for the Study of Comprehensive Schools entitled *Using Assessment Results*, exhorted primary governors to complete detailed worksheets on pupil assessment and school development planning, comparative school data analysis, and understanding 'value added' measures (SCAA/CSCS, 1996). On receiving the worksheet one sanguine governor commented, 'I've spent three years coming to grips with the budget and a range of policy initiatives. I'm now supposed to become an expert on evaluation and testing.'

TO THE FUTURE

The role of school governors will continue to evolve. Whether headteachers will continue to dominate governing bodies in the way that they have in the past remains to be seen (Deem, 1990). Relationships between headteachers and governors (and in particular the headteacher and chair of governors) is likely to range from an uneasy truce at one end of the spectrum, to a firm and consolidated school partnership at the other. Increased professional demands on heads to raise the performance of staff is likely to strengthen the leadership role of the headteacher. At the same time, the role of governors will be sharpened by the increased reliance which headteachers place on them to take on wider battles on the behalf of the school.

The investment of time and energy required to be a governor is also likely to have an impact on governors' expectations about the nature of their role. School governance takes time, on the part of both governors and headteachers, not just for meetings and school visits but for building good relationships which are only achieved by dint of a great deal of hard work and social and political skills. Governors who have invested that energy in the governing body are unlikely to think of themselves as being peripheral to the life of the school. In particular, once they have entered into the wider political field on issues such as testing, resources and school exclusions, they are unlikely to relinquish those interests in the school.

As things currently stand, contradictions are built into the role of head and governor, particularly in relation to school management and quality. There is no doubt that governors bring to many schools a relevant commercial or community perspective and are able to pose good questions to challenge the senior management team and staff. They are involved in working parties, they review standard assessment tasks and examination results, attend moderation meetings and are attached to particular curriculum areas within the school. In many instances, however, governors do not feel that they have the knowledge or confidence to question recommendations from the senior team, and in a small number of instances they may be overstepping the mark.

There is undoubtedly, a need for some reassessment – and possibly redefinition – of the expectation of governors. Governors are not in a position to judge whether the national curriculum is being fully covered or well taught. What they are in a position to say is whether the school is meeting the expectations of the children, parents and the local community. It is through this role that they will be able to exercise their 'oversight' of the school and broaden its accountability base.

Underpinning all the considerations to do with school governance are issues of power: who has it, how it is maintained, how it is used and for whose benefit. The issue of power is linked to that of accountability. The expansion of the role and responsibilities of governors has been couched in terms of making professionals accountable to consumers. In reality, formal mechanisms such as the governors' annual report to parents, have done little to widen the involvement or understanding of parents in the life or work of the school. If accountability is to have some meaning and governing bodies are to become the focus for such accountability, then school governance will need to be defined much more widely than the power settlement in the governing body.

Looking to the future, it seems likely that new accords will be reached and also new conflicts emerge. Headteachers will want a reaffirmation of their professional leadership but they may also grow to recognise, as many have already, that school leadership can be strengthened by meaningful partnership with the governing body. Governors and heads will undoubtedly work to stay together, 'holding on to nurse, for fear of meeting something worse'.

ACKNOWLEDGMENTS

Many thanks indeed to Professor Pat Mahony of the Roehampton Institute, for her helpful insights and analysis of the work of governing bodies.

NOTES

1 'We have given an awful lot of governors aspirations of grandeur. . . . I think that governor power is very much a mixed blessing.' Sir Malcolm Thornton MP, Chair Select Committee on Education (TES, 1993).

2 'There are 350,000 governors which is a brave experiment in local democracy . . . but there are serious issues emerging.' Anthea Millett, Chief Executive of the Teacher Training Agency (quoted in Riley, 1994, pp. 6–7)

REFERENCES:

Allen, F. (1995) The politicisation of school governors, *Management in Education*, Vol. 9, no. 3, June.

Deem, R, (1990) The reform of school governing bodies: the power of the consumer over the producer? in M. Flude and M. Hammer (eds.) *The Education Reform Act 1988: Its Origins and Implications*, Falmer Press, London.

Deem R. (1993) Educational reform and school governing bodies in England 1986–92: old dogs, new tricks or new dogs, new tricks?, in M. Preedy (ed.) *Managing the Effective School*, Paul Chapman Publishing, London.

Earley, P. (1994) *School Governing Bodies: Making Progress?* NFER, Slough.

Ellis, T., McWhirter, J., McColgan, D. and Haddow, B. (1976) *William Tyndale: the teachers' story*, Writers and Readers Publishing Cooperative, London.

Grace, G (1995) *School Leadership: Beyond Educational Management*, The Falmer Press, London.

Inner London Education Authority (1976) *Report of the William Tyndale Junior and Infant School Public Enquiry* (The Auld Report).

Kogan, M. (1986) *Education Accountability: An Analytical Overview*, Hutchinson, London.

Kogan, M., Johnson, D., Packwood, T. and Whitaker, T. (1984) *School Governing Bodies*, Heinemann Educational Books, London.

Mahony, P. (1995) School governance in England and Wales Working Paper, *Effective Leadership in a Time of Change*, The Roehampton Institute, London.

Mahony, P. and Riley, K. A. (1995) Headteachers in the English LEAs: Initial analysis of some themes and issues, Conference Report Edinburgh, March, *Effective Leadership in a Time of Change*, The Roehampton Institute, London.

Millett, A. (1993) Quality in Education: the Challenge for LEAs, Local Government Management Board Conference, June.

Newsam, P. (1994) Last bastion against the mighty state, Governors Guide, *Times Educational Supplement*, 30th September.

Ribbins, P. (1989) Managing secondary schools after the act: participation and partnership?, in R. Lowe (ed.) *The Changing Secondary School,* Falmer Press London.

Riley, K. A. (1994a) *Managing for Quality in An Uncertain Environment*, Local Government Management Board, Luton.

Riley, K. A. (1994b) Uncharted waters to quality, *Times Educational Supplement*, 23rd September.

Riley, K. A. (1994c) *Quality in Education: the Challenge for LEAs. Conference Report*, the Local Government Management Board, Luton.

Riley, K. A., Johnson , H. and Rowles, D. (1995) *Managing for Quality in an Uncertain Climate, Report II*, Local Government Management Board, Luton.

Sallis, J. (1988) Back to the future, The Governors's Guide, *Times Educational Supplement*, November.

School Curriculum and Assessment Authority and the Centre for the Study of Comprehensive Schools (1996) *Using Assessment Results*, May.

Scottish Office Education Department (1994) *School Boards*, Focus No. 3 'Ethos Indicators'.

The Times (1975) Teachers refuse to let managers into classrooms for inspection, 2nd July.

Thornton, M. (1993) Quoted by Nicholas Pyke, TES. Thornton lambastes policy, 8th October, p. 3.

Times Educational Supplement (1996a), September 6th, pp. 4–6.

Times Educational Supplement (1996b), September 6th, p. 15.

Tomlinson, J. (1993) *The Control of Education*, Cassell, London.

2.2

Strategic Management

BRIAN FIDLER

Strategic management is based on a strategic plan. This is a central plan for the whole school which coordinates all its other processes (Fidler, 1989). It thus provides a means of integrating the choices discussed in other parts of this book. This chapter describes the basis of strategic management, the opportunities it opens up and the choices which have to be made to engage successfully in it.

A strategy does not encompass all the activities of a school. It does, however, potentially involve them all. Much of the work of a school is on-going or maintenance. It involves sustaining current efforts. A strategy is concerned with new emphases. This may involve some new activities but almost certainly will involve changes to some existing activities to coordinate them and harness them for the new strategy as indicated in Figure 2.2.1.

Figure 2.2.1 A summary model showing the relationship between strategy and other management functions
Source: Fidler and Bowles, 1989, p. 273.

PLANNING DEVELOPMENT

Developing the whole school can be approached in a number of ways: 'creative muddling', school development planning or strategic management. Each can have its place but the argument of this chapter is that a comprehensive approach to strategic management has much to recommend it.

Creative muddling should not be underestimated if it is achieved by a brilliant strategic thinker in a small organisation which does not use a formal process of strategic management (Barry, 1986). However, it is clear that this approach is very vulnerable because it relies crucially on one individual and his or her continued success.

School development planning (Hargreaves and Hopkins, 1991) as it has evolved has acquired some of the attributes of strategic planning but has substantial differences (Fidler, 1996). The experience should be useful in implementing a strategic plan year by year. The biggest difference is in the analysis stage: the environment and a longer term perspective are much larger features in strategic management. Indeed there should be an overall rationale to a strategic plan which appears to be absent from the individual piecemeal developments which make up most SDPs in practice.

Even a school development plan is not mandatory at the present time. Research evidence shows that not all schools have even a nominal plan (MacGilchrist et al., 1995). Legislation does require some aspects of planning – a finance plan and a staff development plan. Development planning, providing the process has not become discredited in a school, is a useful precursor to strategic planning providing the essential differences are accepted and thinking is freed up for the more fundamental review which leads to strategy.

The present chapter takes for granted that a formal approach to strategy, as described here, is worthwhile for most schools. A discussion of alternative approaches to strategy, their limitations and of the whole concept of strategy as a planning tool is to be found elsewhere (Fidler et al., 1996).

WHAT IS STRATEGY?

Strategy is a rather elusive concept. It originates from usage in military situations where it serves to distinguish an overall plan of action from the tactics which are its constituent parts. It is the broad overall direction that an organisation wishes to move in. A prior, implicit strategy may be divined from the stream of decisions and actions which have been taken by members of an organisation in the past (Mintzberg, 1994). Whittington (1993) identifies a range of approaches to strategy of which the one proposed in this chapter recognises that organisations have multiple goals and that strategy can be planned and used explicitly and prospectively rather than only being apparent in hindsight. However, following Mintzberg (1994) the chapter firmly places emphasis on the strategic element of strategic planning rather than the precision of planning. As Kast and Rosenweig (1970) so aptly put it, the extreme choices are 'extinction by intuition' when there is no planning and 'paralysis by analysis' when planning is taken too far. Thus the approach suggested here is that a broad strategy should be identified first with more detailed planning only of the next stages with regular feedback (Hargreaves, 1995) and correction to ensure that the strategy is on course.

A strategy involves both a strategic aim and the plan for making progress towards that aim. Some typical school strategic aims are:

- raising pupil achievement (for all children or specific under-achieving groups);
- increasing the non-academic (sporting, cultural, artistic, charitable etc.) activities of children;
- increasing pupil numbers;
- increasing parental involvement;
- completing a merger successfully;
- increasing the age-range of the school e.g. by taking on a nursery;
- seeking to be distinctive, for example by taking on a curricular specialism in languages or technology, sport, arts.

A fundamental feature of strategy is that of trying to map out and follow a course of action which meets current demands on a school at the time. This involves trying to foresee, anticipate and influence future demands such that they can be incorporated into its plans. The alternative is to wait until the demands are acute and then react in a piecemeal way.

Thus there are a number of key features which identify a change as strategic. It involves the whole organisation in a holistic way and it is concerned with the longer term (five years or more). It takes account of pressures and influences from outside the school and takes steps to ensure that the planned activity will be sustainable over the medium term. A check-list which helps to decide on whether a change should be regarded as strategic is if it is concerned with:

(a) the whole scope of a school's activities;
(b) the school's long-term direction;
(c) matching its direction to environmental pressures;
(d) devising activities which are sustainable given the school's level of resources

STRATEGIC THINKING

Strategic thinking is a mental attitude which tries to keep long-term objectives constantly in mind and considers all short-term decisions in this long-term perspective. All good headteachers have probably always worked in this way implicitly. When all decisions are consistent with long-term aims and tactics are part of a greater strategy, this is strategic thinking. Strategic thinking and strategic management are complementary. Both are needed. To go through formal strategic management procedures periodically and to ignore such considerations in between would be partial and wasteful. Equally to have strategic thinking going on only in the head of one person is incomplete. Such thinking has not been tested against a formal process and is not easy to communicate to others without a more formal process to relate to. Thus successful strategy requires both a formal process of strategic management and also strategic thinking in the minds of senior managers.

Any selected strategy needs to be borne in mind continuously because decisions have to be made often very quickly on a whole range of issues and these need a guiding steer so that they are consistent and not contradictory. Some of these decisions may have strategic implications and these may not be obvious at first sight. Progress on implementing any strategy will not be straightforward or continuous. There may be reversals, there may be marking time, but this needs to be set in the context of making progress on a strategy in the longer term.

STRATEGIC DECISIONS

In any managerial situation decisions are constantly required on a whole realm of issues. These will vary in their importance and their urgency. As the diagram below shows strategic decisions can either come along in a non-urgent way, be considered and then made or they can be part of a stream of urgent decisions which have to be made very quickly. It is those decisions which have important long-term consequences which are strategic.

		immediacy	
		high	**low**
	high	STRATEGIC	STRATEGIC
importance	**low**	NON-STRATEGIC	NON-STRATEGIC

Figure 2.2.2 Importance and immediacy of strategic decisions

Clearly what is vital is to recognise a strategic decision which comes along as part of a string of other operational decisions which need to be made urgently.

Strategic decisions are those which once made have long-term consequences. They may restrict other possibilities or they may open up options in the future. The first requirement is to recognise a strategic decision and to examine its possible implications. The second, and no less difficult, requirement is to assess these implications and prioritise them against others.

Any decision concerned with new buildings is likely to be strategic, for once built they are expected to last for many years. Thus they may set the context for future decades. Another area of likely strategic decisions is in the appointment of staff. Again these are likely to be with the school for some time and either advance the strategy or represent an opportunity foregone. Other areas of potential strategic decisions are less easy to identify in general terms. Actions which involve alliances with other organisations or engender competition are likely to be strategic as they may start a chain of events with long-term consequences.

Decisions which involve creating a relationship with one or more other organisations are likely to have long lasting effects. Such relationships, whether alliances or competition, cannot be ended and returned to their pre-existing state on demand. Alliances will require actions for joint benefit. Competition once begun is likely to develop in a way which neither party can control. This means that the long-term consequences of a relationship with one or more other organisations are likely to be strategic.

STRATEGIC PLANNING

The major value of a strategy is be able to plan a long-term future for a school. This will attempt to take into account known facts and make some assumptions about influences both inside and outside the school. Compared to a school development plan it is longer term, holistic, outward-looking and pro-active (Fidler *et al.*, 1991; Fidler, 1996).

The value of a strategic plan is that:

- unexpected opportunities and threats can be dealt with in the context of a plan rather than in an *ad hoc* way;
- assumptions on which it is based are identified and hence can be monitored for any changes;
- priorities can be recognised and chosen rather than discovered by default;
- efforts can be synchronised and coordinated to produce a greater effect;
- a sense of purpose can be engendered for all staff;
- new staff are able to make more informed choices about whether they wish to join a particular school.

Such a plan needs to be regularly monitored both for the extent of progress and for any changes in the assumptions underlying it. However, a plan only comes to fruition when it is implemented. The strategic planning process encompasses analysis, choice, and the planning or operationalisation of how to implement the plan. These are elaborated in the next section.

STRATEGIC MANAGEMENT

Strategic management as its name implies involves managing in a strategic way. Thus it requires a continuing emphasis on strategy not a periodic one. The process should be a cyclic one whereby a strategy is devised for a five year period or so and then reappraised in a major way. However, an annual review is needed to check on progress and to see whether any of the assumptions on which the strategy is based have been undermined by, for example, unforeseen changes in government policy or local conditions.

The strategic management process includes planning, implementation and evaluation i.e.

analysis
choice
implementation
evaluation

These are outlined in more detail in subsequent sections of this chapter. Although the process may appear linear in that there is an implicit ordering to the activities, the thinking which guides the process is much more complex. At each stage there is an element of looking forward as well as backwards. If the element of looking forward is too strong it can condition the current stage. This would be undesirable since only the more obvious implications of a previous stage would be carried forward. On the other hand, to carry out each stage without thinking of the consequences for the next stage would be wasteful. For example at the analysis stage, more effort should be spent on obtaining information which is expected to be significant at the choice stage rather than gathering information indiscriminately. If the school is not attracting sufficient pupils for instance, the views of parents and potential parents will be very important even though they are not easy to obtain faithfully. However, the biggest danger is that previously referred to and that is to prejudge and hence narrow the range of choices. This is an extremely tricky tightrope to walk.

THE PRACTICE OF STRATEGIC MANAGEMENT

There are two separate and distinct aspects to strategic management (Figure 2.2.3):

(a) conceptual stages of strategic management (analysis/evaluation, choice, implementation);
(b) operational stages of making decisions about how to devise and implement strategy.

The first set of stages is likely to be similar in all schools. These stages should be identifiable although their extent, their relative priority and the way in which they are carried out may be different in each school.

Differences are likely to be most evident in their operation, or the way in which these stages are carried out, in each school. Factors such as size of school, the prevailing culture, and previous experience of development planning will all play a part in influencing the process. Decisions will be required about the practicalities of how to go about the process and this in turn will reveal institutional values. Decisions will be required about who will be involved, how, when and so on.

PROCESS ISSUES

It should be borne in mind that since strategy is the key to all other management processes, it will involve all staff in its implementation and it will require concerted effort over a number of years to accomplish. Thus at the very least all staff need to understand the strategy and its implications for their work.

Involvement of staff in developing a strategy can be justified either because it is regarded as a fundamental right of all staff regardless of its consequences, or because it leads to better decisions and implementation. The justification, in this latter case, rests on the assumption that staff will be committed to those decisions in which they have played a part. Commitment is the desired end and involvement a means of achieving this end. However, involvement is at most a necessary condition for commitment and certainly not a sufficient condition. For example, staff can become committed through the visionary symbolism of a charismatic leader.

A related advantage of a fairly close involvement of staff with the formulation of strategy is that this will increase their understanding of its rationale and major implications. This should facilitate implementation of the strategy. Since the formulation of strategy takes time it is not likely that involving all staff in all stages will be a good use of time and thus there is a trade-off between the dangers of lack of involvement and the distraction from other vital activities which total involvement would imply.

Over and above these *a priori* considerations, it should be clear that since strategy is such a fundamental part of a school's operations its creation must be integrated and consistent with the way in which other school processes are carried out, and not treated as a separate, bolt-on activity. Thus it will need to be either consistent with the existing culture of the school or seen as an attempt to change aspects of the existing culture.

Thinking here can become very convoluted. Process decisions about how to create strategy are taken before the choice of a strategy is made. The choice of a strategy may indicate that the culture of the school may need to change in order for the school to have a successful future. There is an obvious logical inconsistency here. Those who advocate using the creation of strategy as a way of changing the culture of an organisation need to take account of this dilemma.

Elsewhere (Fidler *et al.*, 1991; Fidler *et al.*, 1996) general patterns of involvement are discussed more fully. A particular issue for larger schools is how to involve constituent parts of the school such as key stage teams, departments, and pastoral teams. Eventually development plans for these groups will need to be consistent with the whole school strategic plan. However whole school plans should be more than the sum of these constituent plans. Two contrasting approaches to this dilemma are

a) grand design (top-down)
b) reconciling the sum of the parts (bottom-up)

The first involves the formulation of a whole school strategic plan and a subsequent exercise of developing group plans within the context of this whole school plan. Indeed it is almost inevitable that the whole school plan can only be fulfilled if individuals and groups within the school play their part. For example if raising pupil achievement is the strategic aim, this can only be accomplished if teachers, individually and collectively, contribute. Although a polarisation between top-down and bottom-up modes of operation can be formulated fairly starkly, in reality, if there is a history of departmental planning and individual staff appraisal a lot of information about the wishes of groups and individuals will be known, albeit as partial and incomplete information.

The second approach tries to incorporate developments proposed by sub-groups within the school into the process in a formal way. This is likely to be more complex and take greater time since a successful plan will require a great deal of reconciling of possibly conflicting proposals from different sub-groups. Time will be required to assess conflicts, to reduce conflicting priorities and to arrive at a meaningful whole school plan. This will require a large investment of time in bargaining and negotiation such that all are committed to the resultant plan and not disenchanted by a failure to have their priorities incorporated.

It should be remembered, particularly in secondary schools, that although individual staff and groups may have particular priorities which do not conflict for them personally, the effect on children of competing priorities may be self-defeating. Any examples of individual subject departments seeking to give their subject a higher profile will be of this kind. And after all the strategy is there to facilitate the education of children and not as a power contest for staff. Thus there is a balance between involvement and encouraging political and micro-political rivalry. Accounts of involvement in the management literature and collaboration in the educational literature usually assume that participants cooperate in the best interests of the organisation. There is, however, no reason to believe that individual interests will always be subordinated to group interests or group interests to whole school interests. Studies of micropolitics identify a range of ways in which individuals seek to use power and influence to promote their own interests (Hoyle, 1986; Ball, 1987).

MODEL OF STRATEGIC MANAGEMENT

Figure 2.2.3 shows a model which incorporates the process decisions involved in carrying out strategic management and also the conceptual stages of strategic management.

Process decisions

The process decisions concern who in the school takes part in the various stages of planning and how these are carried out. The decisions at the three stages involve the following:

1. Getting started – decide how to organise
This stage involves the fundamental decisions about the shape of the whole operation of forming and implementing strategy. The major decisions are concerned with forming strategy such as:

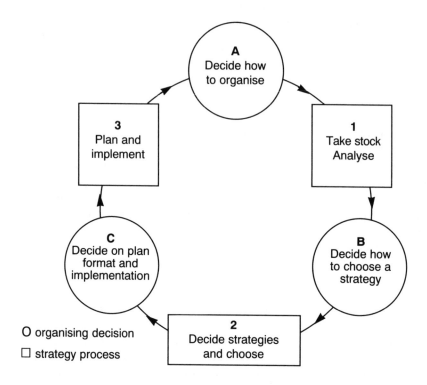

Figure 2.2.3   A basic model of strategic management
(*Source*: adapted from Fidler, 1996 and Fidler et *al.*, 1996)

who takes part?
at what stages?
what evidence is collected?
how long will each stage take?

2.   Choosing – decide how to choose
When evidence has been collected in the analysis of the current strategic standing of the school, decisions are needed about the procedures by which a choice
of strategy will be made such as:

how will accumulated evidence be presented?
how will a positive vision be incorporated?
how will decisions be made?

3.   Plan – decide on plan format and how to implement
Having chosen strategic aims with some broad understanding of how these
will be pursued, rolling plans are required to implement the strategy. This stage

involves decisions about the format of plans and their operation such as:

what will the final format of the plan look like?
how will it be implemented?
who will be responsible for what?
who will monitor and coordinate progress?
when will results be evaluated, how and by whom?

Conceptual strategic stages

1 Analysis or taking stock

This is the stage for taking stock of the present situation and trying to foresee future external influences on the school. It is more conveniently divided into three components (Johnson and Scholes, 1993):

a) The environment Strategy places great emphasis on the organisation keeping in step with its environment. The intention is that there should not only be a fit at the present time but that as far as possible the two should remain in step. Thus an analysis of environmental influences should not only examine the current local and national influences on the school but should also try to anticipate future influences. For example, fewer children in the traditional catchment area and greater emphasis on test results in basic subjects.

For some local sources of external influence on a school there may also be a possibility of the school trying to be proactive and influencing factors in the environment. For example, how the school is currently viewed by its neighbourhood can be influenced by promotional activities of the school. However in the main, the scope for changing the environment may not be great and so the major activity should be recognising current, and anticipating likely growing, influences on the school. These can be classified as opportunities and threats for any future strategy depending on whether they are positive or negative.

For a school one of the most fundamental items of intelligence is future pupil numbers. This involves discovering the number of children in the school's area and assessing future trends. This will also involve acquiring intelligence on the activities of neighbouring schools.

Trying to anticipate future influences should reduce the possibility that any strategy is abandoned half completed because some external imperative has intervened. The scanning of the current environment will be partly based on hard (often numerical) data and partly a product of 'soft' data. In strategic decisions soft data is likely to be particularly valuable. For example, inferences about what other schools are likely to do in the future may be based on a combination of hearsay, chance conversations and knowledge of the people involved. Such soft information will be particularly partial and judgemental. Although more difficult to interpret than more factual material it is likely to prove more valuable, particularly for making informed guesses about the future. Such intelligence gathering, whilst it should never be expected to be wholly an accurate prediction of the future, should improve with experience.

The local environment includes any future clients of the school. Hence what would be acceptable to this group should be investigated as far as possible. As prospective parents are shown round, the questions they ask and the comments they make provide 'soft' information on such matters.

b) Internal resources   Internal resources are those features of the school which can be used to achieve a strategy. These include not only tangible features such as buildings, staff and finance but also such intangibles as reputation. The analysis should cover not only the presence of such resources but also how they are being used or exploited. Thus a school might have untapped potential in, for example, its buildings or staff. It might have further potential in its relationships with local industry or other potential funders.

A realistic assessment of possibilities needs to be made as this will form part of any evaluation of possible future strategies. It is essential not only that all possibilities are assessed but also that over-optimistic assumptions are not made since this would place the viability of any strategy in jeopardy. Strengths and weakness of the school's current operations should emerge from the resource audit.

Surveys of the opinions of staff, parents and pupils will provide data on strengths and weaknesses as perceived by these groups. Such information is essential to the formation of strategy. These opinions will be based upon perceptions of strengths and weaknesses but a more objective analysis may refute the factual basis of such judgements. Cases of this kind throw up issues for the way in which the school promotes itself either to reverse misapprehensions or to highlight unrecognised strengths.

The results of the analysis of environmental factors and internal resources can be embodied in a SWOT (strengths, weaknesses, opportunities, threats) analysis. The figure below gives a summary of actions indicated by the findings:

| | | internal resources | |
		strengths	**weaknesses**
environment	**opportunities**	maximise	remediate/ ignore
	threats	deflect/reduce	minimise

Figure 2.2.4   Actions indicated by a SWOT analysis

This recognises that a combination of an external opportunity and an internal strength represents a growth point whilst an external threat and an internal weakness needs to be reduced. The possibilities offered by the other two positions are less clear. Where opportunities coincide with internal weaknesses it may be worthwhile to seek to deal with the weaknesses or ignore the opportunity. Where there are external threats to internal strengths it may be worthwhile to seek to deflect the threats or allow the internal strengths to decline.

c) School culture The dimension which is missing from a conventional SWOT analysis and which immeasurably reduces its value is an assessment of the prevailing culture in an organisation (Whittington, 1993). As we have seen in Chapter 1.3, culture is a powerful influence on the thinking of school staff and more importantly it is largely an unrecognised one. It has a powerful conditioning effect. Unless cultural influences are made explicit, they may lead to strategic possibilities being pre-judged with the rejection of those that are not consistent with the prevailing culture. This will be particularly disastrous in a failing or near failing school. A failure to question current cultural assumptions condemns the school to more of the same. For some schools, external help may be needed to assist staff to examine a very dominant culture (see Case Study 4 on p. 100).

The effect of the prevailing culture will be self-reinforcing unless attempts are made to stand back and recognise the implicit values and assumptions which are operating. The observations of new members of staff and outsiders are particularly valuable in pointing out actions, habits and ways of seeing the world which are specific to that school. Trying to recognise how the school would appear to a new member of staff or a new pupil helps to bring to the surface those cultural assumptions.

A vital element in assessing the viability of any new strategy will be to compare the values implicit in it with the prevailing values in the school. This will indicate the difficulty of getting the strategy accepted and also the difficulty of implementing it. This represents a key choice: should an attempt be made to change the culture of the school and who should decide this?

The three aspects of strategic analysis are summarised in Figure 2.2.5.

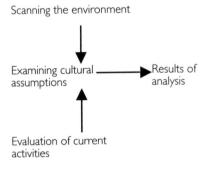

Figure 2.2.5 Summary model of strategic analysis

2   Choice

Having carried out an analysis indicating the school's current strategic position, the next stage is to formulate possible strategies for the next five years or
so. These could be based only on remediating those aspects of current performance which are not reaching acceptable standards, but to do this would be to
miss an opportunity to inject a creative, proactive element into the process. As
Figure 2.2.6 below indicates, strategy should be formed by a combination of
analysis, which is essentially backward-looking, and vision, which is essentially forward-looking.

Figure 2.2.6   Strategy resulting from analysis and vision

A strategy has to deal with issues revealed by the SWOT analysis. These may
be pressing, in which case most other options are precluded. Where pupil
numbers are falling then such considerations have to take precedence because
of their strategic importance. There are fewer options in a school which is
perceived as poor by potential parents (see Case Study 3). A likely order of
precedence in terms of pressing problems may be:

pupil numbers
pupil behaviour
academic achievement of pupils

When these primary issues have been satisfactorily resolved there are likely to
be many more possibilities for future strategies. This means that the choice
stage will take longer, both because there is less urgency and because there are
more options to consider. There will always be a wish to further improve
pupils' performance but if the gains from this are likely to be small because
pupils are working near their assessed potential there may be other possibilities
in terms of giving a broad and balanced educational experience which may
offer a much greater impact, for example through challenging outdoor group
activities.

Case Study 3: What next?

A new headteacher was appointed to a primary school. The school could accommodate 300 pupils but there were only a little over 100. The strategic goal was to increase pupil numbers. The strategy involved both improving work within the school and also improving parental and community perceptions of the school. There were some inadequacies in the teaching methods but another factor was that the school had acquired a poor reputation. Parents in the former catchment area became increasingly interested in surrounding schools. This led these schools to promote themselves in the area

The school strategy involved a review of internal processes. This led to some changes to existing operations such as team teaching and an integrated day. But the other aspect of the strategy was to seek parental views on the school and as a result of this to begin to promote the school in the local community. One aspect of this was to invite parents and potential parents into school to see classrooms for themselves rather than rely on neighbourhood gossip.

Pupil numbers began to rise. However, an emerging perception of visiting parents was that the school was achieving great progress with special needs children. This is beginning to be known in the neighbourhood.

The previous strategy has now virtually been accomplished in a five year period. Two very different strategies for the future present themselves. On the one hand, the school could seek to acquire a reputation for special needs and attract such children in greater numbers. On the other hand, the school could try to attract a more balanced intake. Strategic objectives now are more numerous and more difficult to decide upon.

Some possibilities for secondary emphases when the primary issues have been dealt with are:

academic curricular emphases e.g. technology, languages, sport, creative arts
creative use of IT
music performances
art displays
drama performances
sport performances
charitable work
varied work experience
preparation for adult life

Although the primary and secondary issues are presented as independent ideas, in practice they may be interrelated. Enrolment below expectations may be due to poor behaviour and poor results. Poor behaviour may be partially due to an unstimulating curriculum and poor teaching. Thus they are presented individually and in an order of precedence for heuristic reasons rather than

Case Study 4:   A strategic dilemma

A prestigious boys grammar school has a well established set of traditions. Its exam results are exemplary and places at the school are contested. Staff are highly qualified and long-serving. Many were pupils of the school. Another local grammar school begins to offer a wider choice of sports. Some able boys are attracted to this school by the prospect of football rather than rugby during the winter season.

The dilemma is clear. If the traditional school does not change it risks the prospect of a trickle of able pupils turning into a torrent who go elsewhere. In time this may depress its examination record. However, part of the attractions of this school are its traditions. If rugby, which is seen as a cornerstone of these traditions, is changed what else is sacrosanct? Such symbolism is likely to be more potent because of the long-serving and traditionally minded staff.

Does the school stick to its traditional sports and risk losing able pupils or does it change its traditions in order to appeal to the preferences of eleven year olds and undermine staff and parental expectations of stability?

suggesting that they should, or could, be tackled linearly.

Forming a strategy is an opportunity to make a move forward towards a vision of an improved future. Substantial steps towards this vision should be possible – it should not be some idealised picture that is unachievable. For example, a vision could be of a much greater degree of self-selected learning by pupils in the future, whilst its embodiment in a strategy could be something like a multimedia centre bringing together library and computing resources leading to a greater degree of directed self-study by older pupils. The possibilities are endless and will need to suit each school and its situation in its current state of development. But it is the opportunity to skip steps in incremental development and make a bold and imaginative leap forward.

Other means of formulating strategies are by considering strategic issues (Bryson, 1988) and by identifying a single goal (Fidler *et al.*, 1996). The strategy may be refined by using cost–benefit analysis to examine alternative ways of achieving the same objectives as the strategy requires.

3   Evaluating choices

To make a valid choice a number of possible strategic options should be formulated. These could be radically different or they could be alternative emphases on a common theme. There are three tests which should be used to choose between options and to apply particularly stringently to the preferred option. These are (Johnson and Scholes, 1993):

suitability
feasibility
acceptability

Suitability involves assessing the proposed strategy for the extent to which it deals satisfactorily with issues raised by the SWOT analysis. In particular are any issues raised by clients – parents and children – being addressed (and being seen to be addressed) sufficiently rigorously? The test of feasibility asks whether the strategy has a good chance of being put into practice. Are the assumptions on which it is based sound, has implementation been subjected to detailed logistical analysis and contingencies considered? Finally, the test of acceptability asks whether groups who play a part in the decision to accept the strategy and, also, those groups who will be required to implement the strategy will find the strategy acceptable. Much preparation will be required to make more radical strategies acceptable.

Strategic implementation

Having chosen a strategy, the final step is to implement it. Implementation should not be considered for the first time after a strategy has been chosen but should have been considered in detail at the formulation stage and been checked at the evaluation stage for its viability. Thus problems involved in implementation – for example resources, cooperation of others, staff preparation – should have been largely foreseen.

A strategic plan is likely to have a number of sub-plans (Fidler et al., 1991, 1996). The most fundamental is that concerned with the school's organisational structure and decision making. This identifies any changes to the school's customary ways of working which will be necessary – how are we going to work together to achieve our strategy? The main plan will concern the curricular changes which the strategy incorporates – what is the contribution to children's learning? There are then subordinate plans for:

- staffing (how will staff be recruited and trained to carry out the strategy?);
- finance (how will resources be deployed?);
- marketing (how will support be built up?).

There should also be plans for constituent units within the school which are consistent with the overall plan for the school. If a strategy is to be effective it should influence the day-to-day work of teachers and other staff. Thus it should influence the plans for development of sections of the school and the development plans of staff.

MANAGEMENT OF CHANGE

All the precepts involved in managing a change (Chapter 1.4) should apply to implementing a strategy. It can be expected to have implications for the work of staff and their development and training and future appointments. It can be expected to have implications for spending patterns and finance. It can also be expected to have implications for the school's organisational structure (Fidler

1992, 1997). This covers the formal allocation of roles and responsibilities, the way decisions are made and the systems and procedures in an organisation.

In addition because the strategy will involve the whole school, is long term and responds to environmental pressures, it may involve large scale, and even radical, change. It can be expected to have an impact on the culture of the organisation. Organisational culture has been discussed in Chapter 1.3 and also earlier in this chapter. However, there are some choices which strategy throws up which deserve a brief discussion here in the context of planning change.

It is not difficult to identify situations where a need for a change in a school's culture may be indicated. One such example is where a secondary school finds itself in a developing competitive situation initiated by other schools when it has previously eschewed competition. Another example is where a primary school which has previously had very little parental involvement, and a strong element of professional initiative, wishes to respond to demands from parents for more involvement.

One approach is to regard the values and assumptions which underlie culture as the guiding stars in the formation of strategy. This essentially takes culture as a given. Inevitably any change will affect the culture but this would not be the prime aim of the change. Dilemmas are posed here because it may be difficult to reconcile an unchanged culture with a successful future for the school.

An alternative approach recognises that a need to attempt to change the organisational culture may become apparent as a result of the analysis stage of strategic planning. Dilemmas then concern an ability to bring about change, the morality of attempting to do so and a consideration of who should be involved in any decision to change.

A third approach uses the planning of strategy as a means of changing the culture of the organisation. The ways in which staff work together on the stages of strategic planning and the way decisions are made can have such an impact. All the dilemmas about changing culture apply here also and in addition there is the conundrum which has been posed earlier of beginning to change culture before the cultural assumptions underlying a successful strategy have been examined.

All the foregoing applies irrespective of whether the view is taken that culture can be managed and changed or only influenced.

CONCLUDING DISCUSSION

Strategic planning offers schools the opportunity to seize the initiative in their own development. At the least it should help ensure a more secure future. However, it can do far more. It offers a school the possibility of fulfilling the wishes of its stakeholders whilst taking account of external opportunities and constraints. There are two principal limitations – one situational and one conceptual.

The situational limitation is that the process has to recognise and accept the current strategic position of the school. This will signal requirements for the future and also impose limitations on what is possible in a five year period. The related conceptual limitation, particularly for those who come to strategy for the first time, is of having sufficient confidence in the process and being able to judge what is possible. On the one hand there will be an inevitable temptation to play safe and not attempt too much and to move slowly in small incremental steps. On the other hand expectations can be built up by the process which are unrealistic.

Experience from schools (Fidler et al., 1996) shows that the early stages of the process take a great deal of time if they are to involve and touch all staff. A very fine judgement is required to keep the process moving but not to move too quickly so that those who are not so immersed in the ideas are left behind. A longer term perspective is required by which the first application of these ideas is regarded as a formative learning experience by which judgements can be refined for the next time they are used.

REFERENCES

Ball, S. (1987) *Micropolitics of the School: Towards a theory of school organization*, Methuen, London.

Barry, B. W. (1986) *Strategic Planning Workbook for Nonprofit Organizations*, Amherst H Wilder Foundation, St Paul, MN.

Bryson, J. M. (1988) *Strategic Planning for Public and Nonprofit Organizations: A Guide to Strengthening and Sustaining Organizational Achievement*, Jossey-Bass, San Fransisco, CA.

Fidler, B. (1989) Strategic Management in Schools in Fidler, B. & Bowles, G. (eds) *Effective Local Management of Schools*, Longman, Harlow, Essex.

Fidler, B. (1992) Job Descriptions and Organisational Structure in Fidler, B. & Cooper, R. (eds) *Staff Appraisal and Staff Management in Schools and Colleges: A Guide to Implementation*, Longman, Harlow, Essex.

Fidler, B. (1996) School Development Planning and Strategic Planning for School Improvement in Earley, P., Fidler, B. & Ouston, J. (eds) *Improvement Through Inspections?: Complementary Approaches to School Development*, David Fulton, London.

Fidler, B. (1997) Organisational Structure and Organisational Effectiveness in Harris, A., Bennett, N., & Preedy, M. (eds) *Organisational Effectiveness and Improvement in Education*, Open University Press, Buckingham.

Fidler, B. & Bowles, G. with Hart, J. (1991) *ELMS Workbook: Planning Your School's Strategy*, Longman, Harlow, Essex.

Fidler, B. with Edwards, M., Evans, B., Mann, P. and Thomas, P. (1996) *Strategic Planning for School Improvement*, Pitman, London.

Hargreaves, D. H. (1995) Self-managing schools and development planning – chaos or control?, *School Organisation*, Vol. 15 no. 3, pp. 215–27.

Hargreaves, D. H. & Hopkins, D. (1991) *The Empowered School: The Management and Practice of Development Planning*, Cassell, London.

Hoyle, E. (1986) *The Politics of School Management*, Hodder & Stoughton, London.

Johnson, G. & Scholes, K. (1993) *Exploring Corporate Strategy* (3rd edition), Prentice Hall, Hemel Hempstead, Herts.

Kast, F. E. & Rosenweig, J. E. (1970) *Organization and Management: A Systems Approach*, McGraw-Hill, New York.

MacGilchrist, B., Mortimore, P., Savage, J. & Beresford, C. (1995) *Planning Matters: The Impact of Development Planning in Primary Schools*, Paul Chapman Publishing, London.

Mintzberg, H. (1994) *The Rise and Fall of Strategic Planning*, Prentice Hall, Hemel Hempstead, Herts.

Whittington, R. (1993) *What is Strategy and Does It Matter?*, Routledge, London.

2.3

Managing the Curriculum and Assessment

HUGH BUSHER AND KEITH HODGKINSON

THE CURRICULUM: A CONTESTED AREA

A school's curriculum is made up of far more than the academic subjects taught. What is incorporated depends on what values and beliefs powerful people hold about how society ought to be structured. The national curriculum (NC) in the UK acknowledges this when it asserts that a school's curriculum will be adequate if it is broad and balanced and promotes 'the spiritual, moral, cultural, mental and physical development of pupils at the school and of society; and prepares pupils for the opportunities, responsibilities and developments of adult life' (Education Reform Act, 1988, Section 1, paragraph 2).

Lawton (1989) points out that a curriculum acts as a vehicle for transmitting cultural messages in a society, such as how children can be inducted into society in preparation for their future adult economic and social roles. As different groups of people in society hold different views about what should be taught through the school curriculum, who controls the structure, content and values of the curriculum can determine what views of society and of its future development are taught to pupils. For this reason the curriculum has become a strongly contested arena between national and local government, lay people and professionals, since the publication of the first Black Papers in Education in 1969. For example, requirements by the UK central government in 1994 that school assemblies and religious instruction should be of a mainly Christian character represent value choices by influential people in the Conservative Party about what is the dominant culture of the UK and, so, what pupils should learn. Not surprisingly some minority religious and ethnic groups have objected to such choices especially in those areas where they form a majority of the local population.

In 1988 the UK central government established a national curriculum to ensure that all children had the same opportunities at school and parents knew what educational opportunities to expect from schools. It defined subject syllabuses in great detail, leaving teachers with only the more technical tasks of implementing them. Particularly in primary schools this deprived teachers of their role of curriculum construction within the contexts of individual schools. Chitty (1993, p. 8) claimed the main purpose of the NC was social engineering:

to fit the school curriculum more closely to central government's views of the needs of the national economy; and to make teachers more accountable to a lay constituency through school governors. Not until the Dearing Review (1994) was more flexibility given to schools to meet identified local needs. It encouraged headteachers and school governors to use up to 20 per cent of the school week in whatever way seemed appropriate.

Leadership of the curriculum, then, is fragmented. Apart from central government, for example, headteachers have to ensure that the national curriculum is implemented in their schools, while local education authorities (LEAs) and school governors supervise this, often by requiring schools to construct development plans. In smaller schools headteachers are likely to be powerful in influencing the shape, structure, pedagogy and resourcing of the curriculum. In larger schools heads of department may develop powerful semi-autonomous baronies using claims to expert subject-specialist knowledge to legitimate their hegemony. Within these frameworks, teachers have to implement the curriculum within the resources available in ways which meet the educational needs of the pupils. The last requires the exercise of professional judgement by all teachers. This necessarily, but potentially creatively, leads to micropolitical tensions as teachers' different sets of values co-exist uneasily within a school's organisational framework and limited resources.

The national curriculum specifies a framework for pupils aged 5–16 years in LEA maintained and grant-maintained (GM) schools. These are the ages for compulsory schooling in the UK since 1972. The national curriculum establishes detailed programmes of study in three core subject areas (English, mathematics, and science) and several foundation subject areas, such as modern foreign languages, design and technology, history, geography, and physical education (PE). These curricula have been drawn up and modified from time to time by subject working parties appointed by and giving advice to the Secretary of State for Education through the National Curriculum Council (NCC) which was originally set up to co-ordinate the NC. Religious education (RE) also has to be taught but its syllabus is agreed within each LEA through Standing Advisory Councils on Religious Education (SACREs). In addition, schools are supposed to develop a range of cross-curriculum themes and skills, such as personal and social education; economic awareness; environmental understanding, which will help students relate different subjects to the adult world of work or unemployment as well as to each other.

The curriculum for each subject has been given a linear structure throughout the years of compulsory schooling, although some teachers contest the admissibility of this shape for their subjects. Pupils' year groups are now numbered from Year 1 to Year 11 across the primary–secondary divide, rather than being numbered within each phase of schooling as happened previously. Within this linearity the curriculum is segmented into four key stages (5–7 years; 7–11 years; 11–14 years; 14–16 years) at the end of each of which pupils are supposed to have achieved certain levels of performance. The first two key stages fit within existing notions in the UK of primary education, the latter two within that of secondary schooling. In those middle schools which serve pupils from 10–14 years old, this structure tends to emphasise divisions between different age groups of pupils rather than encouraging a sense of corporate school identity. It also faces teachers with a difficult job in balancing first year pupils' learning needs against those of preparing them for the Key Stage 2 Standard Assessment Tests (SATs).

Each subject area is divided into a series of strands or attainment targets which have to be studied throughout the stages. Pupils are expected to perform at different levels according to their age within fairly tightly defined bands of achievement. Syllabuses, lesson plans and tests have to be related to these attainment targets and levels as well as to the content prescribed in the programmes of study. Originally there were ten levels of performance, assuming that the last level would measure the performance of the most able pupils at the end of Key Stage 4. However, since the acceptance in 1994 that the General Certificate of Secondary Education (GCSE) will provide the certification for pupil performance at the end of Key Stage 4, the number of levels of performance has been reduced to eight, with eight being the top level of performance expected of pupils by the end of Key Stage 3.

Pupils' performance is measured at the end of each key stage by nationally constructed tests (SATs) which have been introduced gradually since 1990. These results are set alongside teachers' assessments of pupil performance, using whatever forms of testing and monitoring of performance they do within their schools. The creation of the SATs was supervised by the Schools Examination and Assessment Council (SEAC), an advisory body to the Secretary of State for Education like the NCC, until it was merged with the NCC in 1994 to become the Schools Curriculum and Assessment Authority (SCAA), recreating the Schools' Council of the 1960s and 1970s under new management. Some teachers wonder why the latter was ever scrapped.

In the national curriculum central government has placed emphasis on subject specific teaching, a pattern common in secondary schools, rather than on teaching subjects in combined packages or topics. This has made the implementation of the NC particularly difficult for primary schools which have traditionally and successfully taught many subjects through an integrated topic approach. This last has been seen as a means of making pupils aware of the cross-curriculum links in knowledge rather than of the artificial boundaries created by academic study which secondary schools have tended to emphasise.

Fletcher-Campbell, Tabberer and Keys (1996) point out how difficult it is especially for small primary schools to match the curriculum structure required by the NC because of the few staff they have and the resource level differentials they face compared with secondary schools. The latter are sustained by the age-weighted pupil formula which substantially controls levels of funding for schools under the Local Management of Schools (LMS) introduced in 1988. It means in some smaller primary schools some teachers having responsibility for co-ordinating more than one subject, as well as teaching their own class, raising problems of role strain for them. It underscores the importance of curriculum co-ordinators inducting non-specialist colleagues into the working syllabuses and relevant resources and materials which they have prepared.

The emphasis on single subject teaching – science being defined as a single subject, as is design and technology – and the extent of the NC syllabuses creates a variety of challenges for teachers. First they pose time pressures on teachers and pupils trying to learn subjects adequately. Second, they raise questions about the range of materials and equipment which schools need to have available at any one time. Third they make it more difficult for teachers to provide adequate support in large classes to pupils with learning difficulties, especially if there is no learning support assistant available to help. Fourth, they militate against the maintenance or development of cross-curriculum links, although the NC expects schools to teach these through the themes referred to earlier. Fifth, they ask teachers to teach a much wider range of knowledge than formerly, sometimes in areas of knowledge with which they have little familiarity. This poses challenges for schools creating programmes of staff development as well as for subject co-ordinators trying to give special-ist support to non-specialist colleagues.

The extent of the core and foundation subject syllabuses, despite the Dearing Review (1994), faces teachers with difficult choices about the effective development of pupils' personal and vocational education, despite the emphasis placed on both of these by central government rhetoric. It leads teachers and pupils to question the value of, say, work experience programmes which are supposed to help Year 10 pupils make vocational choices. These are often arranged in the summer term at the very time when teachers may have more time for Year 10 pupils because older stu-dents have begun to take their public examinations.

The introduction of SATs has caused teachers many dilemmas and led to much resentment (Ball and Bowe, 1992). The introduction of Key Stage 2 tests into the primary schools faced many teachers with reduced teaching time for the intensified NC syllabuses and created supervisory problems of managing large classes of pupils under formal examination conditions in rooms which had not been designed for such activities. It was claimed in some primary schools that many pupils were nervous about the formality of the occasion, raising questions about how accurately their SAT performance would reflect their real abilities. Teachers also resented the results of the formal SATs ini-tially being given more weight than their own professional assessment (Teacher Assessments) of pupil performance, a situation moderated in 1994 to give parity of weight between types of assessment. Teacher Assessments are usually arrived at through internal school testing and the marking of pupil coursework over many weeks, arguably a much sounder basis for judgement than the single occasion pencil and paper SATs.

Teachers in many secondary schools in the Midlands perceived SATs as a serious infringement on their teaching time with pupils and thought that it told neither them nor their schools' parents anything about the pupils' capacity to perform which they did not know already from the regular internal test which they administered. It seemed to many of these teachers a waste of scarce time and effort to mark such tests, resulting in a boycott of the Key Stage 3 SATs in 1994. Only with the introduction of external markers for SATs in 1995, i.e. the injection of further resources into schools, were teachers freed from this potential addition to their already multi-tentacled duties. However, schools are still faced with the dilemma about how to manage the publication of SAT results so as not to demoralise pupils or alarm parents unnecessarily, while continuing to give parents and pupils essential feedback on student performance.

The introduction of the NC has also generated divisions amongst teachers, particularly in primary schools, as they identify increasingly with the strong subject boundaries of the NC. Further, a new layer of hierarchy is beginning to emerge in primary schools either formally or informally, with the teacher responsible for preparing pupils for key stage SATs able to gain more resources and class help than other teachers. With the publication of league tables for SAT results as well as GCSE results since 1996, headteachers cannot afford not to bias their allocation of school resources in this way. This, ironically, at a time when research in management is suggesting the key importance of better teamworking and flatter hierarchies to improving school effectiveness.

MANAGING THE CURRICULUM IN PRIMARY SCHOOLS

In reducing and simplifying the national curriculum the Dearing Review (1994) raised primary teachers' hopes that they would enjoy greater flexibility and be able to make more positive choices in reorganising their teaching. They re-planned their curricula to meet the now much clearer guidelines on hours per year per subject and were initially much encouraged by the suggestion that they 'double count' time in some subject areas. Examples of this are English across the curriculum, and information technology (IT) taught *through* other subjects which in turn makes further managerial demands on the IT Co-ordinator. Teachers also have wide choices over which subject elements will be used for their Teacher Assessments at ages 5 and 11. Primary schools are thus encouraged to decide their own local priorities within the national curriculum.

A summary of the Dearing Review's 1994 recommendations

- the existing national curriculum for 5–14 year olds be streamlined to release a day a week (20 per cent of the teaching) for schools to use at their own discretion:
- the reduction in curriculum content for this age group to be concentrated outside the core subjects;
- allowing schools more flexibility to offer a wider range of academic and vocational options for 14–16 year olds;
- a reduction in the workload of teachers by simplifying the national curriculum and reducing demands for testing and recording;

- the ten level scale of attainment to be simplified and run only until the end of Key Stage 3;
- the national curriculum subjects to be reviewed in one go for September 1995;
- no further change to the national curriculum for five years after this.

Within each subject there are other opportunities for constructive decision making. The history study units, for example, specify concepts, terminology and skills with only broad content outlines. At Key Stage 1 the content of 'Areas of Study' is unspecified and very much open to local interpretation, whilst at Key Stage 2 there are choices to be made from the list of study units ('Victorians' or 'Britain since 1930') and even within the study unit 'Invaders' (DFE, 1995). More imaginative topics can create links with geography programmes of study or make full use of local site opportunities and field trips in the summer term. Such decisions help to enable teachers to maintain integrated work and help children to develop cross-curricular understandings.

Curriculum development is increasingly linked with decisions over positive staff deployment within each school. Job-sharing is one option bringing greater curriculum flexibility, and there is increased use of classroom assistants to provide time for teachers to develop their expertise (Fletcher-Campbell, Tabberer and Keys, 1996). Reorganised mixed age classes encourage teacher collaboration and joint curriculum planning. Partly in response to government concern about weaknesses in teachers' subject knowledge (Alexander, Rose and Woodhead, 1992), confirmed by research on the three core subjects (Bennett and Care, 1993; Summers, 1994), schools are increasingly experimenting with differentiated subject expertise among teams of teachers with split, streamed classes typically in Year 5 and Year 6. Within the East Midlands at least there is evidence of increasing use of such options, typically in English and mathematics, over that recorded only three years ago (Webb, 1993).

The retention of such progressive views of curriculum responsibility are most clearly seen in small schools where the tensions are greatest and staff deployment is more problematic. Here there is increasing use of job-sharing to spread the load, as in the following examples from Leicestershire villages:

School (1): 19th century building, CofE, Maintained
Number on roll (1995/6): 95
Staff: 4.0
Headteacher: Mid-career, ex-inner city deputy, one year in post

Post	Curriculum responsibility
Headteacher .6	English, history
1.0 (Deputy)	maths, geography, PE
1.0	technology, music, assessment
.6	science, IT, SEN
.4	RE, library
.4	Art

School (2): 18th century, CofE Aided
Number on roll: 76
Staff: 3.3
Headteacher: Very experienced, in post 20+ years

Post	Curriculum responsibility
Headteacher .8	English, RE, assessment
1.0 (Deputy)	music, art, technology
.8	geography, history, PE
.7	maths, science, IT

In both schools English obviously has the highest subject priority with assessment clearly targeted, but there are questions about the status of the other responsibilities, particularly mathematics. In school 2, the mathematics/science/IT part-timer was 'a mathematics graduate'. For both schools, subject combinations seem to be a result

---

Case study 5:   Curriculum leadership in a large primary school

This traditionally styled school takes 521 children from mixed private housing on the edge of a medium-sized town in the Midlands. Staffing is stable and experienced.

Curriculum management is complex with weak co-ordinator power. Overall curriculum responsibility is shared by the head and deputy although whole school planning is done by the school's curriculum committee which maintains the balance between broader curriculum goals and the fragmented subject contributions. All curriculum planning is related to the curriculum sub-committee of governors and is driven by the school's rolling development plan. Curriculum co-ordinators for English, mathematics, science/technology, music and special educational needs (SEN) are remunerated at above the Main Scale and all have appropriate specialist and/or graduate qualifications, but budgets are delegated to four age-group teams of staff (Pre-school, Reception/Years 1/2, Years 3/4 and Years 5/6). At this level there is good team-building and growth of teacher confidence through shared planning.

Specialist teaching is developing slowly. The Year 5/6 classes are setted for mathematics where 'at times the Year 5/6 staff operate as a mathematics department' (headteacher). At this stage, too, science/technology, IT, music, dance and games are modularised which allows use of extra staff to reduce class sizes. These limited forms of subject specialisation give several advantages, claims the head. Crucially they lead to improved mathematics scores on NFER tests through greater consistency and structure in whole school mathematics teaching and closer matching of task levels to pupils' abilities. Additionally teacher confidence is increased and children are better prepared for secondary school mathematics teaching. But specialisation increases problems with timetabling scarce resources ('a source of tension for the first time'), and Key Stage 1 teachers 'feel pushed out'. Most co-ordinators are indeed Key Stage 2 teachers.

of serendipity and opportunism rather than any conscious planning of staff development. Even in larger primary schools, though, headteachers are still expected to play a central role in overall curriculum development through long-term planning (OFSTED, 1995). Although the full planning and implementation process 'involves whole staff participation', successful curriculum management still requires 'strong and enthusiastic leadership, good co-ordination . . . through a senior manager, either the headteacher or deputy . . .' (SCAA, 1995, p. 6). The tension between centralised curriculum development and full staff participation can be seen in the case study of a larger primary school.

Unlike secondary schools where subject departments are well organised with a history of considerable devolved power, middle management in primary schools is still developing under the patchwork of curriculum co-ordinators (CCos), also variously called subject leaders, managers or co-ordinators (OFSTED, 1994; West, 1996). Their role is historically and geographically variable, and problematic in terms of relationships with the headteacher, deputy head, governors and OFSTED inspectors. In PE for example a recent survey found that it was the head rather than the PE Co-ordinator who controlled the PE budget and the research enquiry itself was answered by the head in most cases, by the deputy in 12 per cent and by the CCo in only 29 per cent of the schools (Evans *et al.,* 1996). The OFSTED report, *Primary Matters* (1994) offered comprehensive guidance on the delineation of the CCos role covering in-service training (INSET) attendance and in-house leadership, resource provision and maintenance, long-term and medium-term planning of topics and subjects, documentation for teaching and inspection, and advising teachers. Through the process of writing job descriptions for appointments, promotions and appraisal, headteachers have enormous freedom to determine the roles of their CCos and crucial decisions have to be made on the limits of their managerial responsibility. Larger schools clearly have greater opportunities for establishing subject tenure and for delegating power and responsibilities. But should the CCos control their own budgets? Are CCos directly answerable to governors for their work? What is the relationship between CCos and the heads of each key stage? Does the head or the relevant CCo write documentation for OFSTED inspection, and who is responsible for the inspection response? What is the role of the CCos for Special Needs children (SENCOs) and the nature of their relationship to other class teachers and CCos? (See Dean, 1996.) Who controls subject priorities within each successive school development plan, and how will this be managed, resourced and audited? Does the CCo have a wider quality assurance remit throughout the school? Is there a role for a co-ordinator of co-ordinators?

Individual headteachers have established their own local solutions to these real dilemmas with the result that curriculum development is being achieved on locally negotiated agenda reflecting local power relationships, often piecemeal as schools 'eat the elephant bit by bit' (Webb, 1993). Thus the effectiveness of the CCo 'system' is extremely difficult to gauge on a national level and their potential has been underestimated (Edwards, 1993). This patchiness has already been seen in the way in which small schools particularly are struggling to match their staffing to national curriculum subject priorities. The current regime of identifying the schools' and individual teachers' subject strengths and weaknesses through the processes of inspection reports and assessment league tables drives the movement for more subject specialisation. On the other hand, problems of staff replacement and development mean that in most primary schools, teachers' versatility and collegiality are of greater long-term value.

And yet it is clear that with the imminent withdrawal of LEAs from effective INSET, future primary school improvement, curriculum change and staff development are all intimately tied in with the success of the CCo system. The track record of this patchwork system is not encouraging. Surveys of practice have found that CCo's have been most successful in short-term, lower order outcome tasks concerned with 'serving colleagues' needs' whereas higher order outcomes aimed at improving teachers' skills, knowledge and classroom practices were much more rarely attempted (Reynolds and Saunders, 1987; Kinder and Harland, 1991). Wider pedagogic implications identified in the current 'primary debate', such as the prospects for specialised subject teaching, whole class or group teaching, and the sharpening of cognitive processes in asking open questions, were 'not being exploited' (Edwards, 1993). OFSTED has suggested that improved teaching standards depend very much on the active monitoring of the classroom performance of individual teachers. Given the time constraints on CCos it is likely that only the headteacher can fulfil this role over which teachers are sceptical if not cynical. Yet arrangements for paired observation and collegial debriefing linked perhaps to individual action plans may prove to be much more effective in raising confidence and standards than top-down management styles, but such strategies require more widespread training in observational and mentoring skills. Outside of initial teacher training programmes there is no tradition of teacher evaluation and co-teaching in the UK that does not carry threats or explicit rewards. It is not sufficient simply to rely on staff turnover to generate curriculum change: long-term strategies for promoting significant and continuous training and self-development are desperately needed. The careful creation of such an open learning culture is a major task facing the primary school manager. There is perhaps much to learn from our American colleagues who have developed the concept of the 'Professional Development School' in collaboration with higher education institutions over several decades.

Perhaps most English primary schools are too small, too isolated and too defensive for such an enterprise. In regions with strong LEA loyalty and support and some demographic stability, some local groups of primary schools have formed strong collegial development groups to provide curriculum change (Busher and Hodgkinson, 1995, 1996). Headteachers were conscious of subverting central government's attempt to introduce open competition and took a pride in using the opportunity to reformulate their deeper professional commitment. Within the clusters some smaller primary schools are subsidised by their secondary schools, and elsewhere there is discussion and some action on the prospects for employing peripatetic specialist teachers between isolated villages. Thus the pressures of the national curriculum and assessment are inadvertently bringing together schools which should be competing for children and resources, although where there are falling rolls it is highly problematic how long these strategies can be sustained.

MANAGING THE CURRICULUM IN SECONDARY SCHOOLS

The impact of the national curriculum

Many of the facets of the national curriculum mirror commonplace secondary school practice in England and Wales: the emphasis on a subject centred curriculum; the concern with regular testing of pupil performance; the requirement that the curriculum should be driven by the formation of skills and concepts as well as by content; the prescription of a particular content. For the last, teachers are familiar with preparing pupils for public examinations, the syllabuses and tests for which are constructed by employees of the five Examination Boards for England and Wales within guidelines laid down by the Secretary of State since 1986. Nonetheless the implementation of the national curriculum caused secondary school teachers a great deal of extra work, much of it initially at the same time (1986–1990) as the introduction of the new GCSE syllabuses. Campbell and Neill (1994) pointed out how much the national curriculum increased teachers' hours of work through extra preparation, professional development and administration. Foreman and Busher (Foreman, 1995) found that of the 128 primary and secondary school teachers they surveyed in the East Midlands over 50 per cent had introduced new materials or topics.

The impact of the curriculum working parties of the NC has been profound not only in bringing some subject areas together but in splitting some subject areas asunder. Some teachers have viewed this as a loss of autonomy in curriculum decision-making. Others have welcomed it, particularly where the educational views of the working parties have coincided with their own. The new syllabuses have meant that many teachers have had to prepare and teach aspects of subjects with which they were unfamiliar. For example, the introduction of balanced science syllabuses is facing many teachers with the need to become generalists when formerly they specialised in only one science, although many science teachers have welcomed this (Foreman, 1995). In those schools in areas such as Leicestershire where teachers had developed integrated humanities syllabuses, the national curriculum syllabuses have made continued integration very difficult. The result of years of co-operation developing cross-curriculum links for sound pedagogical reasons is now threatened just when the NC is encouraging schools to teach specified cross-curriculum themes such as IT, environmental awareness, personal and social education, and economic and business understanding.

Curriculum and assessment choices for senior staff

Bennett (1995) suggests that people in positions of leadership need to give direction to the other people with whom they work. The direction they give depends on their vision of what can be achieved in the contexts in which they find themselves. Subsumed within that vision in schools are particular educational and social values. Brighouse (1991) like many other people currently writing about leadership, distinguishes it from the managerial functions of working with other people to plan, organise, co-ordinate, produce and evaluate the work of a particular entity, whether whole-school or subject or pastoral unit (department).

Alternatively, leaders might be viewed as the servants of the people with whom they work whose function it is to help them realise their separate and independent visions and judgements within the frameworks laid down by society. While this perspective might be particularly appropriate in professionally staffed organisations, such as schools, whose members have to work with considerable autonomy, it is also relevant to a school's primary beneficiaries or students who are encouraged through their education to develop personally. Such a perspective contains an unresolvable but creative tension between social structures and individuals' needs to develop personal social and educational values.

Interestingly SCAA recognises the importance of this latter perspective in its 1996 initiative to encourage developing understandings of citizenship amongst pupils. Crucial to this development will be the choices which senior staff make about the culture of a school, the values which it sustains and how these are symbolised, perhaps through the active participation of students, teachers and school governors, as well as, more conventionally, through teaching in classrooms. For example, the development of an annually debated code of conduct for students and teachers is a route taken by some schools as a means of beginning to empower pupils to take responsibility for their own lives and those of others around them, i.e. to begin to become responsible citizens at least within the community of the school. The structuring and use of assemblies is a further area of practice through which values are imparted, and therefore about which choices have to be made, as are also the use of tutor or form periods.

Perhaps nowhere more clearly are the choices and values of a school shown, and therefore of its senior staff in particular, than in the way in which pupils with different educational needs are treated. These tensions are as sharp in the development of multicultural education as they are in the teaching of pupils with special educational needs and behavioural problems. In this context, the recent white paper, *Self-Government for Schools* (DFEE, 1996), proposing to give schools greater opportunities for selecting pupils can only be seen as socially divisive. It will give more choice to some – those who appear to have particular gifts who may be wanted by several secondary schools – while denying it to others without those gifts. Such inequities will be compounded by those social class and family factors which currently limit the freedom of some pupils to go to schools of their or their parents' choice.

The choices facing teachers are painful. For example, a policy of full integration of pupils with learning disablities into mainstream classes may enhance those pupils' self-images but it may also increase teachers' organisational and curriculum differentiation problems so possibly diminishing the quality of education for other pupils in the classroom. In turn this raises awkward philosophical problems about the balance of gain and good that might arise from such a policy. If learning support staff are available to help teachers and pupils develop the curriculum it raises questions about to which pupils or to which areas of the curriculum they should be allocated, unless funded and designated by an LEA for certain pupils. Should such staff confine their work only to those pupils identified by a school's SENCO or be expected to give support generally to pupils who need it if the class teacher is busy? To what extent can such part-time staff be reasonably expected to be integral to subject departments' curriculum planning and development? If they are not so engaged then to what extent are they disempowered from shaping the processes of teaching and learning and what impact will this have both on them and on the pupils and teachers whom they support? In some cases a sense of disengagement or disenfranchisement by learning support staff can lead to serious and enervating tensions for teachers and pupils.

At a whole school level, senior staff face a series of related choices about the structuring of a school's pupil population. One aspect of this will be to decide whether streaming, setting or mixed-ability teaching best serve the interests of the pupils and make work feasible for the teachers. In making such choices they will be making visible their educational and social values about under what conditions they think pupils learn and teachers teach more effectively. To some extent the decisions they make will be limited in the short term by various resource factors: the rooms available (particularly specialist classrooms); the availability of learning support materials, such as computers and textbooks; the number of staff who can teach certain subjects. Of course they may be able to gain more flexibility by persuading existing staff to teach their subsidiary areas of expertise, albeit with support from the relevant heads of departments, or hire part-time staff temporarily. The last option, however, does not seem particularly popular with only 9 per cent of teachers being on temporary contracts (*The Guardian*, 19 August 1996).

Another aspect is balancing the opportunities for a general academic education with the needs of many pupils for more specific vocational training. Schools recognise this by running work-experience schemes for their older students. However, providing a wide range of vocationally oriented exam courses is often beyond their resources. Tensions between the need for vocation-specific and general education become particularly acute for many students after Year 9 and may be sharpened if General National Vocational Qualifications (GNVQs) develop at Level 1 as a credible option to GCSEs: i.e. as vocationally oriented school-based, rather than industry-based courses to be taken by post-14 year old students. Even at present, it faces schools with major problems of timetabling Year 10 and 11 pupils for compulsory or core GCSE courses, optional or half GCSE courses and more vocational courses such as those run by the Royal Society of Arts (RSA). Such choices in timetabling are seriously affected by the need for a school to staff the NC for pupils in Years 7 to 9.

In the latter part of the 1980s co-operation between secondary schools and Further Education (FE) Colleges under the Technical and Vocational Education Initiative (TVEI) helped to reduce tensions between the provision of vocational and general education by making available to Year 10 and 11 students a jointly provided curriculum that was more vocationally oriented but still academically rigorous. Since then the incorporation of Further Education Colleges in 1992 and the impact of LMS in promoting secondary school competition has largely destroyed such opportunities. The development of viable GNVQ vocational courses for pupils in Years 10 and 11 is unlikely to diminish the tensions in this debate. Indeed it may well enhance it, if incompatible structures between GCSEs and GNVQs force students after Year 9 to opt largely for one or the other, either a general education based on the national curriculum or a series of quasi-vocational training courses defined by superficial work-specific competencies. One can only speculate on the impact of social class and family background on pupils faced with such choices.

It is not only in structuring the curriculum that senior staff have to make choices. They also have to do so in arranging the assessment of pupils' performances and communicating the outcomes to parents. Although what is communicated is regulated by legislation and government circular, how that assessment is carried out and in what form the outcomes are conveyed is largely left to teachers to decide. At the end of each key stage of the NC schools have to enter pupils for SATs, state created exams, alongside which are placed teachers' assessments of how pupils have performed. For secondary schools this only involves teachers with Key Stage 3 SATs, for children aged 14 years, since GCSE stands in place of Key Stage 4 tests. However, the timing of the GCSE examinations imposes constraints on when non-GCSE pupils in a secondary school can be examined, since teachers of Year 11 pupils will want to give their pupils the experience of trial GCSE examinations sufficiently early in the year to allow them time to compensate for any poor performances before the real exams. As those same teachers will also be teaching other year groups, they will not want to be marking Year 11 trial exams as well as those of other year groups. The school, then, has to create an examination timetable for all year groups to take account of this and to allow the parents of each year group in the school to receive regular feedback about their children's performances.

The dilemmas do not end with such simple organisational matters. More complex choices arise in deciding how to construct feedback on pupil performance so that parents can understand it and pupils can benefit from it. It raises questions about what should be the balance in assessing pupils' work, whether classroom exercises, interim course tests or end of year exam, between formative guidance for future development and summative judgement on what has been achieved. To ensure coherence of practice across the school, then, senior staff will need to help departments to implement common policies on testing and marking pupils work, on recording the outcomes and on discussing the outcomes with pupils and parents. In turn this leads to contentious questions about how reports are constructed and the importance of helping pupils to develop criteria for evaluating their own work through, perhaps, involving them in the construction of personal records of achievement. However, the last is a very time consuming activity, particularly if carried out in every subject area more than once a year. In turn, then, this raises questions about what should be the balance between learning and assessment for pupils and teachers in the course of a school year.

The work of head of department in co-ordinating the curriculum

Heads of subject departments in secondary schools form part of a group of people sometimes referred to as middle managers. Even the curriculum-oriented posts display considerable differences. While some teachers with a single responsibility point may have oversight of part of the work of a department, other teachers with three or four additional points may be responsible for the work of an entire subject (e.g. mathematics) or group of related subjects (e.g. modern foreign languages) and several staff both teaching and support.

None the less these posts have characteristics in common: overseeing an aspect of the curriculum, if not a whole subject area; having responsibility for the work of other adults; contributing to the work of the whole school; supervising the use of finance and other resources (Bennett, 1995). However, Bennett points out that only the most senior of the middle managers have any influence over whole school policy, the rest working almost entirely within their own sections of the school.

Within the framework of the national curriculum and the Local Management of Schools (LMS), which was introduced by the Education Reform Act (1988), heads of department have had to work to help their colleagues meet the new curriculum requirements, but to do so in a cost effective way, at the very least saving as much of the former curriculum materials as possible and applying them in the new context. Such parsimony has been necessary not only to keep within the limited financial resources that have been available for introducing change but also to limit the pressures on teachers' time and to maintain their morale. The imposition of the national curriculum has made some teachers feel that their professional judgement is under attack (Foreman, 1995).

The introduction of these national initiatives in England and Wales have led to a fundamental shift in the way teachers work and schools are managed. To make the national curriculum work, teachers have needed to work more in teams than formerly – a shift in traditional cultures in secondary schools (Bennett, 1995, p. 52). These changes in the policy framework of education have brought about a more bureaucratic approach to teaching and increased emphasis on organisation and hierarchy. This is seen most clearly in the emergence of regular cycles of department and school meetings in secondary

Case Study 6:   Curriculum leadership in a secondary school

Constable (1995) offers an analysis of how a head of department (HoD) used the processes of development planning to bring about change in a science department. The following is loosely based on that. The science department needed to develop new modules of work to meet the national curriculum programmes of study. Rather than leave teachers to do this individually, duplicating time and effort, the head of department preferred to use a collaborative approach, getting certain colleagues to develop certain modules which lay within their areas of expertise.

At a July department meeting he persuaded colleagues to agree to this programme of curriculum development on grounds of efficient use of resources and expertise. In addition he asked that module co-ordinators make open to collegial scrutiny their work in progress, partly to validate the quality of work and partly to develop a sense of there being a departmental team. However, some teachers were reluctant to make their work open to such scrutiny because of fear of criticism. To address this, the head of department and a colleague undertook the construction of the first module, creating a sequence of topics and collecting together suitable materials. A curriculum grid is a useful way of summarising what is involved in such a module. This specifies the allocation of time to each topic in the module; the sequence of topics covered and their contents, skills and concepts; the materials to be used for each topic; the pupil activities involved in each; the form of assessment for each; and the NC Attainment Targets and levels of attainment envisaged for each.

They presented the draft package at an October department meeting for colleagues to comment on constructively, i.e. would the module package work, not could it be done differently. After this the HoD and his colleague tried out the topics of their module on the pupils when these were relevant to the pupils' studies. There seemed no point in rushing into duplicating the module for colleagues to use if it was going to need substantial modification soon after publication.

Within six months of the original decision of the department, the HoD was able to present his colleagues with a module that had been trialled and offered them a means of teaching part of the national curriculum for which the department had previously had a few scattered resources. Again colleagues were invited to comment on the final draft version of the module before it was duplicated on a sufficient scale to be used by every teacher in the department as they needed it. As a result of this approach, other teachers now were willing to help to construct modules of work for the department, submitting them, too, to peer review during their construction. Members of the department were learning to develop qualities of professional trust and co-operation that could lead towards more collaborative working when facing the educational challenges for which they, as teachers, were responsible collectively.

schools, on the agenda of which aspects of the national curriculum are often an item (Foreman, 1995), and the introduction of a four yearly cycle of school inspections by the Office for Standards in Education (OFSTED). The latter in effect lays down guidelines about what aspects of departmental work should be monitored if a department is to be effective, thereby delineating the work of a head of department.

OFSTED expect heads of department to monitor the standards of achievement of pupils, the quality of learning, and the quality of teaching. In addition they expect to find managed:

- the organisation, planning and delivery of the national curriculum;
- the assessment, recording and reporting procedures used to raise the quality of pupils' work;
- the deployment of teachers and the support they are given, particularly if they are not specialist subject teachers;
- the efficiency with which resources are used and made available to pupils;
- the quality of the accommodation and how it is used.

(OFSTED, 1992)

This emphasises the internal and administrative functions of heads of departments rather than their networking or boundary management functions. The latter, for example, include micropolitical ones of representing the department to the rest of the school, especially the senior management team, and liaising with wider professional networks such as subject associations and public examination boards. In stressing hierarchy and control, ironically, it mitigates against the development of teamworking in curriculum development which both Bell (1993) and Constable (1995) indicate as of key importance in bringing about change. Both thought the creation of a culture of support and co-working more important for the development of professional competence and self-esteem among staff and pupils. Constable looked at change through collaboration in the implementation of a departmental development plan to meet the needs of GCSE in a science department, Bell at the development of a pastoral curriculum in a school. On the other hand Bennett (1995) points out that many heads of department do seem just to carry out the administrative functions of management without the more inspirational ones of leadership.

CONCLUSION

Managing the curriculum in any school is essentially concerned with creating an effective provision of learning opportunities for pupils. A key figure in creating such an environment is the curriculum co-ordinator or head of department. Research into departmental effectiveness offers a broader view than OFSTED on what may be involved in this. Sammons, Thomas and Mortimore (1996) suggest that those departments which are effective exhibit:

- high teacher expectations of pupil performance whatever are the starting points for pupils;
- an emphasis on academic performance and stress on effective preparation for that;
- shared visions or goals which included belief that school is primarily a place for learning and teaching;
- clear leadership in which the head of department provides a clear sense of direction but encourages team-work through involving teachers in decision-making;
- good relationships with an effective senior management team which provided support to a department.

Harris and Jamieson (1995) offer a similar, if longer list of criteria for effective departments. They, too, found that effective departments emphasised the importance of pupils through organising teaching effectively and through having a shared vision which encompassed change through collaborative styles of management. None the less, they suggested that effective departments kept careful scrutiny of departmental results and uses of resources.

Emerging from this brief discussion is the importance of curriculum co-ordinators working with their colleagues and encouraging their colleagues to work with each other for the benefit of the pupils. This is borne out by the evidence from micropolitical perspectives on leadership, such as that of Blase and Blase (1995). They stress the importance of person-oriented approaches to management by heads of department, improving pupils' learning opportunities through facilitating staff development. In part, this is by fostering more open participation in decision-making: what Hargreaves (1990) calls genuine collegiality. Similarly Brown and Rutherford (1996) found evidence of successful heads of department leading through working with their colleagues to create a web of social networks. These valued the qualities and expertise which each member of staff could bring to a department or subject area. They were, however, focused on particular visions of how education could be improved, usually stemming from a curriculum co-ordinator's values and professional expertise, constrained by national and local demands on a school and on the curriculum. To elaborate on Hughes' (1973) categorisation, effective curriculum leaders need to be leading professionals as well as chief executives and institutional politicians, at least within their subject area, and to be extended professionals (Hoyle, 1975), too, who concern themselves with personal relationships as well as curriculum structures inside and outside a school.

REFERENCES

Alexander, R., Rose, J. and Woodhead, C. (1992) *Curriculum organisation and classroom practice in primary schools: a discussion paper.* DES, London.

Ball, S. and Bowe, R. (1992) Subject departments and the implementation of National Curriculum policy: an overview of the issues, in *Journal of Curriculum Studies*, 24, 2, pp. 97–115.

Bell, L. (1993) The management of pastoral care in two secondary schools in Busher, H. and Smith, M. (eds) *Managing Educational Institutions: Reviewing Development and*

Learning, Sheffield Papers in Educational Management, Sheffield, Sheffield Hallam University for BEMAS.

Bennett, N. (1995) *Managing professional teachers,*   London, Paul Chapman Publishing.

Bennett, N. and Care, C. (eds) (1993) *Learning to teach*, London, Routledge.

Blase, J. and Blase, J. (1995) The micropolitical orientation of facilitative school principals and its effects on teachers' sense of empowerment. Paper given at the American Educational Research Association (AERA) Conference, San Francisco, April.

Brighouse, T. (1991) *What makes a good school?* Stafford, Network Educational Press.

Brown, M. and Rutherford, D. (1996) Leadership for school improvement: the changing role of the head of department. Paper given at the British Educational Management and Administration Society Research Conference 25–27 March, Robinson College, Cambridge.

Busher, H. and Hodgkinson, K. (1995) Managing inter-school networks: across the primary-secondary divide, *School Organisation*, 15, 1, pp. 329–40.

Busher, H. and Hodgkinson, K. (1996) Co-operation and tension between autonomous schools: a study of inter-school networking, in *Educational Review*, 48, 1: pp. 55–64.

Campbell, R. and Neil, S. (1994) *Teacher Commitment and Policy Failure*, Harlow, Longman.

Chitty, C. (ed) (1993) *The National Curriculum – is it working?* Harlow, Longman.

Constable, H. (1995) Developing teachers as extended professionals in Busher, H. and Saran, R. (eds) (1995) *Managing Teachers as Professional in Schools*, Kogan Page, London.

Dean, J. (1996) *Managing special needs in the primary classroom*, Routledge, London.

Dearing, R. (1994) *The National Curriculum and its Assessment: Final Report*, School Curriculum and Assessment Authority, London.

DFE (Department for Education) (1995) *History in the National Curriculum*, HMSO, London.

DFEE (1996) *Self-Government for Schools* (White paper), HMSO, London.

Edwards, A. (1993) Curriculum co-ordination: a lost opportunity for primary school development? *School Organisation*, Vol. 13, no. 1 pp. 51–9.

Evans, J., Penney, D., Bryant, A. and Hennink, M. (1996) All things bright and beautiful? PE in primary schools post the 1988 Education Reform Act, *Educational Review*, Vol. 48, no. 1, pp. 29–40.

Fletcher-Campbell, F., Tabberer, R. and Keys, W. (1996) *Comparative costs: perspectives on primary-secondary difference*, NFER, Slough.

Foreman, K. Teacher Professionality and the National Curriculum in H. Busher and R. Saran (eds) *Managing Teachers as Professional in Schools*, Kogan Page, London.

Galton, M. (1996) *Crisis in the primary classroom*, David Fulton, London.

Hargreaves, A. (1990) Contrived Collegiality: The micropolitics of teacher collaboration in J. Blase (ed) *The Politics of School Life*, Sage, New York.

Harris, A. and Jamieson, I. (1995) How to be effective: a 10 point guide to what marks out the departments where pupils achieve most, *Times Educational Supplement*, School Management Update p. 11, 10 Nov. 1995.

Hoyle, E. (1975) Leadership and Decision-making in Education in Hughes, M. (ed) *Administering Education: International Challenge*, Athlone Press, London.

Hughes, M. (1973) The Professional-as-administrator: the case of the secondary school head, in Peters, R. S. (ed) *The Role of the Head*, Routledge and Kegan Paul, London.

Kinder, K. and Harland, J. (1991) *The impact of INSET: The case of primary science*, NFER, Slough.

Lawton, D. (1989) *Education, Culture and the National Curriculum*, Hodder and Stoughton, London.

OFSTED (1994) *Primary Matters*, HMSO, London.

OFSTED (1995) *Annual Report of Her Majesty's Chief Inspector of Schools, Command Papers 122 and 284*, HMSO, London.

Reynolds, J. and Saunders, M. (1987) Teacher responses to curriculum policy: Beyond the 'delivery metaphor', in Calderhead, J. (ed) *Exploring teachers' thinking,* Cassell, London.

Sammons, P., Thomas, S. and Mortimore, P. (1996) Improving school and departmental effectiveness. Paper given at the British Educational Management and Administration Society Research Conference 25–27 March, Robinson College, Cambridge.

School Curriculum and Assessment Authority (SCAA) (1995) *Planning the Curriculum at Key Stages 1 and 2,* SCAA Publications, London

Summers, M. (1994) Science in the primary school: The problem of teachers' curricular expertise', *The Curriculum Journal,* Vol. 5, no. 2, pp. 179–94.

Webb, R. (1993) *Eating the elephant bit by bit: The National Curriculum at Key Stage 2.* Association of Teachers and Lecturers, London.

West, N. (1996) *Middle management in the primary school,* David Fulton, London.

2.4

Markets and Marketing

CHRIS JAMES AND PETER PHILLIPS

Arguably, the main underpinning intention of education legislation in the last decade has been to establish a market in education in England and Wales (Demaine, 1988; Maclure, 1992; Whitty, 1989). Although the market remains partial and imperfect (Bash and Coulby, 1989; Miliband, 1991), one consequence of the legislation has been the increased priority given to the marketing of educational organisations. Educational marketing has become an important aspect of educational management.

This chapter explores key aspects of educational marketing focusing essentially on the choices educational managers can make as they respond to and seek to influence those who are themselves making choices in relation to schools. The chapter begins with a review of the assumptions that underpin market theory which is followed by a critical analysis of the education market. There is then a section which explores how schools collect data about their own 'market' and considers how schools respond to – or are prevented from responding to – competitive pressures. The issue of school choice and some of the implications for school marketing are analysed in the following section. The final section outlines the different aspects of the practice of educational marketing in schools as defined by the marketing mix.

THE MARKET AND EDUCATION

In essence, markets are devices to facilitate the exchange of goods and services with individuals entering the market place to perform such exchange transactions. Miliband (1991) considers that two types of argument can be advanced for the market as a distributive mechanism. Firstly, there is a moral argument based on the notion that the exercise of choice and not to be constrained in that choice are fundamental rights. Secondly, the market produces the most optimal outcome and generates an overall increase in the quality of goods and services. It is argued that the market environment presses producers to make improvements which in turn raise educational performance (see for example, Chubb and Moe, 1990).

Schotter (1990) has identified a number of assumptions on which market theory is based.

Individualism – the individual is free to act in a way which is not coerced or interfered with by the state.
Rational self-interest – individuals act either in an instrumental fashion (that is they act in a way that is most likely to satisfy a particular need or set of needs) or they explore a number of possible means and outcomes.
Utilitarianism – the rational individual calculates how much use or satisfaction might result from a particular course of action.
Laissez-faire and the invisible hand – the free and rational self-interest of individuals will generate consequences beneficial to everyone as they seek to maximise their own position.
A *minimal but strong state* – the state must not interfere with the operation of the market or attempt to coerce the decisions of individuals.

Competition is at the heart of market theory. For perfect competition there must be buyers and sellers who have perfect knowledge of market events. Buyers and sellers operate independently and sellers are free to enter or leave production. Also for perfect competition, sellers must be able to supply what-ever is needed to meet demand and the product or service is the same every-where (Bash and Coulby, 1989).

A consideration of the assumptions on which market theory is based in relation to education and the prerequisites for perfect competition points up quite clearly that the education market is not perfect. For example, it is unclear who the buyers are, whether there are many of them and whether they have perfect knowledge of the school they are choosing. Are the buyers the children? Their parents? Or are they others in the community such as industry, com-merce or higher education? How easy is it for those doing the choosing to be certain of the use or satisfaction they will gain from the school of their choice? How rational is the process of choice? How can buyers – say parents – and schools operate independently when partnership between schools and parents is so important (Tomlinson, 1991)? Clearly the education market is 'heavily conditioned' (Woods, Bagley and Glatter, 1996, p. 13) and is best described as a quasi-market (Le Grand and Bartlett, 1993).

MARKETING AND EDUCATION

Metherell (1991) defines marketing in an educational context simply as finding out what people want, then providing it and letting them know. Pardey (1991) uses similar themes to underpin a model of educational marketing aimed at the development of a market orientation within the organisation. He defines a marketing orientation as 'anticipating what the client will need, identifying what they do need, and satisfying those needs' (p. 14). Arguably, a marketing orientation contrasts with a product orientation where the emphasis is on producing the same product regardless and then promoting and 'selling' the

organisation's products. A marketing orientation places customer need anticipation, identification and satisfaction at the centre of the organisation's activities and in educational marketing sits more comfortably with educational
values than does a product orientation. In education, anticipation and identification of needs (that is, scanning and interpretation of the market (Bagley,
Woods and Glatter, 1996a)) and responsiveness to those needs in competitive
arenas (Woods, Bagley and Glatter, 1996) are key notions in these conceptions
of marketing. Competitive arenas are 'areas of varying sizes and natures within
which schools draw from a largely common population of parents and children' (Woods, Bagley and Glatter, 1996, p. 11). According to Glatter, Johnson
and Woods (1992) 'Producer responsiveness determines the extent to which
under market pressures, quality is enhanced in accordance with the wishes of
consumers' (p. 9). In terms of the choices for the educational manager, challenges arise in distinguishing between clients' wants and needs and deciding
how to meet identified needs in ways which do not conflict with the manager's
own educational values.

Scanning and interpreting the market

As part of a wider study, Bagley, Woods and Glatter (1996a) have explored the
scanning and interpretation strategies which schools adopt in order to discover
parental perspectives on schools. They conclude that formal scanning and
interpretation in relation to parents is not a high priority in the schools they
studied. The schools in their study gave this aspect of marketing much less
attention than promotional activities and the managers in the schools were
more concerned to monitor the actions of competing schools than to discover
the preferences of users directly. The schools rely heavily on informal information gathering but nonetheless, Bagley *et al.* conclude that their findings place
'a major question mark over claims that schools immersed in a market culture
will be more 'consumer responsive' (p. 133). The findings of Bagley *et al.*
support those of James and Phillips (1995) that marketing practice in schools is
relatively unsophisticated and that many educational managers see marketing
primarily as promotion. Although Bagley *et al.* were unable to find evidence of
schools using formal ways of identifying client needs, they do cite other examples of successful scanning and interpretation activities (for example, Harrison, 1991; Bush, Coleman and Glover, 1992). There are examples from
elsewhere of the value of the *process* of formal data collection activities in
enhancing parental involvement (Williams, 1996).

School responsiveness in a competitive arena

Potentially, schools can respond in a range of ways to the pressures of a
competitive arena. Woods (1994) outlines a framework for consideration of
the kinds of responses schools *can* make to the quasi-market.

1 *Competitive responses* which have the overall purpose of maintaining the numbers of pupils in the school. Within these responses are substantive changes – for example to the curriculum, teaching methods and organisation and environmental scanning. There are also promotional activities which are actions intended to raise the school's profile and/or improve its image.
2 *Income-enhancing responses* in order to secure income over and above the school budget based on formula funding.
3 *Efficiency-increasing responses* which have the intention of getting the most out of the school budget and concentrating resources on the core educational activities.
4 *Political responses* in order to influence politicians and or officials to the benefit of the school.
5 *Collaborative responses,* the purpose of which is to obtain benefits from working in cooperation in achieving aims of the above responses or to eliminate or reduce competition.

Although it might be expected that schools could choose to exercise a wide range of response options within this framework, Bagley, Woods and Glatter (1996b) have found that responsiveness is restricted and that they are constrained by 'the history, locality and community in which they are situated' (p. 47). These constraints form a number of 'barriers' which inhibit the choices of schools in responding in competitive environments. In summary, they are as follows:

Reputation – a poor reputation is notoriously difficult to change and can make it very difficult to attract parents.
Locality – nearness to home and convenience for travel are core factors influencing parental choice.
Finance – unpopular schools will have a smaller budget with which to compete with teaching skills, curriculum depth and educational environment offered by their more popular – and better off – rivals.
Senior management attitudes – managers may be resistant to being guided by consumers rather than their own sense of professionalism.
Competitor schools – the preference of managers to be more influenced by local competitors than the needs of parents will impact on true responsiveness.
Government policies – may override developments in the market brought about by responsiveness to market need. For example, the creation of City Technology Colleges and schools becoming grant-maintained and receiving a financial bonus for so-doing will distort the market and influence responsiveness.
Differential responses to groups of clients – a school's response to one group may be at the expense of its response to another group.

Bagley, Woods and Glatter (1996b) give a helpful classification of barriers to responsiveness which is set out in Table 2.4.1.

Table 2.4.1   Classification of barriers to responsiveness

Internal	External
Producer domain	*Consumer domain*
School personnel – their perspectives, motivations competencies; includes professional and ethical objections to responsiveness and competition	Existing and prospective parent and pupil perspectives, preferences and needs
Availability of developed methods for scanning and interpreting the market	Local population/community perspectives, preferences, needs
Inadequate funding	Socio-economic/ethnic character of local population/community
	Micro-environmental domain Socio-economic/ethnic character of local area
	Local history
	Local social policy (housing, etc.)
	Local education policy (admissions, funding, etc.)
	Macro-environmental domain Government social policy (housing, etc.)
	Government education policy (funding, grant-maintained schools, City Technology Colleges

Source: Adapted from Bagley Woods and Glatter, 1996b.

CHOOSING A SCHOOL

It is a truism that a key purpose of educational marketing is to optimise the number of pupils entering the school and remaining in the school. Influencing pupil choice at the point of entry is very important since evidence suggests (James and Phillips, 1995) that parents of children attending state schools are generally reluctant to exercise the 'exit option' (Hirschman, 1970) and move their children to another school if they are dissatisfied. The research literature on the factors influencing choice – which is dominated by explorations of choice of secondary school – reveals a complicated picture. Within this picture, there are three important themes: who chooses, the negative factors influencing choice and the positive factors influencing choice.

Who chooses?

Who chooses the school is a complex matter. Government policy has focused on parents as choosers, for example through the Parents Charter, and early research centred on how different social backgrounds influenced choice. However, more recent research (for example, David *et al.*, 1994; Gorard, 1996) has indicated that the intergenerational models where both parents and children to various extents are involved in the choice decision are more appropriate. These intergenerational groups are referred to here as families.

Hunter (1991) proposed a model where pupils choose under the influence of their parents. Coldron and Boulton (1991) confirm that children's choice factors are important, a view confirmed by West, Varlaam and Scott (1991). West and Varlaam (1991) conclude that the interaction between parents and children on the matter of choice is so close that it may be difficult to distinguish between parents and children in the decision-making process.

Gorard (1996) describes a three step model to explain the choice process.

Step one – parents alone decide on the type of school (for example, fee-paying or state, single-sex or co-educational).
Step two – parents alone consider some options within the type they have chosen.
Step three – parents and the child reach a satisfactory agreement.

Any or none of the three steps can be omitted giving theoretically eight different ways of choosing. In practice, Gorard suggests that only five different models are in play and the titles he gives them indicate different levels of engagement and empowerment.

Eclectic – (steps 2 and 3). These families are perhaps ideal consumers – 'alert clients'. They are able to consider schools of different types and involve their child with informed guidance.
Fatalist – (step 1). These families may decide on a fee-paying school at an early point or if they decide to use state schools are prepared to use the school allocated to them.
Child-centred – (steps 1 and 3). These families leave the choice to the child and most commonly use state schools.
Parent-centred – (steps 1 and 2). The parents decide. Typically those in this group use fee-paying schools.
Consumerist – (steps 1, 2 and 3). The members of this group use all three steps in the decision-making process and only seriously consider one type of school.

Choice criteria

The outcomes of research into the reasons why schools are rejected or why they are chosen give an unclear and inconsistent picture (Smedley, 1995). A number of factors apparently have influence: socio-economic status, geographical area, ethnicity and contextual factors such as the number and variety of options available (Smedley, 1995). Gorard (1996) suggests that different choice criteria are more relevant at different stages of the process. In step one (see above) where parents decide on the type of school, factors such as parental convenience, tradition, school size, pupil safety are important. During step two when parents consider options within the type of school chosen, important influences include the advice of their child's current school, local reputations of schools and school-based literature (when matters like provision and outcomes are important). In step three, during which parents and child reach a satisfactory agreement, extra-curricular activities, pupil happiness and convenience are important factors. Welfare and outcomes (examination results) are also important in this third stage. There is evidence that although school choice is a significant matter for parents (Webster *et al.*, 1993) over three-quarters of parents only realistically consider one or at most two schools (Yorke and Bakewell, 1991).

Reasons for rejecting schools

Reasons for rejecting schools are generally more consistent than are positive factors and there is evidence that avoiding a school is significant in school choice (Alder, 1993; West and Varlaam, 1991). Reputation is an important factor and Smedley (1995) considers that 'repeatedly, parents say they would not send their children to a school with a "bad reputation"' (p. 97). He suggests that a bad reputation is characterised by poor discipline, badly-behaved students and abysmal examination results. Fenton (1995) lists discipline, location and appearance as important negative factors. 'Highly visible' schools are most at risk of acquiring a bad reputation, for example, those schools whose pupils are seen around the town centre or where pupils have to travel to school through a residential area (Thomas and Dennison, 1991). Fenton (1995) suggests that the reputation or 'embedded image' may be very enduring and difficult to change and that it acts early in the decision process.

Reasons for making positive choice

Research into the reasons why parents and children positively choose particular schools is very variable and is complicated considerably by socio-economic status, gender and ethnicity. Despite the complexity, Smedley (1995) considers there is one over-riding criterion: 'above all, parents want their children to go to schools where they will be happy'. He suggests that parents therefore choose on the basis of process criteria which are to do with for example, pupil–teacher relationships and whether the child's friends attend the school rather than product criteria such as examination results. His view is supported by several research studies (Stillman, 1986; Coldron and Boulton, 1991; Alder, 1993). Among the process criteria cited are the child's own preference, siblings or other relatives attending the school, good discipline, caring teachers/school (Smedley, 1995; Fenton, 1995). Factors such as school proximity and ease of access which are associated with process factors are also important (Smedley, 1995).

Academic standards (typically characterised by examination results) are an important consideration for parents and there is evidence that they act as a 'gating' or 'threshold' factor (Stillman and Maychell, 1986; Fenton, 1995). That is, other considerations come into play once the academic standards criterion has been met. Academic standards have been shown to be consistently important for one group, those of high socio-economic status who are considered to be 'active choosers' (Echols *et al.*, 1990; Yorke and Bakewell, 1991; Coldron and Boulton, 1991; Hunter, 1991). In contrast, Thomas and Dennison (1991) found that academic standards were not significant for working class parents. Such analyses rely on clear definitions of class and relative uniformity within those class groups. Nonetheless, Smedley (1995) considers there is sufficient evidence to suggest that 'schools consider carefully who are their target population for marketing and whether their approach needs to be varied with different client groups'.

THE PRACTICE OF MARKETING IN SCHOOLS

Much of the educational marketing literature is characterised by suggestions, guidance and strategies based on marketing models taken from non-educational settings. Typically, these are service marketing models and although the nature of services (Cowell, 1984) and service marketing (Lovelock, 1988) is problematic, these models do provide a useful framework of ways in which school can respond in a competitive arena.

In essence, service organisations are those where the activity or benefit that the organisation offers to others, the service, is essentially intangible (see for example, Cowell, 1984; Gronroos, 1980; Lovelock, 1988). So, unlike goods, services 'cannot be seen, tasted, felt, heard or smelled before they are bought' (Kotler, 1986, p. 681). Although some authors stress a 'goods-service continuum' (see for example, Rathmell, 1966; Shostak, 1977) the notion of intangibility remains an important distinction.

There are a number of key variables which can be controlled in order to shape marketing practice. These are categorised as the marketing mix and activities within these variables enable the organisation to move from 'where it is' to 'where it wants to be' in terms of responding to client need. The marketing mix represents the domains of marketing practice and as such it offers a framework for the analysis of the practice of marketing (James and Phillips, 1995).

The marketing mix can be separated into different components (see for example, Christopher and McDonald, 1991; Cowell, 1984). Within the marketing mix for services there are seven components:

product
place
price
promotion
people
processes
proof.

This model of service marketing is often referred to as the 'Seven Ps' (Cowell, 1984). The number of components is sometimes contested (see Gray, 1991) and it has to be accepted that much of the practice of educational marketing is integrated and any particular marketing activity may encompass several components. However, the 'Seven Ps' offer the most detailed framework for considering the choices that educational managers can make in their responses to the market.

Product – the services being offered to the market

The product in education is consistently described as the range of services provided by the school, college or university (see for example, Barnes, 1993). Primarily, the services provided by schools are the courses offered to students but the services will extend beyond the curriculum. Frequently cited examples of other services include twilight computer clubs, restaurant meals for adults, consultancy for businesses and contract research programmes, care of children while parents work and so on (see Gray, 1991; Marland and Rogers, 1991; Stott and Parr, 1991). Consideration of the product includes the product range – the range of goods or services offered; product benefits – how those who use the service benefit; product life – a recognition that products have a finite life-cycle; product quality – the service's strengths and the demands of the market.

Case Study 7:   Getting the Price Right

Highvale is an 11–18 mixed comprehensive school. Steve Jackson, the head-teacher, has been in post since 1985. Since the advent of LMS, Steve has paid particular attention to the price element of the marketing mix in two ways.

The first concerns the funding that each pupil carries in the form of age-weighted pupil units when they join the school or if/when they leave. Steve considers himself lucky that very few pupils exercise the 'exit option' other than at age 16 – unlike the neighbouring independent school where apparently, there are frequent movements in and out at any stage. So for Steve maximising admission at 11 and retention at 16 is crucial. Because of this he has invested heavily in promoting the school, for example through open evenings, well in advance of those transfer points.

Secondly he is very keen to get value for money from the school's non-pupil support services. For example, since he seriously embarked on his version of compulsory competitive tendering he reckons to have made considerable cost savings. He says, '*I have almost halved my grounds maintenance budget costs and knocked about 10 per cent off the cleaning bill which was over £55,000 a year*'. He concedes that the cost-cutting decisions are not a straightforward ones. For example, rather than cut the school catering costs he has gone for improved quality. Also, on any matter where there are clear health and safety concerns such as electrical work he still uses companies on the LEA list. Nonetheless he considers that the savings he has made have been considerable and have been ploughed back into the school in the form of additional teaching and support staff.

Price – the resources needed by customers to obtain the goods/services

The price element of the marketing mix has two components: costing and pricing. In costing, the key task is to match institutional spending and benefits to the customer. Pricing (fixed in schools as 'age-weighted pupil units' for each student) is concerned with ensuring that recipients are charged sums in line with the institution's objectives (see Case Study 7).

Place – the location and accessibility of the services

Important aspects of 'place' in service marketing include: the appearance and condition of the service location; the care of the customers – actual and potential – and other visitors to the service location; first contact and accessibility. The nature of the first contact (what it is and how easy it is) is important.

The challenge of improving the 'place' can be daunting and can require creative and 'radical thinking. Improvements might range from the simple and inexpensive to the more complicated and potentially costly. In a school setting, an example of the former would be a telephone answer machine which received messages *and* gave explicit information (such as emergency contact numbers) in use outside normal hours when the school office was not staffed. An example of the latter would be where the head and other senior staff routinely hold 'clinics' at off-site venues such as local primary schools, or the local welfare club. This attempt to improve accessibility is potentially expensive not solely because of the time used but because of the cost incurred following up quickly all enquiries, complaints and so on. Choosing to improve the 'place' has cost implications and since the improvements do not directly impact on the pupils' learning the educational manager can be presented with dilemmas and value-conflicts (see Case Study 8).

Promotion – the activities which communicate the benefits of the services to potential customers

Promotion can be used to inform the market and persuade those in it to choose the service that is being offered. This is best done by identifying the key feature which will appeal to the market, the unique selling proposition (see for example, Gray, 1991), and supporting this message through the design and content of publicity material. Important aspects of this element of the marketing mix include the following.

Communication
The promotion part of marketing is the aspect which most people understand and come into contact with. In its simplest form, promotion is the communication between the producer and the customer. Promotional material should:

- attract   ATTENTION   of potential customers
- arouse   INTEREST   in the product

Case Study 8:   Improving the Place

In recent years, Wendy Jenkins and the staff at Whitefields Primary have put a particular effort into improving the reception area for visitors to the school and they have developed and refined the procedures for dealing with visitors and prospective parents. The reception area, which Lesley thinks has always been 'OK', is now more welcoming and there are better signs to guide visitors who do not know the school. The display of pupils' work in the visitors' area is now changed regularly and has particular themes and/or focuses on topical events. For example, around the time of Armistice Day, the display featured pupils' writing and artwork on a 'war' theme. The display is changed regularly and is managed by a *'two-person team'* the deputy and one of the nursery nurses who has turned out to have a real flair for display work and is an endless source of good ideas. They both 'volunteered' when the matter was discussed at a staff meeting. There are now better notice boards in 'public areas' – again with displays of pupils' work. These displays are also regularly changed. A main aim for Wendy in improving the 'place' component of her marketing practice was *'cost-effectiveness'*. She admits that in managing the improvement, some colleagues had to be *'won over'*. She was careful not to be seen spending money on improving facilities for visitors which could have been spent on facilities for pupils. The response to the improvements from all the staff and the pupils for that matter has in fact been very positive. *'It's improved their sense of pride in the school'* and the high quality of the displays is regularly commented on by visitors.

Another area where Wendy considers the school to be more visitor-friendly is in out of hours telephone access. The phone is now staffed from 6.00am to 6.00pm. Outside office hours, it is the duty caretaker's responsibility. Wendy has experimented with an answer-phone but ensuring that there was a response to all messages proved too difficult to ensure. She considered that *'one message not followed up out-weighed a hundred that were'*. Wendy has decided that her school is not large enough to make it worthwhile installing the touch-tone system for redirecting calls which the local comprehensive is considering .

- create   DESIRE   for its benefits
- prompt   ACTION   from potential customers

These features are usually referred to by the acronym 'AIDA'. Marland and Rogers (1991) add 'conviction' to the list to give the acronym AID(C)A. It is included to prompt the question 'How do you convince the viewer/listener/ reader that what you are saying is true?'

Promotional tools
Stott and Parr (1991) identify the three main types of promotion.

Advertising – using television, cinema, radio, posters and the press. Important considerations here include: cost, target market, timing and consistency of the advertising medium with the ethos of the organisation. Generally, advertising as a way of promoting state schools is not widely used possibly because it might reveal a weak competitive position or it might not be deemed to be a wise use of resources, or it might commit all those in the competitive arena to competitive advertising. Also arguably, advertising is not consistent with the values of many educational managers.

Public Relations (PR) – through newspapers and other means. The aim of press PR is to achieve editorial coverage which can be secured by building up trusting relationships. Used in this way it can be a reinforcing mechanism and is cheaper usually than advertising. Non-press PR includes special events in the school calendar together with receptions and/or exhibitions. The claim that whilst advertising costs money PR is free is not true although typically PR is very cost-effective. Some of the PR mechanisms will involve consultation processes and all social events can be important components of the school's PR portfolio. Off-site displays may be of limited use on their own but coupled with other kinds of exposure are positive. Exhibitions can also be useful but there are cost implications in terms of time, effort and money. In a school context maintaining a customer orientation requires regular consultation with parents and others (for example, employers) about improvements which can be made.

Outreach material – includes all material which is produced to communicate with a specific audience. Examples include the prospectus, leaflets, letters, Christmas cards, direct mail, promotional videos and any 'giveaways' (such as pens, carrier bags, badges, etc.). There are important design considerations the elements of which can collectively help to establish a corporate identity (Case Study 9).

People – over 90% of 'services' personnel come into contact with customers

The 'people' element of the marketing mix is concerned with those involved in delivering the service and with their interaction with customers receiving the service. Important considerations include the following.

The people are the service. Gray (1991) claims that any service industry is to a substantial extent the people who deliver it. For example, 90 per cent of service staff have direct contact with the customer in contrast to only 10 per cent in manufacturing organisations. In organisations, the values and practice of those providing the service must be consistent with the those of the organisation (as expressed, say, in the mission statement).

Good motivation is good organisation. Service industries need both organisation structures and staff motivation policies. There is a need for training, involvement, staff development and incentives to motivate staff.

Quality and codes of conduct. Gray (1991) makes the point that in service industries, the staff codes of conduct replace the quality control systems used

Case Study 9: Promoting the School

Forest Down is one of six comprehensive schools in a small to medium-sized city. The headteacher, Lesley Hobson views the school as being in a very competitive environment. There are a number of private schools in addition to the other 'very good' state schools. Although the school has always ('for as long as anyone can remember') produced a prospectus, the format of the prospectus has changed recently. In the late eighties/early nineties it became a 'glossy' which Lesley in fact considered to be quite expensive. In the last couple of years the school has produced a very 'straightforward' brochure – in black and white. Lesley explained the change: the new brochure 'gives the basic information, everything's there, but we now think that a glossy brochure does not promote the school well enough to warrant the expenditure'. Parents who specifically request information receive a pack which includes for example, the relevant school handbooks, the latest copy of the parents' newsletter and photocopies of recent press articles. Lesley has concluded that this kind of pack gives a much more vivid picture of the school. The money saved on the brochure has been put into other promotional tools such as staffed exhibitions at the city's schools fair and very importantly the parent's newsletter.

Lesley thinks that the parent's newsletter is one of the most cost-effective promotional tools: 'informed parents are the school's best promoter'. The use of the newsletter is not without its problems, though. The content needs to be current, relevant and well-produced. Lesley, along with senior staff have also worked particularly hard at getting the 'voice' of the newsletter right. They have also tightened up the 'pupil post' method of distribution and each newsletter now has a return slip built in (and follow up for non-returns). Parents are informed of the newsletter publication schedule so that they know when to expect them. Lesley considers that the school is 'very close' to sending out personalised newsletters with the parents' individual personal addresses and name on each letter. Lesley recognises that when this move is implemented, the distribution of the newsletter at form tutor level may have to be sharpened up in some cases. For Lesley the parents' newsletters have added value because they also give proof of service.

in manufacturing as the quality bench-mark. He asserts that education is no exception in this regard.

Corporate strategy. Since all service organisations are wholly dependent upon the success of their marketing, the marketing function is the central management function. When this is the case a 'marketing strategy', and a 'corporate strategy' are one and the same. Again schools are no exception in this regard.

Processes – the operational system by which marketing is managed within the organisation

This aspect of the marketing mix, the process of marketing, is concerned with the management of marketing within the organisation. It should not be confused with other marketing activities and is not part of the marketing strategies and tactics. In educational settings, Shreeve *et al.* (1989) suggest that the management of marketing should be the responsibility of one individual who has a co-ordination role. This person could be a 'freelance' (for example, a parent), a member of staff or the chair of governors (Marland and Rogers, 1991) although given its importance there is a good case for arguing that the management of marketing should be a senior management function.

Marketing can have significant financial implications. Pardey (1991) suggests that the budget should be determined by reference to the strategies required to achieve the objectives set for the school's marketing operations. All resources should be included and will be controlled most effectively by delegating responsibility for them to those who will be involved in achieving the objectives. Linking the responsibility for operations and budgets together and setting up clear lines of accountability can make the management more effective.

An important and challenging aspect of the management of marketing is engendering of a market orientation in the organisation. Those with this management responsibility in schools can draw on other management systems such as total quality management (Murgatroyd and Morgan, 1993; West-Burnham, 1992) and other management frameworks (see for example, Hargreaves and Hopkins, 1991; Murgatroyd, 1989). There are clear links here between those management systems and frameworks and the processes element of the marketing mix.

Proof – what actual evidence is there to confirm that customers have received service appropriate to their needs?

The proof of the sale of a manufactured product is easily obtained and unambiguous. The proof of a service – and the benefit from it – is less easy to obtain. Education is no exception to this 'service problem'. This element of the marketing mix is therefore to do with all the physical evidence that supports service delivery and any physical items which may go with the service.

CONCLUDING COMMENTS

This chapter has explored important facets of educational marketing and the choices educational managers can make as they respond to those who are making choices in relation to schools. If we take educational marketing to be the process of anticipating and identifying the needs of the actual and potential clients, satisfying those needs and informing the clients, those responsible for educational marketing in schools are faced with a daunting task. This task is complex and challenging because of the multiplicity of different clients, the wide and often conflicting needs of those clients, the problematic nature of need identification and because of the value conflicts that educational managers often have to face in marketing their schools.

REFERENCES

Alder, M. (1993) An alternative approach to parental choice, *National Commission on Education Briefing Paper No. 13*, London. National Commission on Education.

Bagley, C., Woods, P. and Glatter, R. (1996a) Scanning the market – school strategies for discovering parental perspectives, *Educational Management and Administration*, Vol. 24, no. 2, pp. 125–38.

Bagley, C., Woods, P. and Glatter, R. (1996b) Barriers to school responsiveness in the education quasi-market, *School Organisation*, Vol. 16, no. 1, pp. 45–58.

Barnes, B. (1993) *Practical Marketing for School*, Blackwell, Oxford.

Bash L. and Coulby, D. (1989) *The Education Reform Act: Competition and Control*, Cassell, London.

Bush, T., Coleman, G. and Glover, D. (1992) Life after opt-out, *Times Educational Supplement*, 4 December.

Christopher, M. and McDonald, M. (1991) *Marketing: An Introduction*, Pan Books, London.

Chubb J. and Moe, T. (1990) *Politics, Markets and America's Schools*, Brookings Institution, Washington, DC.

Coldron, J. and Boulton, P. (1991) 'Happiness' as a criterion of parents' choice of school, *Journal of Education Policy*, Vol. 6, no 2, pp. 169–78.

Cowell, D. (1984) *The Marketing of Services*, Heinemann Educational, Oxford.

David, M., West, A. and Ribbens, J. (1994) *Mother's Intuition? Choosing Secondary Schools*, Falmer, London

Demaine, J. (1988) Teacher's work, curriculum and the new right, *British Journal of Sociology of Education*, Vol. 9, no. 3, pp. 247–63.

Echols. F., MacPherson, A. and Willms, J. D. (1990) Parental Choice in Scotland, *Journal of Education Policy*, Vol. 5, no. 3.

Fenton, M. (1995) The embedded image: does school marketing make a difference? *Management in Education*, Vol. 9, no. 3, pp. 10–11.

Glatter, R. G., Johnson, D. and Woods, P. A. (1992) Marketing, choice and responses in education. Paper presented at the British Educational Management and Administration Society Research Conference, University of Nottingham, 6–8 April.

Gorard, S. (1996) Three steps to heaven? The family and school choice in Wales. *Educational Review*, Vol. 48, no. 3, pp. 237–52.

Gray, L. (1991) *Marketing Education,* Open University Press, Buckingham.

Gronroos, C. (1980) A service-oriented approach to marketing services. *European Journal of Marketing*, Vol. 12, no. 8, p. 589.

Hargreaves, D. and Hopkins, D. (1991) *The Empowered School: the Management and Practice of Development Planning,* Cassell, London.

Harrison, P. (1991) Pupils must come first, *Times Educational Supplement*, 31 May.

Hirschman, A. O. (1970) Exit Voice and Loyalty: responses to decline, in *Firms, Organizations and States*, Cambridge, MA: Harvard University Press.

Hunter, J. B. (1991) Which school? A study of parents' choice of secondary school. *Educational Research*, Vol. 33, no. 1, pp. 31–41.

James, C. R. and Phillips, P. (1995) The practice of educational marketing in schools. *Educational Management and Administration*, Vol. 23, no. 2, pp. 75–88.

Kotler, P. (1986) *The Principles of Marketing,* Prentice-Hall, Englewood Cliffs, NJ.

Le Grand, J.and Bartlett, W. (eds) (1993) *Quasi-markets and Social Policy*, Macmillan, London.

Lovelock, C. H. (1988) Classifying services to gain strategic marketing insights, in C. H. Lovelock, (ed) *Managing Services: Marketing Operations and Human Resources,* Prentice-Hall, Englewood Cliffs, NJ.

Maclure, S. (1992) *Education Reformed*, Open University Press, Milton Keynes.

Marland, M. and Rogers, R. (1991) *Marketing the School*, Heinemann Educational, Oxford.

Metherall, C. (1991) Space for Marketing, *School Governor*, Feb/Mar pp. 20–1.

Miliband, D. (1991) *Markets, Politics and Education: Beyond the Education Reform Act,* IPPR, London.

Murgatroyd, S. (1989) KAIZEN: school-wide quality improvement, *School Organisation,* Vol. 9, no. 2, pp. 241–60.

Murgatroyd, S. and Morgan, C. (1992) *Total Quality Management and the School,* Open University Press, Buckingham.

Pardey, D. (1991) *Marketing for Schools,* Kogan Page, London.

Rathmell, J. M. (1966) What is meant by services?, *Journal of Marketing,* Vol. 30, no. 4, pp. 32–6.

Schotter, A. (1990) *Free Market Economics,* Basil Blackwell, Oxford.

Shostak, G. L. (1977) Breaking free from product marketing, *Journal of Marketing,* Vol. 41, no. 4, pp. 73–80.

Shreeve, R., Thorp, J. and Rickett, J. (1989) *Marketing Hertfordshire Colleges,* Herts County Council/Ware College Marketing and Information Unit, Ware, Herts.

Smedley, D. (1995) Marketing Secondary schools to parents – some lessons from the research on parental choice, *Educational Management and Administration,* Vol. 23, no. 2, pp. 96–103.

Stillman, A. (1986) Preference or choice? Parents, LEAs and the Education Act 1980. *Educational Research,* Vol. 28, no. 1, pp. 3–13.

Stillman, A. and Maychell, K. (1986) *Choosing Schools: Parents, LEAs and the 1980 Education Act,* Windsor, NFER-Nelson.

Stott, K. and Parr, H. (1991) *Marketing your School,* Hodder and Stoughton, Sevenoaks.

Thomas, A. and Dennison, B. (1991) Parental or pupil choice – who really decides in urban schools. *Educational Management and Administration,* Vol. 19, no. 4, pp. 243–51.

Tomlinson, S. (1991) A New Partnership: Home-School Contracts. in A. Ross and E. Tomlinson (eds) *Teachers and Parents: New Roles,* IPPR, London.

Webster, A., Owen, G. and Crome, D. (1993) *School Marketing: Making it Easy for Parents to Select your School,* Avec Designs, Bristol.

West, A. and Varlaam, A. (1991) Choosing a secondary school: parents of secondary school children, *Educational Research,* Vol. 33, no. 1.

West, A., Varlaam, A. and Scott, G. (1991) Choosing a Secondary School: pupils' perceptions, *Educational Research,* Vol. 33, no. 1, pp. 22–30.

West-Burnham, J. (1992) *Managing Quality in Schools: a TQM Approach,* Longman, Harlow.

Whitty, G. (1989) The new right and the national curriculum: state control or market forces?, *Journal of Educational Policy,* Vol. 4, no. 4, pp. 329–41.

Williams, T. (1996) Parental Views and Expectations. Unpublished MSc Dissertation, University of Glamorgan.

Woods, P. A. (1994) School response to the quasi market in J. M. Halstead (ed.) *Parental Choice and Education,* London: Kogan Page.

Woods, P. A. Bagley, C. and Glatter, R. (1996) Dynamics of competition – the effects of local competitive arenas on schools. in, C. Pole and R. Chawla-Duggan (eds) *Reshaping Education in the 1990s: Perspectives on Secondary Schooling,* Falmer Press, London.

Yorke, D. and Bakewell, C. J. (1991) Choice of secondary school, *International Journal of Educational Management,* Vol. 5, no. 2.

2.5

Managing Staff

VALERIE HALL

On average 75 per cent of a school's budget goes towards teachers' salaries. They have always constituted a major expenditure, but responsibility for managing the costs of employing staff has only recently been required of schools. The effect has been as governments intend when they decentralise budgets; to focus school managers' thinking about how they manage staff to achieve optimum performance in the most cost-effective way.

The shift towards school-based management has been accompanied by a shift in the language used, both in and outside education, to describe the processes involved. The term 'human resource management' (HRM) has been accepted more readily in non-educational settings but is daily gaining currency in education (see, for example, Riches and Morgan, 1989; O'Neill, 1994; Seifert, 1996). Until it entered the vocabulary, managing staff conventionally referred to the ways in which teaching and teaching support staff were, among other things, recruited, selected, developed, monitored and motivated. Many of these processes were shared between the LEA and schools, with LEAs holding the majority of the relevant budgets and providing many of the personnel services necessary. As schools assumed greater control, so the concept of HRM has assumed a greater relevance for integrating these different personnel management functions. However, describing people as 'human resources' continues to be controversial for those commentators like Bottery (1992), who prefer to see people as 'resourceful humans'. Generally, the culture of education is suspicious of philosophies and practices transplanted from other work settings, driven by different values about people and products. HRM does, however, embody the tensions with which this volume is concerned, between managing for autonomy and managing for accountability. My purpose in this chapter is to show how the concept of 'strategic human resource management' (SHRM) can be both liberating and constraining, as a strategy for managing people in education.

DEFINING THE TERMS

Riches and Morgan (1989, pp. 2–3) define HRM as follows:

The HRM approach seeks to start from a consideration of what the strategies of an organization might be and then asks how the human resources can help formulate and accomplish those strategies, and what human development and motivation is required to meet those ends.

HRM's focus on the links between managing staff and achieving the organisation's strategic objectives differentiates it from earlier 'personnel' models. These were seen to atomise rather than integrate staff management functions. Key people management tasks were the responsibility of one individual or department rather than diffused through line management structures. Now, in autonomous schools, all teachers have some management responsibilities and, as such, share in 'managing' each other. Personnel strategies were also mainly reactive and *ad hoc*, rather than proactive and strategic. In contrast, SHRM addresses organisational and individual needs together so that meeting individual needs complements rather than clashes with meeting the school's needs. After all, the ultimate goal of HRM in schools is to improve the quality of the learning environment for young people.

The problem with using SHRM to describe managing staff arises, as we shall see, from the conflict between the values underpinning human resource strategies, as advocated by central government, and those which inform the management philosophies and behaviour of many of those in education. Both parties are concerned to improve standards in education. For government, this is achieved through management practices that prioritise control rather than development and liberation. In DES circular 7/91 (p. 3) the Secretary of State states his aim: 'to build on the progress that has already been made towards pupil-led funding and delegated management so as to increase schools' control over resources and thereby improve the standards of education which they provide.'

Resources, of course, include human resources i.e. the people who make up the staffs of schools and colleges. School-based management provides opportunities for schools to review their approaches to managing staff. It also creates a new, and for many uncomfortable, agenda in relations between those who have a primary responsibility for management and their colleagues. Recent research on effective schools has confirmed the potency of transformational leadership, in which the leading professional role is reinstated alongside the chief executive (Bolam *et al.*, 1993). These same transformational qualities are in conflict with the pressures on school managers now to make hard executive decisions about people. In this chapter I will look at the ways in which the constraints of government expectations of how people in schools should be managed (as human resources) can be transformed by the choices open to school managers within an SHRM approach to support and enhance the performance of 'resourceful humans'. The chapter begins by proposing a model for reviewing SHRM approaches to managing people in schools; then considers each of the human resource management strategies in turn to determine their potential for liberating or constraining staff performance. It concludes by showing how a particular view of SHRM allows managers to combine accountability and freedom for the benefit of the school.

THE CONTEXT FOR SHRM IN SCHOOLS: CONSTRAINTS, DEMANDS AND CHOICES

As an approach to managing people, SHRM is subject to the constraints, demands and choices that shape and reflect managers' responses in schools. Human resource management involves People, Philosophies, Policies and Practices (the '4Ps', as I see it). The people to be managed vary between schools and, as individuals and groups, within schools. People, children and adults are at the heart of any educational enterprise. They have different expectations and needs and very different responses to attempts to 'manage' them to achieve the school's purposes. Similarly, different managers hold different beliefs about managing people, depending on their preferred explanations of human action, and their philosophies and principles influence the policies and practices they devise. Policies represent both formal and informal agreements about how things are done in the school. While school staffs sometimes question the cry that frequently goes out 'We need a policy on that', they provide a necessary framework for action. Practices describe what actually happens when staff are, for example, recruited, selected, developed, appraised. In other words, they are the realisation in action of the philosophies and policies that guide how staff are managed.

Subsequent sections consider each of these in turn. First I want to consider the scope and impact of the constraints, demands and choices with which managers in schools are faced. This framework comes from Rosemary Stewart's (1982) research on managerial work and behaviour. She defines constraints as the factors, external or internal to the organisation, that limit what a jobholder can do. Demands are what anyone in a job has to do i.e. what must be done. Choices are the activities that a jobholder can but does not have to do. This framework, applied to HRM in education, shows how decisions about HRM strategies emerge from the tension between constraints, demands and choices facing managers in autonomous schools. It is sometimes suggested that increased levels of stress among school managers are the outcomes of too many demands within too many constraints. Yet recent studies of school leaders (e.g. Grace, 1995; Hall, 1996) show many headteachers as welcoming the opportunities delegated budgets bring to manage staff creatively. For them decentralised budgets represent challenges and choices within demands and constraints.

The constraints on school managers as employers fall into four categories: legal, technical, financial and contextual. Legal constraints arise from legislation governing employment. Technical constraints relate to the managers' own capacity for carrying out their management responsibilities. Delegated budgets mean financial constraints as well as creative opportunities. They have to be managed within a context of competition with other schools in the market place, i.e. the contextual constraints within whose parameters school managers have to operate, whether in maintained or grant-maintained schools and colleges.

Many of these constraints are not specific to managing staff in education. Legal constraints arise from the different employment laws such as:

- Sex Discrimination Acts 1975 and 1986;
- Equal Pay Act 1970 and 1984;
- Race Relations Act 1976;
- Employment Protection (Consolidation) Act 1978;
- Health and Safety at Work Act 1974;
- Employment Acts regulating the ways employers and trade unions could act in dispute.

Teacher-specific legislation includes:

- Teachers Pay and Conditions Act 1987;
- Education Reform Act 1988;
- School Teachers Pay and Conditions Act 1991 (which set up the School Teachers Review Body).

Seifert (1996, p. 23) provides a useful summary of the impact of legislation on the employment of teachers. He points to the problematic nature of the ambiguous relationship between school managers (heads and deputies) and the employers (governing bodies, LEAs, DFE officials and ministers):

> The first point is that managers, whether they are heads or LEA officials, are answerable to the employer. Managers, in this sense, are the agents and representatives of the employer, and, as far as employees and their unions are concerned, decisions by managers reflect employer policy and have the authority of employer support . . . This represents an important aspect of both state employment and collective bargaining: that managers are required to carry out the policy of the employer but they may be subject to strong countervailing influences from their own profession, their own union, their own service culture and their own expectations of being a head teacher and/or LEA official.

The 1989 teacher regulations require a school to have a head and teachers who are qualified. Beyond that, 'at any school . . . there shall be employed a staff of teachers suitable and sufficient in numbers for the purpose of securing the provision of education appropriate to the ages, abilities, aptitudes and needs of the pupils'. Once these provisions have been met, school managers are then faced with the explicit and implicit 'demands'; which arise from the different regulations including:

- instituting proper appointment procedures (recruitment and selection);
- providing an induction programme for new staff;
- deploying staff effectively and efficiently;
- providing opportunities for training and development (including coaching and mentoring);
- review the staff performance, potential and development needs through appraisal systems and OFSTED inspections;
- gaining staff commitment through managing the school's culture;
- managing staff reductions (through retirement, redundancy, redeployment, etc.);
- ensuring fair systems for carrying out all its human resource management functions, including grievances, disputes and dismissal.

The scale of the task of managing schools today is clearly daunting. The capacity of individual and groups of school managers to meet these demands depends on the support available to them, their own opportunities for development and the personal strengths they bring to the job. If managers have to deal with all these 'demands' in managing people, who manages the managers and gives them support in the task? What choices do they have in how they 'manage'? As Figure 2.5.1 suggests the choices are about personal philosophies, policies and principles and preferred strategies or processes.

MANAGING PEOPLE: SOME PHILOSOPHIES

Managers' personal philosophies about education and managing people provide the guiding principles for their management actions. For example, are staff to be valued as 'resourceful people' or 'human resources' and treated accordingly? These contrasting perspectives which place a different value on the 'people' to be managed, are captured in Storey's (1987) distinction between 'hard' and 'soft' normative models of HRM. The 'hard' model is associated with utilitarian instrumentalism: ends are more important than means. The 'soft' model reflects developmental humanism: means are as important as ends. Yet, in the context of managing schools, both the means and the ends are people. In Figure 2.5.1, I suggest some differences in approaches to managing people that arise from these contrasting philosophical positions. I would argue that how managers in education go about selecting, motivating and developing staff will be influenced by the beliefs they have about people as people and people as employees. For example, favouring contracts that make staff easily expendable demonstrates sharply drawn boundaries in perceptions of people's personal and professional identities, i.e. taking a 'hard' line.

The dichotomies represented in Figure 2.5.1 are, of course, simplistic particularly in their implication that the 'soft' approaches are less controlling than the 'hard'. People-centred programmes like Investors in People (which many schools are becoming involved in) can seem as manipulative in their attempts to gain staff commitment as 'hard' approaches. The dichotomies also oversimplify by failing to capture the dynamic interplay between the rights and responsibilities of employers and employees. We need to hear the accounts of all involved to understand fully how management strategies (whether hard or soft) are worked out in practice. However, Figure 2.5.1 does provide a framework for reviewing the different values that underpin the choices managers make in carrying out HRM processes, as we shall see.

An example of how constraints, demands and choices come together is in the ways in which school-based management can lead to the creative deployment of staff. It allows decisions to be made at the level of the school about, for example, the creation and allocation of posts of responsibility in primary schools or whether or not to have subject department heads in secondary schools. The study by Mortimore *et al.* (1994) of what they call associate staff, i.e. all the people working in schools who are not teachers, shows how the

'HARD'	'SOFT'
Systems-led	People-led
Market-led	
Cost effectiveness	Effective learning
Improblematic goals	Diverse goals, 'visions'
Periphery workers = variable cost	All workers important
Selection to 'fit'	Something to offer
Targeted development	Development for all
'Accountable' appraisal	'Development' appraisal
Human *resources*	*Resourceful* humans
People – means to an end	People – ends in themselves
Control, compliance, 'fit'	Consensualism, mutuality, commitment
Training for now	Development for the future
Strategic concern	Excellence ethos
Mechanistic	'Organic'
Uniformity	Flexibility

Figure 2.5.1 HRM: Which philosophy?

constraints of school-based management led to the 'demand' for new ways of distributing responsibilities and workloads, often away from teachers and towards other staff. Decisions about new or modified roles reflect choices about who is suitable to carry out which tasks. For example, many school secretaries in primary and secondary schools have taken on the equivalent of a bursar's job. In some cases, their pay and status has increased accordingly, though this is dependent on the senior managers' beliefs about how people should be rewarded. Purchon's (1991) study shows that many school secretaries felt overworked, underpaid and undervalued. In contrast, Gittins (1989) reports his school's decision to employ a bursar with the experience and status of a senior manager in the school. These divergent responses suggest that, in making choices about deploying staff, different perceptions of men's (bursar) and women's (school secretary) may have a part to play. Mortimore and his colleagues explain the disproportionate number of women among associate staff in their studies as 'related to the nature of contracts and conditions of service offered with the posts' (p. 181). Their questionable justification of lower rates of pay and less favourable conditions of service is that the posts offer women, who have been out of paid employment for domestic reasons, a route back into the job market.

This is just one example of the tensions for managers in schools in managing people for accountability and freedom in the context of autonomous schools As Seifert (1996, p. 6) points out, management in schools has always been 'the simultaneous exercise of power over colleagues in the interests of employers and pay masters, and the exercise of power for colleagues to achieve the shared values and co-operative spirit required to stimulate a team of dedicated professionals.' The tension for managers in schools is thus in the tension of management itself, in the context of teaching as a profession. Elsewhere (Hall, 1997) I have written about the mismatch between pedagogic and managerialist cultures and the impact on management roles. Education managers' credibility in their role depends on keeping in touch with education's central tasks; learning and teaching. This inevitably influences their approach to managing staff, particularly teaching staff. While, on the one hand, they are being forced to consider total and unit labour costs, they are also driven by their commitment to professional collegiality.

For some commentators, these tensions constitute polar opposites and cannot be reconciled. Enjoying what Grace (1995) calls the 'new playing field' of school management in response to educational reform is tantamount to selling out on educational values, in his view. The new managerialism, in which people are seen mainly as resources, fails to challenge the values informing the reforms. Yet my own study of women heads at work (Hall, 1996) showed how they aimed to transform the constraints of new responsibilities into a form of entrepreneurialism that was ethically based. Their strategies for 'bringing out the best in staff', a key function of HRM, reflected other research evidence about what effective school managers do (Blase and Kirby, 1992). They demonstrated a resistance to the government's economic and political imperative to get more for less (Seifert, 1996) and its implicit attempts to transform their consciousness, values and behaviour as well as the headship role itself (Grace, 1995).

Management styles relate to the values individual managers hold about people. In managing staff in their schools, heads have had to adjust to the constraints and demands of changed relationships with their governing bodies. Whatever principles inform a head's choice of human resource management strategies, there is no guarantee these will be shared with the governors who are now joint partners in the school management enterprise. In spite of changes in their statutory powers, research suggests that most heads remain 'in charge' (Grace, 1995, p. 77). The power of 'interference' from governors, when it does come could be, according to Grace, represented as 'an appropriate and long overdue move towards a more democratic and consultative culture of school leadership' (p. 84).

In the rest of this chapter I want to explore the issue raised by HRM in education from two perspectives. First, I will look at the ways in which the different personnel processes are transformed by an SHRM approach that is underpinned by values that liberate, albeit seeking accountability within constraints. Second, I will consider the workplace culture of schools and its contribution to effective staff performance. How far can it be 'managed' and through which strategies?

MANAGING PEOPLE: WHO ARE THEY?

Picking up my theme of the '4Ps' of human resource management (people, philosophies, policies and practices) my starting point is the defining characteristics of the people they concern. One possible approach to managing people in education would assert that they are no different from employees in any other field of work and can be understood and 'managed' in exactly the same way as factory workers in Detroit or health workers in Japan. Yet such an approach ignores the interplay between the meanings of work for employees both individually and in terms of the central purpose of the work itself. For most staff working in education (reflected in the majority of the staffing budget being spent on teachers' salaries), supporting children's and adults' learning is a primary motivation for working in this field, alongside the need to earn a living. Others, such as teaching support staff, governors, external support staff, may bring different meanings to their work relationship which may require different responses from schools as employers.

Managing staff in education is, however, mainly about managing professionals. Busher and Saran (1995, p. 1) introduce their discussion of new concepts of teacher professionality by referring to a vision in which:

> schools moving into the twenty-first century . . . are rapidly becoming centres of learning, not just for students but for all involved with the institution, including staff (both teaching and support staff), parents and members of the local community . . . This visionary view of schools points to an entirely new setting for the work of teachers, support staff and governors. It has implications both for the management of teachers in schools and for understanding teacher professionality and staff development.

Employers ignore at their peril the impact on individual performance of an employee's 'professional identity', including their identification through trade union membership, with the profession's collective interests. Ozga's pessimistic view that effective management of people will become managerialism reflects this concern. Within this model, which resembles the 'hard' model I described earlier, teachers would be deskilled, disempowered and conflict would reign. HRM becomes, in her view, a tool for controlling, not liberating teachers as professionals. (Ozga, 1995, p. 34). Beresford (1995, p. 74), however, argues the need for teachers, through their teacher unions, to seek ways of challenging the rational–economic model for managing people in education and reinstating an alternative human relations model (resembling the 'soft' model described earlier). In his view, this model, based on teachers' responses is more likely to achieve the school management conditions under which teacher unions suggest effective professionals should operate: 'While the goals of academic achievement and good pupil behaviour are paramount, cordial as well as professional relationships amongst staff are clearly represented, but are developed collaboratively by all staff rather than being the sole preserve of a hierarchical management team.' In these alternative perspectives lie the possibilities of SHRM approaches in education that take account of the relationship between people's experience of work and its primary purpose. HRM in education is about managing professionals and associate staff and others who have a stake in running the school i.e. governors, parents and the wider community. Its philosophies, policies and practices need to reflect this central concern.

The other challenge is in managing diversity and recognising the need for and needs of different groups of staff within a framework of justice and equity.

Recruitment and selection, for example, are about attracting 'the best person for the job'. Employers, including those in education, have historically worked within narrow boundaries in defining 'the best person for the job'. The disproportionately low number of women in senior educational management posts and teachers from ethnic minorities are testimony to this narrowness of vision. The same myopia encompasses discrimination on the grounds of disability and sexual orientation. In spite of Equal Opportunities legislation and other initiatives, school managers' attitudes to these different groups of workers are still influenced by age old stereotypes. The process has been reinforced by the 'hard' thrust of school-based management systems that push schools to prioritise 'efficient' use of resources over 'fair'. For example, few women returning to work after maternity leave, will find after-school child care facilities available. Many, who have been out longer, will be forced into jobs at a lower status and pay than previously.

MANAGING PEOPLE: HRM PRACTICES

How, then, do schools go about their personnel function? How far can and does it reflect their concerns for the particular characteristics of staff in schools and the need for HRM strategies that are fair and acknowledge diversity? Are the strategies used aimed at controlling or liberating people's performance at work? Figure 2.5.2

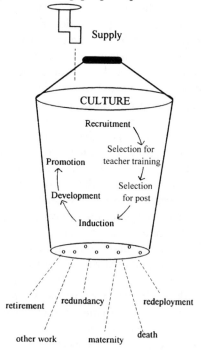

Figure 2.5.2   The flow of staff in education

shows the different HRM processes as they relate to teachers' career cycles. Many of the issues it raises apply equally to teaching support staff, although employers continue to see their work more as a job rather than a career. This is to the disadvantage of both employers (who fail to get the best from these staff) and employees (who fail to get the best from their jobs).

Recruitment of people into education is the starting point for a quality teaching workforce. Schools necessarily work within the constraints of national factors relating to teacher supply and shortages over which they have no influence. In responding to the need for new staff they have considerable room for choice in education systems where teachers are not allocated centrally. Autonomous schools may have responsibility for initial teacher training. They will certainly be responsible for attracting teachers to specific posts. A strategic view of recruitment starts from the institution's present and future staffing needs and seeks to meet these within a set of practices that are fair and efficient.

Although individual schools and colleges may be constrained in the extent to which they can influence strategic recruitment practices, there are some possibilities open to them. Dodds (1993), for example, stresses the need for regional structures, As well as national, to aid supply and recruitment. In his view all the changes planned for education will require more, rather than fewer, teachers. Yet transferring responsibility for recruitment to individual schools may be too big a burden for them to bear. He concludes:

> No doubt many will try to grapple with the problem but some of the employment issues are too large for the size of the present employer units. No large successful employer in the commercial or industrial world leaves such matters to their outlet units. In order to provide the necessary requirement of a proper recruitment and retention strategy for the teaching force some regional organisation will have to be established. The future supply of teachers depends on it.
>
> (p. 27)

Even at school level, strategic approaches to recruitment are possible. In the context of the School's Development Plan and anticipated movements of existing staff, they need to take account of:

- how many and what types of people are required;
- which of these needs can be satisfied by transfer and development of existing staff and where staff need to be recruited externally;
- anticipated problems in recruitment (for example, due to the school's location or the higher wages offered by other local employers);
- the need for a recruitment timetable, so that posts do not remain vacant unnecessarily.

Effective recruitment practices take account of the wide range of groups who might be attracted to a post (e.g. women returners, ethnic minority teachers) and the best ways of reaching them. The problem for schools managing this process is in being prepared to devote the necessary finances and having the appropriate expertise to do it properly. Advertisements can be costly; developing job descriptions and person specifications are skilled activities. Yet the cost of getting it wrong and appointing a staff member who 'fails' (for whatever reason) is enormous. Local Authority handbooks provide advice on proper appointment procedures, including the appropriate placement of well-worded advertisements. The freedom that responsibility for recruitment brings to schools is in the possibilities it allows for precise targeting of the kinds of people they are looking for. A vacancy on the staff allows them to consider:

- whether it needs to be filled or whether the work could be reorganised, relocated or redistributed;
- the nature of the job to be filled and the kind of person wanted;
- whether someone should be recruited from inside the school or outside;
- whether the incentives (e.g. pay, promotion, support in post) are appropriate for the kind of person sought;
- whether the process is non-discriminatory and based on objective criteria for viewing the qualifications for the job rather than the sex or race of the applicant.

These 'demands' for a fair system of recruitment and selection have been contradicted, to some extent, by financial constraints. An HMI Report to the DFE (1992) described some outcomes of school-based management as the appointment of younger, less experienced staff, increases in the use of non-teaching staff and more part-time teachers. These trends appear to confirm the fear of budget priorities leading to the creation of a 'peripheral' workforce in schools which is both cheaper and more expendable. Seemingly contributing to the flexibility of a school's strategic plan, such measures potentially reduce both the commitment of staff and their employment security and prospects. Where they are based on a recognition of all employees' needs for flexibility, particularly women combining work and family, then they have a humanistic as well as pragmatic basis. When flexibility is synonymous with casualisation, then people and their rights as employees are under threat.

If recruitment is about attracting the right kinds of applicants for a post, then selection is about finding the best person for the job. Budgetary constraints apply here too as well as technical constraints, since there is an even greater need for those responsible for selection decisions to know what they are doing. The biggest change, since the POST Project completed its review of headteacher selection in Britain in the eighties (when only one LEA had a headteacher job description), is in the existence of job descriptions for staff at all levels (Morgan et al., 1983). In some cases, these reflect the growth of a concern for identifying the competencies associated with skilful performance. Earley (1992), Esp (1993) and Jirasinghe and Lyons (1996), for example, all provide well-researched examples of competency-based approaches to school management, with implications for how managers are selected and developed. The Teacher Training Agency's (1995) current proposals for training and development are based on competencies identified at each stage of a teacher's career. In spite of these moves, questions remain about the reduction of the skills, qualities, knowledge required for effective teaching to seemingly mechanistic competences. They appear to fit more with controlling approaches to human performance. Yet they can provide a basis for a much more systematic approach to selection that considers:

• what the job consists of (job analysis and job description of key tasks and activities);
• what knowledge, skills and values are required to perform it effectively (job and person specifications);
• which selection methods are most likely to lead to 'the best person' being chosen.

More systematic approaches to selection provide a powerful mechanism for school managers to bring people on to the staff who will be committed to the school's values or bring new and challenging perspectives. Once more, how managers use selection will depend on whether they are seeking 'human resources' or 'resourceful humans'. The strategy or process is led by the philosophy and principles. In either case, objective selection processes require using measurable standards to judge applicants, rejecting stereotypes and using selection methods that are reliable and valid. Equitable approaches, as well as being morally appropriate, ensure that the best available people have equal access to all jobs and positions, as well as receiving equal treatment in post.

All these requirements apply as much to selecting non-teaching as teaching staff, whose contribution to the life of the whole school is crucial. Appointing the wrong person as cook or caretaker can have devastating repercussions for the whole school. As Figure 2.5.2 suggests, recruiting and selecting the right staff are only two of the processes through which schools seek to accomplish their organisational objectives through their staff. Providing support for individual teacher development is equally important, whether at the induction stage (first two years in-post), the in-service stage or transitional stage (promotion, redeployment, retirement). Getting support for development right means having appropriate systems in place for performance review, including monitoring, inspection and appraisal. The spectre of development for accountability or freedom raises its head yet again, as school managers grapple with the constraints of training budgets, the demands of performance review systems and the possibility of choices about learning events and learning environments. On the one hand they are exhorted by central government to monitor closely and get rid of failing teachers. OFSTED inspections not only play havoc with a staff's morale (Ouston *et al.*, 1996), but also require heads to respond to their identification of failing teachers as well as failing schools. On the other, they are seduced by the principles of 'the learning organization' in which, as Kath Aspinwall shows elsewhere in this volume, all staff cooperate in collective learning.

Reporting on her research into continuing professional development (CPD) for teachers, McMahon (1996) contrasts the government's dissatisfaction with the outcomes of CPD with teachers' own perceptions of its impact on their performance. The DFEE's concern is that it is not delivering maximum value for money, estimated at some £400 million a year. She comments:

> This may sound like a paradox to teachers who have worked exceptionally hard in recent years to cope with change on an unprecedented scale. New curriculum and assessment procedures have been implemented; schools have learned to manage their own budgets and to work more closely with their governing bodies; individual staff appraisals and OFSTED inspections have been introduced. All these changes have required teachers to gain new knowledge and skills, acquired through programmes of in-service teacher education, largely funded through the GEST budget. The structures for providing CPD have also improved; individual and school needs can be identified through appraisal and development planning; schools have their own INSET budgets and five non-contact days are available for development activities. Surely, this is evidence that the provision of CPD is at least satisfactory? Well, it depends on what the various stakeholders think CPD is for.

(p. 5)

School managers are faced with choices about the relative priorities of individual and institutional development needs, within funding constraints that emphasise on-the-job training to meet immediate deficiencies in the balance of staff skills and knowledge in organisations. The literature abounds with models for developing teachers' performance (e.g. Oldroyd and Hall, 1991) but its prescriptions for holistic approaches conflict with the harder training models. Within a SHRM approach that prioritises accountability to people as well as the organisation, CPD would aim to meet the changing nature of development needs at different stages of a teacher's career, as well as the immediate needs of the organisation.

Bennett (1995) proposes ways for middle managers in schools to address the tension between manager as agent of the headteacher's or school's vision and coordinator of the professional activity of their team. Levine's (1989) research (in the United States) into how school principals 'promote adult growth' in schools, demonstrates the value of viewing teacher development as a life-long learning process. Learning happens most effectively when the individual is involved in the process as a whole person. One way around the dilemma of prioritising individual and school needs may be in refusing to see them as dichotomous. If, as I suggested earlier, there is an overlap between education's central purpose and the meaning of work to those working in education, then there is greater scope for synchronicity of individual and school needs than exists in, for example, banking or manufacturing. Most teachers consider students's needs as paramount, even when these may be different from their own as employees. The creative manager recognises and works with this commitment within a collaborative rather than conflict approach that drives people apart.

Appraisal provides potentially a route into understanding the relationship between individual and school needs but the potential of appraisal systems in education for identifying development needs is muddied by their accountability purposes of performance, potential and reward review. ACAS (booklet

11) suggests that appraisals regularly record an assessment of an employee's performance, potential and development needs. In this way, they provide an opportunity to take an overall view of work content, loads and volume; and to review what has been achieved during the reporting period and agree objectives for the next. Well-documented negotiations between teacher unions and the government led to an appraisal scheme that recognised accountability (it was compulsory and included observation of teaching) as well as development principles. The dominant message from government, to use appraisal for control purposes, is reflected in OFSTED's concern that headteachers have avoided linking appraisal, even indirectly, with pay and promotion, despite encouragement in the Circular to consider such links. The continuing resistance to an appraisal scheme in education which would like to control performance through pay means that its professional development purposes have been lost sight of. Many schools conduct a ritualistic version of appraisal, to satisfy DFEE requirements, but reserve the 'real' review for staff development interviews conducted outside its specifications. Unsullied by links to merit pay and redundancy, these interviews aim to be supportive and developmental. They help individual teachers identify strengths and weaknesses that can be tackled through appropriate staff development. They should, of course be culture free and operated in such a way that women and ethnic minority teachers among others have the same access to development opportunities as others. Thompson (1989) and Shakeshaft (1993) have made cases for a consideration of the effects of gender on the appraisal process, particularly since senior managers in education are more likely to be men. However, such interviews uncoupled from the appraisal process lose their strategic potential as far as the school is concerned. DES Circular 12/91 states:

In the majority of schools, the links between appraisal and the School Development Plan (SDP) were undeveloped. In 80 per cent, some element of linkage was apparent, but in only a third of schools was the link an established one – strong and clearly in compliance with the Circular. In these schools, there was a clear attempt to reconcile and align individual targets with those of the SDP, particularly as exemplified in departmental objectives. It was comparatively rare for the headteacher's analysis of appraisal targets to provide the feeding of common concerns into the SDP.

(p. 17)

In only a third of schools was there a clear attempt to reconcile and align individual targets with those of the SDP (p. 17). The report concludes that, 'if it is to be effective, the national appraisal scheme needs to address a number of current weaknesses in accountability, as well as meeting individuals' professional development needs' (p. 25).

Mentoring presents similar problems to appraisal since management posts in education are held mainly by men and teaching posts by women. Potentially valuable from an organisational point of view, it can help identify, develop and motivate people with the potential to fill key roles in the future. Mentors are identified as experienced and trusted advisers who play a variety of roles in helping a less experienced colleague manage and advance their career. They can help solve real problems and create learning opportunities from the individual's experience. From their senior positions they can provide insight into the workings of the organisation's culture, often hidden to the uninitiated. Yet there are many issues around choice of mentor, including those relating to cross-gender mentoring. Achieving a balance between intimacy and distance means careful selection of partners is crucial.

MANAGING THE CULTURE

Emerging from this consideration of the different HRM strategies available to managers in schools is the powerful influence of the culture of the school as workplace. Elsewhere in this volume, the editors argue that the effective articulation of an appropriate culture is an essential precondition for exercising organisational choice within a world of autonomy and constraint. Here I will concentrate on what I will call the eight 'C's' of workplace culture: Commitment, Conditions of Service, Communication, Consultation, Creativity, Collaboration, Conflict, Control. Together they form a tightly woven context for HRM practices. I will look at whether workplace cultures can be managed, why it might be desirable, examples of school managers' attempts to do so, and the implications for underperforming teachers. Influenced by the Harvard Business School model of HRM (Beer *et al.*, 1984), HRM outside education has thus become associated with the creation and maintenance of a strong organisational culture. The notion has a particular resonance in education, where research suggests close links between types of school culture and school effectiveness.

In contrast to this emphasis on corporate cultures, writers like Hargreaves (1994, p. 166) talk of the content and form of teacher cultures: the 'way we do things around here' and 'the patterns of relationship and forms of association' that characterise relations between teachers and their colleagues. He is concerned to highlight the dangers of the culture of collaboration (another version of corporate culture) if it is 'contrived' and at the expense of individual teacher autonomy. Within an HRM perspective both these approaches to managing culture, individualistic and collaborative, are potentially about controlling people. Encouraging individual autonomy limits the possibilities for collective action although it may also enhance individual employees' creative potential. Cultures of collaboration if contrived may inhibit individual creativity though they can also achieve a synergy that transcends what any one individual could produce.

The first question we have to ask about culture is whether it can, in fact, be 'managed'. Is it something an organisation is or has? Hargreaves' definitions above suggest a view that a school is a culture and attempts to manipulate it may be more damaging than fruitful. Yet initiatives such as Total Quality Management (TQM) and Investors in People (IIP) are predicated on the belief that the culture of schools can be changed, alongside the behaviour of these who work in them. They claim to gain employee commitment through

---

Case Study 10:   Gaining staff commitment: contrived or chosen?

Headteacher John Roe was convinced that the Investors in People (IIP) Programme was just the boost to morale Sandy Lane School needed. The programme's emphasis on senior management's commitment as a starting point led him to believe that consultation with staff first about the school's involvement was inappropriate. He assumed they would be pleased at the funding for development it offered. As a result, he barely listened to his senior colleagues' concerns that, unless staff were involved from the beginning, it might backfire. Having secured what he thought was their agreement to go ahead with the project, he was dismayed when they failed to support him at the governors' meeting. They joined in the governors' attack on the idea, implying the head had not consulted either the wider staff or his senior management team. As a result, relations were strained for some time among team members and the IIP scheme did not go ahead. John Roe felt angry at the school's failure to benefit from the development opportunities for all staff that it provided.

Meg Evans, headteacher of Seaview Comprehensive, was also enthusiastic about IIP's possibilities. She worked hard to sell it to staff, capitalising on the career ambitions of a head of faculty who was keen for a whole school responsibility. Staff were asked to volunteer to join a working party to take the scheme forward. The programme offered the possibility for reviewing goals, structures and reviews, where these had become stale. Everything started with the volunteer working group, including the bursar and the caretaker. No-one was pressured and time was made available where necessary. It was a public exercise in which people's tasks and responsibilities were openly discussed.

---

involvement and empowerment but is this just rhetoric to obscure control? There is no doubt that the schools in Murgatroyd and Morgan's (1993) study of TQM benefited from the initiative. Similarly, as Case Study 10 suggests, Investors in People can succeed in inspiring some school staffs towards improved performance. The problem is that they both represent top-down models for managing culture that potentially conflict with notions of teacher empowerment through teacher-led collaboration and collegiality. Meg Evans got away with it by consulting widely first; John Roe didn't. Advocates of these corporate approaches point to their capacity for gaining and retaining staff commitment, focusing individual contributions and linking them to overall strategy. The question remains whether they succeed in changing culture only at the level of visible behaviour while values and assumptions remain intact. How far are the behaviours generated based on internalised values? Fullan (1993) has asked the same question in the context of schooling and arrived at a similar answer: that a concern with the ends (behavioural compliance) might be the best answer since a change in values is so much harder to achieve. This is particularly true of equalities work in organisations, which so often succeeds in altering the policies but fails to challenge the values and assumptions underpinning them. There may be changes to what Schein (1992) calls the 'artefacts' of organisational cultures including publicity that reflects equality issues, the gender balance in the workforce, family-friendly policies and equality goals. The harder task is changing values (e.g. about the value of the contribution of different groups to the organisation) and assumptions (e.g. that one group's career aspirations are different from another's).

Part of managing culture includes managing the different incentives that motivate people to perform well. These include pay, conditions of work, fair HRM systems and involvement in decision-making. What appears simple in motivating employees in other work contexts becomes complex in education, where a causal link between pay and performance cannot be assumed. At a time of multiple changes when high morale is most necessary in schools, it also appears to be a time when it is at its lowest ebb. Faced with the need to implement a multiplicity of mainly imposed changes, many teachers feel threatened, over-burdened, ill-equipped and generally stressed at the ways their job is changing. A survey of over 3,000 teachers by Varlaam, Nuttall and Walker (1992) showed that 'job satisfaction' and 'good relations with pupils' provided the strongest motivation for teachers but serious demotivators were teachers' perceived low public image in the media and the need for improved pay. Varlaam *et al.*'s data suggests that many teachers no longer value the reward of making a difference – the professional satisfaction of teaching itself. Nor do they feel valued by society.

Within this somewhat gloomy picture of staff morale in education, it might be anticipated that pay could provide a greater incentive to enhanced performance than it did in previous decades. This was certainly the thinking behind the government's delegation to school managers of budgets to manipulate grading and promotion structures at school level. The problem with incentive payments and other forms of performance-related pay (PRP) is in the conflicting evidence about their strengths as motivators. Fidler (1992) reviews a range of PRP schemes to determine their usefulness and acceptability in the educational context. He notes the range of approaches, not all of which are as backward looking, evaluative and divisive as many in the teaching profession fear. He distinguishes 'pay as motivation' (with its symbolic as well as material impact) from 'payment by results'. He concludes that 'if teachers are to be paid by results at all, it should be on the basis of as direct a measure of their own efforts or performance as possible' (p. 307). Tomlinson (1992, p. 2) also argues that performance-related pay is part of a necessary change to school and college culture, if standards are to be raised significantly without a massive and possibly wasteful input of new resources. The strategy of rewarding teachers for the quality of their work has been welcomed more in GM schools and CTCs than in maintained schools, where there is little evidence of them using their budgets in this way. In spite of Fidler's optimism, what many see as the potentially divisive nature of PRP is antipathetic to the collegiality that continues to characterise staff relations in schools. In practice, where incentive payments are used, it is often in a mainly *ad hoc* manner, leading to accusations from non-recipients of unfairness. Even more divisive are some head-teachers' negotiations for salary top-ups for themselves. Sinclair and Seifert (1993, p. 9) conclude from their research on industrial relations in schools that 'financial constraint, deep mistrust of many aspects of the reform process and relative inexperience in handling industrial relations issues would make the measuring of performance and its forthcoming link with pay a damaging activity for schools.'

Pay is just one possible motivator. Conditions of service are another. School managers' discretion over some of these, such as the working environment, equal opportunities, job sharing is greater than others, such as hours and leave. Most aspects of Conditions of Service are covered by legislation or national agreement. Teaching staff are subject to the provisions of the School Teachers' Pay and Conditions Document supplemented by the Burgundy Book. The National Joint Council for Local Authorities, APT and C Purple Book and White Book set out the conditions for most other staff. Some recent events involving violence against staff by pupils and intruders have led to a tightening of security arrangements to make schools safer places to work in. Concerns about health hazards such as the effects of asbestos have led to substantial changes in the material environment, including the demolition of contaminated swimming pools and other buildings. In managing people strategically, attention to the physical environment and its impact on physical and mental health is as crucial as attention to managing tasks and careers.

Another high profile issue within Conditions of Service is hours of work. As we saw earlier, school managers are seeking more innovative uses of teaching support staff in order to improve their schools. These innovations extend to creating more part-time posts and more casual contracts for both teaching support and teaching staff. However creative the resulting use of labour is, it also runs the danger of undermining the professional status of teachers. At the same time the ever-expanding role of teachers, to include in most cases management responsibilities too, means longer hours, often combined with larger classes. This is where creativity becomes a key component of managing the culture; using creative and critical problem-solving methods involving staff to arrive at acceptable and innovative solutions.

Managing the culture must include sharing with staff the concerns of the school. The constraints on sharing are likely to be greater where the concerns relate to staff themselves. Many aspects of pay, performance, promotion, grievance are confidential and appear to require decisions behind closed doors. This, in turn, contributes to the widening gap between managers and the rest of the staff that already threatens, as a result of managers' preoccupations with the school's performance in the marketplace and teachers' concerns with the classroom and student learning. My own research on headship (Hall, 1996) and Senior Management Teams (Wallace and Hall, 1994) leads me to conclude that 'wise' school managers aim to keep boundaries as permeable as possible, through creating an atmosphere of openness, honesty and trust. As the

---

Case Study 11:   Managing redundancies

Bill Smith's school is suddenly faced with the need to make someone redundant. Cutting staffing is the only way they can make the huge savings their depleted budget requires. The decision to cut the staffing budget comes from the governors but he knows they will expect him to identify the appropriate person. His first source of support would normally be Sheila, his deputy, but he has insisted that she disassociate herself from management on this issue and join the staff in their discussions. Bill is steeling himself to look 'very coldly' at whether the children are getting value for money. He knows he will have a fight with the unions defending their members, as they see it, against management's arbitrary actions. Bill is reluctant to lose any of the General Assistants, but his staff governors are pressuring for the cuts to be in that area. Even though it is the governing body's responsibility to set the criteria for selecting for redundancy, if no-one volunteers, he knows the decision will ultimately rest with him. He has spent some sleepless nights going over and over the different options available to him. He relies heavily on the Local Authority's personnel office and the school's adviser for guidance on procedures. He does not want to put a foot wrong within employment law, but he also wants to handle the matter fairly, with the children's interests the priority. The adviser warns him against using the redundancy as an opportunity to identify less competent staff. In the end, there is an uncomfortable showdown with the union representatives who accuse him of being Machiavellian. Then an older member of staff decides to retire, since she has only a year to go anyway. It is not Bill's preferred solution but it provides a way out of the seeming impasse that has been reached on this particular issue.

---

contrasting examples of introducing IIP (in Case Study 10) show, failure to communicate and consult widely can stymie potentially powerful initiatives for improving performance.

The remaining '4Cs' of workplace culture: Communication, Consultation, Conflict and Control, provide some clues as to how these boundaries can be made more permeable and obstacles to achieving this. Each of these processes includes constraints, demands and choices too extensive to be dealt with here. For some, too much communication is a constraint. These staff would prefer fewer managers to make the decisions and only inform them on a 'need to know' basis. This perception is particularly difficult for managers who choose to work collaboratively and transparently. Decisions about people also involve issues of confidentiality, thereby limiting the free exchange of information. Consultation reputedly enhances employee commitment but it is also time consuming and raises issues about the relative powers of the consultor and those consulted.

Teacher unions play a key role where HRM issues are concerned. Union representatives have specific knowledge of the vast array of employment and other laws governing employer–employee relationships in schools. Many of their interventions are as a result of senior managers' ignorance (leading to inappropriate action) of how they 'should' rather than want to behave. Responding to budget cuts by making staff redundant is a particularly thorny area, as far as headteachers and union representatives are concerned. The example in Case Study 11 illustrates this well. Headteachers' claims that the curriculum and the children must come first clash with union concerns about the rights of their members. In this case, the conflict that arises is with an external body (the union), as well as the staff members concerned. The way in which relations between senior staff and union representatives are managed internally can do much to reduce conflict which might otherwise lead to disciplinary, grievance and other disputes. For some, the involvement is more ritualistic than real; the union representatives receive rather than influence decisions about staffing. Others' involvement may extend to regular formal meetings in which they contribute to the decision making.

Control, in the form of disciplinary procedures, has a particular resonance in schools where discipline is central to achieving the school's task. Such procedures can be triggered by staff's inappropriate behaviour or misconduct (e.g. criticising a colleague in front of students, being inappropriately intimate with a student); or by their incompetence, that is, consistently underperforming. Then, the choices the senior manager might want to make in response to this challenge to the norms of the school's culture are constrained by the complexity of the written procedures to be followed and the union's involvement. The increasing codification of teacher's jobs means that heads and governors can more easily identify underperforming or misperforming staff. Their responses will depend on the priority they give to sanctions, rather than support, as ways of changing behaviour.

MANAGING STAFF: HIGHLIGHTING THE CHOICES

The purpose of the approach to managing people outlined here is to get the best from staff in order to achieve the school's strategic goals, represented in improved opportunities for learning. Autonomous schools are both constrained and liberated in managing staff, but I want to conclude by focusing on the positive implications of de-centralised decision-making for human resource management. It enables choices to be made about guiding philosophies and principles for HRM policies and practices. These philosophies will be based on values and beliefs about the rights and responsibilities of employers and employees and the role of managers in working to achieve results with and through other adults. After all, how adults behave at work provides role models and influences young people sorting out their own beliefs and values. What schools need, as employers, is a statement of shared values and educational objectives to inform their management of people and performance. The cynicism that so often accompanies the generation of policies to guide action obliterates their positive role in clarifying processes and procedures. Every component of SHRM needs a policy to provide a framework for action. Selection, induction, development, promotion, health and safety, staff welfare are just some HRM processes requiring guiding principles. Choosing which principles will inform good practice in each of these areas becomes more possible, when decision-making rests with schools. For example, a key principle might be a school's commitment to orienting all its newly appointed staff. Good practice arising from this principle would be identification of a 'mentor' for each new member of staff and provision of an induction programme to socialise new staff into the unfamiliar environment. Whatever the principles, their power rests in providing a framework for action that liberates rather than constrains staff performance. In this way, managing staff in autonomous schools successfully balances management accountability and management for freedom.

REFERENCES

Beer, M., Spector, B., Lawrence, P., Quinn Mills, D. and Watson, R. (1984) *Managing Human Assets*, Free Press, New York.

Bennett, N. (1995) *Managing Professional Teachers*, Paul Chapman Publishing, London.

Beresford, J. (1995) Teacher Union Perspective on the Management of Professionals, in H. Busher and R. Saran (eds) *Managing Teachers as Professionals in Schools*, Kogan Page, London.

Blase, J. And Kirby, P. (1992) *Bringing out the best in teachers*, Newbury Park, CA: Corwin Press.

Bolam, R., McMahon, A., Pocklington, K., and Weindling, D. (1993) *Effective Management in Schools*, London: HMSO

Bottery, M. (1992) *The Ethics of Educational Management*, Cassell, London.

Busher, H. and Saran, R. (1995) (eds) *Managing Teachers as Professionals in Schools*, Kogan Page, London.

Department of Education and Science (1991) *Local Management of Schools: Further Guidance* (Curriculum 7/91) London: DES.

Dodds, J. (1993) The Work of TASC in B. Fidler, B. Fugl and D. Esp (eds) *The Supply and Recruitment of School Teachers*, Longman, Harlow.

Earley, P. (1992) *The School Management Competencies Programme* 3 Vol. School Management South, Crawley.

Esp, D. (1993) *Competencies for School Management*, Kogan Page, London.

Fidler, B. (1992) Performance related pay in local government and public sector organisations: lessons for schools and colleges in B. Fidler and R. Cooper (eds) *Staff Appraisal and Staff Management in Schools and Colleges: A Guide to Implementation*, Longman, Harlow.

Fullan, M. (1993) *Change Forces*, London: Falmer Press.

Gittins, C. (1989) A Bursar in a School in B. Fidler and G. Bowles (eds) *Effective LMS* Longman, Harlow.

Grace, G. (1995) *School Leadership: beyond education management: an essay in policy scholarship*, Falmer Press, London.

Hall, V. (1996) *Dancing on the Ceiling: A Study of Women Managers in Education*, Paul Chapman Publishing, London.

Hall, V. (1997) Management Roles in Education in T. Bush and D. Middlewood (eds) *Managing People in Education*, Paul Chapman Publishing, London.

Hargreaves, A. (1994) *Changing Teachers, Changing Times: teachers work and culture in the post-modern age*, London: Cassell.

HMI (1992) *The Implementation of Local Management of Schools: A report by HMI* 1989-92, London: HMSO.

Jirasinghe, D. and Lyons, G. (1996) *The Competent Head: A Job Analysis of Heads' Tasks and Personality Factors,* Falmer Press, London.

Levine, S. (1989) *Promoting Adult Growth in Schools: The Promise of Professional Development,* Allyn and Bacon, Boston, Mass.

McMahon, A. (1996) Continuing Professional Development Report from the Field, *Management in Education,* Vol. 10, no. 4, Sept–Oct.

Morgan, C., Hall, V., Mackay, H. (1983) *The Selection of Secondary Heads,* Open University Press, Milton Keynes.

Mortimore, P. and Mortimore, J. with Thomas, H. (1994) *Managing Associate Staff,* Paul Chapman Publishing, London.

Murgatroyd, S. and Morgan, C. (1992) *Total Quality Management and the School,* Buckingham, Open University Press.

Oldroyd, D., and Hall, V. (1991) *Managing Staff Development: a handbook for secondary schools,* London, Paul Chapman Publishing.

OFSTED (1996) *The Appraisal of Teachers 1991-1996: A Report from the Office of Her Majesty's Chief Inspector of Schools,* London: OFSTED.

O'Neill, J. (1994) Managing Human Resources in T. Bush and J. West-Burnham, (eds) *The Principles of Education Management,* Longman for the Educational Management Development Unit, Harlow.

Ouston, J., Earley, P., Fidler, B. (eds) (1996) *OFSTED Inspections: the early experience,* David Fulton, London.

Ozga, J. (1995) Describing a Profession: Professionalism, Deprofessionalisation and the New Managerialism in H. Busher and R. Saran (eds) *Managing Teachers as Professionals in Schools,* Kogan Page, London.

Purchon, V. (1991) Working more for a lot less money – school secretaries, *Times Educational Supplement,* 7th June.

Riches, C. and Morgan, C. (eds.) (1989) *Human Resource Management in Education,* Milton Keynes, Open University Press.

Schein, E. H. (1992) *Organisational Culture and Leadership* (2nd edn), Jossey-Bass, San Francisco.

Seifert, R. (1996) *Human Resource Management in Schools,* Pitman, London.

Shakeshaft, C. (1993) Women in Educational Management in the United States in J. Ouston (ed) *Women in Education Management,* Longman, Harlow.

Sinclair, J. and Seifert, R. (1993) Money for value?, *Managing Schools Today* Vol. 2 (9).

Stewart, R. (1982) *Choices for the Manager: a guide to managerial work and behaviour,* Maidenhead: McGraw-Hill.

Storey, J. (1987) Developments in the management of human resources: an interim report, *Warwick Papers in Industrial Relations,* 17, IRRU School of Industrial and Business Studies, University of Warwick.

Teacher Training Agency (1995) Corporate Plan, London: TTA.

Thompson, M. (1989) Appraisal and equal opportunities, in A. Evans and J. Tomlinson (eds.) *Teacher Appraisal: a nationwide approach,* London: Jessica Kingsley.

Tomlinson, H. (ed) (1992) *Performance-related pay in education,* Routledge, London.

Varlaam, A., Nuttall, D., Walker, A. (1992) *What Makes Teachers Tick: a survey of teacher morale and motivation,* Centre for Educational Research, London

Wallace, M. and Hall, V. (1994) *Inside the SMT: Teamwork in Secondary School Management,* Paul Chapman Publishing, London.

2.6

Managing Resources

TIM SIMKINS

As was demonstrated in Part 1 of this book, the movement towards school self-management in England and Wales has, in fact, involved a mixture of centralising and decentralising elements. The major focus of the decentralisation of power to schools has been in the area of resource management. For both LM and GM schools this has involved:

- providing every school with a block budget designed to meet all recurrent expenditure, although schools are free to supplement this budget through their own income generation activities;
- requiring this budget, established by the LEA for LM schools and by the central government for GM schools, to be based upon a formula with at least 80 per cent of the total allocation based on the number of pupils and their ages in each school;
- placing the responsibility for managing this budget with school governors;
- in addition, giving governors the responsibility for all major aspects of personnel management, including appointment, discipline, dismissal and, within regulated limits, remuneration, and also for the management of the school premises and for undertaking small capital works.

The main differences between LM and GM schools in the area of resource management relate to the employment of staff and large capital works where, in each case, GM schools exercise powers which are retained by the LEA for the LM sector. This chapter will explore the consequences of these changes for processes of resource management in schools.

THE CONSEQUENCES OF LM AND GM FOR RESOURCE MANAGEMENT

Resource management in relation to the school needs to be considered as a system within which resources are transformed into educational outcomes through a number of stages (see Figure 2.6.1). Initially *financial resources* are generated through various income generation processes to produce a budget. Secondly, decisions must be taken about the kinds of *real resources* which are to be purchased with the financial resources available. Third, these real resources need to be deployed among the *activities* of the school – the core curricular activities and those supporting activities such as the establishment and maintenance of a suitable environment and the provision of appropriate management and administrative systems – to produce learning and other *outcomes*.

Each of these stages of the transformation processes involves choices and, as Figure 2.6.1 shows, a major consequence of self-management has been that many more of these decisions are now located within the school. Prior to the establishment of LM and GM schools, major decisions about the deployment of real resources – particularly teaching and non-teaching staff and premises costs – were located within the LEA. This left a relatively small area of financial discretion within schools. Now, in contrast, schools themselves must determine how their financial budgets are to be translated into staff complements, expenditure on premises, supplies, services and so on. This means in essence that schools now have a much wider range of choice about the resources they purchase and the ways in which they deploy these.

A number of caveats need to be noted here, however. First, compared with commercial organisations, schools still have limited power to influence the total quantum of financial resources available to them, especially through the

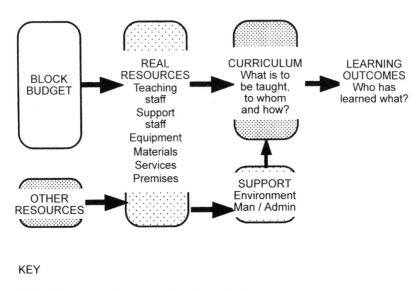

KEY

▨ Main area of resource choice for school prior to LM/GM

▨ Main additional areas of choice after LM/GM

☐ Area still outside school's control

Figure 2.6.1 Changing frameworks for resource choice

block LM or GM budget. Secondly, increased freedom to determine how resources should be deployed has been accompanied by a much wider range of regulations, advice and incentives designed to constrain schools in the choices which they actually make. Some of these do not relate specifically to resource management (see Chapters 1.1 and 1.2), but there is now fairly extensive guidance about good practice in the area of resource management (for example, Audit Commission/Ofsted, 1993; Audit Commission, 1996) enforced through processes of school inspection and audit.

Finally, we should not underestimate the importance of choices in resource use which were available to schools prior to LM and GM. In particular, decisions about the deployment of particular resources among curricular and other activities have always been taken at school level. The new need to manage large financial budgets and to make major personnel decisions should not deflect from a clear understanding that ways in which non-financial resources, in particular staff and pupil time, are utilised remain critical determinants of the quality of educational experience and outcomes which schools provide (Knight, 1989).

THE PURPOSES OF RESOURCE MANAGEMENT

Resource management in education as elsewhere is only a means to an end. In education, perhaps more than anywhere else, it is important to keep this point in mind, because we know so little about the relationship between the ways in which resources are managed and deployed and the educational outcomes which result. Yet it is just because it is so difficult to make a link between particular decisions about resource use and the learning outcomes which are achieved by individual pupils, pupil groups and whole school cohorts that we need to think clearly about the principles and assumptions upon which such decisions are made. The wider range of resource management responsibilities placed on schools by LM and GM makes this point even more important.

Ofsted (1995a, p. 121) defines the efficient school, as one which 'makes good use of all its available resources to achieve the best possible educational outcomes for all its pupils – and in doing so provides excellent value for money'. While helpful as an overall statement of purpose for resource management, this form of wording fails to distinguish between a number of concepts which are conventionally considered to be distinct. These include 'the three E's' which the Audit Commission (1985) defines as follows:

Economy: the purchase of a given standard of goods or service at lowest cost.
Efficiency: the achievement of given outcomes at least cost.
Effectiveness: the matching of results with objectives.

To these must be added a fourth 'E': *equity* – the fair distribution of resources among individuals and groups. It is up to each school to determine exactly how these terms are to be interpreted within the regulatory and resource constraints within which it operates (Simkins, 1994, 1995). However, Figure 2.6.1 helps us to identify the kinds of choices which are involved in pursuing these ideals:

- how far will the school seek to supplement its block budget with other financial resources and how will it do this?
- what types and quantities of real resources will the school purchase with its financial resources?
- how far can economy be achieved in the purchase of real resources?
- how will the school's resources be deployed between those activities which contribute directly to pupils' learning, i.e. curriculum provision and learning support, and those which contribute to other activities?
- can the proportion of resources available to deliver the curriculum be enhanced through more efficient resource use in other areas of expenditure?
- how can curricular resources – the time of teaching staff and non-teaching staff, equipment, materials and space – best be deployed to maximise the effectiveness of pupil learning and ensure that appropriate standards of equity are achieved?

Taken together these questions represent a formidable resource management agenda. Arguments for the delegation of resource management responsibilities to schools emphasise, among other things, the potential for such delegation to enhance achievement of the 'three E's' in particular (the official literature on LM and GM has very little to say about equity) through giving those closest to the needs of the client the power to deploy resources in the most appropriate way. However, these potential benefits are not inevitable. They depend on how schools carry out the tasks of resource management.

RESOURCE MANAGEMENT TASKS

There is now considerable emphasis on the development of 'rational' approaches to the management of resources. They are embodied, for example, in Ofsted's approach to managing 'the efficiency of the school' (Ofsted, 1995a), and in much of the writing on school development planning as well as that on resource management more specifically (Thomas and Martin, 1996). There are other ways of understanding resource management in organisations than those which embody the rational model (Simkins, 1989), but since the rational approach is now so dominant and also because it presents a clear framework for the management of resources, we will use it to underpin the argument of this chapter.

Figure 2.6.2 provides an idealised model of the resource management process. At its heart lies the operational cycle of resource management comprising five key activities (Simkins and Lancaster, 1988):

- the *mobilisation* of financial resources through the block LM/GM budget, supplementary forms of income (such as lettings, sponsorship and PTA activities); of real resources through processes of staff recruitment and motivation strategies, purchasing policies, and so on; and of parental and other voluntary support;

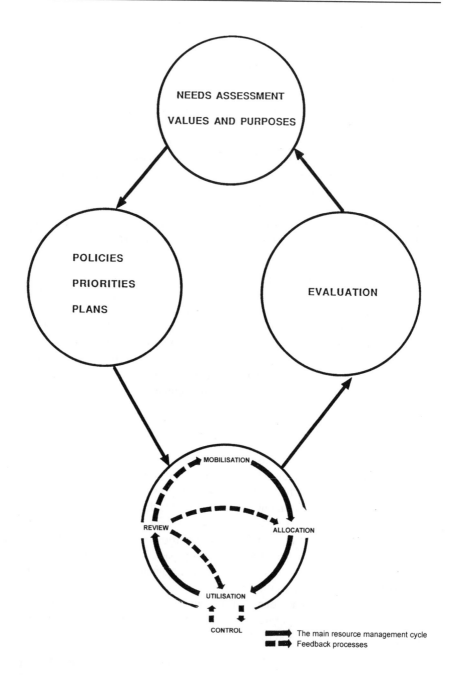

Figure 2.6.2 The resource management cycle

- the *allocation* of these resources among various aspects of the school's work through the production of the annual budget estimate, or some analogous document such as, in the case of school staffing, the timetable;
- the *utilisation* of resources in the work of the school – teaching, pastoral support, curriculum and staff development, management and so on;
- processes of *control* to monitor whether the activities undertaken and the resources expended correspond to those which have been planned or authorised; and finally
- the *review* of the outcomes of the current year's expenditure to feed forward into decisions about resource mobilisation and allocation for the coming year.

These activities take place over time in the form of one or more annual resource management cycles. For schools there will be at least two of these – the financial budgeting cycle and the staffing/timetabling cycle – but there may be others. In many schools these *operational cycles* dominate the resource management process. In a sense this is understandable and inevitable: no organisation can exist without making adequate and regular arrangements to ensure that it obtains and utilises the resources necessary for it to carry out its major activities. In a number of ways, however, a resource management process which does not go beyond this is seriously lacking. The operational cycle should be managed within the context of a *strategic cycle* which, as Figure 2.6.2 indicates, provides a longer-term policy framework for the management of resources. Resource management, of course needs to be concerned with both the operational and strategic cycles: they need to be related to each other, and each needs to be supported by appropriate administrative systems. The school, therefore, needs to organise itself to undertake three key tasks in relation to resource management: *strategic planning and evaluation, budget management* in relation to the activities in the operational cycle, and *financial administration* in relation to the day-to-day running of the financial control system in the school and providing the information required to support the other activities.

OPERATIONAL MANAGEMENT: RESOURCING THE CURRICULUM

Prior to the implementation of LM and GM, the two most important areas where schools had considerable autonomy were in the allocation of staff time through the timetable and of 'capitation' – those financial resources (rarely exceeding 5 per cent of the total budget) available for use at the school's discretion for purchasing curriculum and other resources. It was in these areas that the school had the opportunity to manage resources systematically in pursuit of its curricular and other objectives. These areas remain of central importance and the ways in which a school goes about them can tell much about the ways in which resources and educational purposes are linked.

With respect to staff deployment, schools are faced with critical choices in relation to their policies about the length and utilisation of the school week, the proportion of that week for which teachers will be expected to teach and the ways in which classes are to be organised. Each of these decisions establishes a succession of 'resource envelopes' which constrain the decisions which follow, so that once the length of the day and the staff contact ratio have been established, reductions in class size for one particular group of pupils or curriculum area can only be attained at the expense of increases elsewhere. The timetabling process – perhaps the quintessential component of operational resource management in a school – depends on explicit or implicit choices about all of these things. Questions of the length of the school week and class size have been the subject of recent studies by Ofsted (1994, 1995b) and remain controversial, especially the latter (Mortimore and Blatchford, 1993; Bennett, 1996), but schools need to take clear positions on them which they embody in their staff deployment strategies.

The deployment of resources to support the curriculum also needs careful management. Although relatively insignificant in relation to a school's overall LM or GM budget, the 5 per cent or so of what was once 'capitation' funding has the power to make a good deal of difference in the classroom. Knight (1993) argued that there were essentially only four main ways in which such resources could be allocated:

- 'incrementalism': basing this year's allocation primarily on last year's, once account has been taken of the overall sum available for allocation;
- 'benevolent despotism': basing allocations primarily on the professional judgement of the headteacher or senior management team;
- 'open market': basing allocations on the quality of bids made by those to whom the resources are to be allocated;
- 'formula': basing allocations on some quantified measure of needs such as pupils or pupil-periods taught, perhaps weighted in some way to reflect the differential costs of areas of activity.

While this categorisation has a good deal of face validity, the range of possibilities is wider than this, with a number of rather different approaches possible under each of the headings (Simkins, 1986). In determining an appropriate approach, four choices have to be made:

- what kinds of information are to inform the decision – informal soundings, formal bids or quantitative data?
- how open is the process to be – centripetal flow to senior managers only, bilateral flow between senior managers and budget holders, or multilateral flow among senior managers and budget holders?
- what criteria are to be used – incremental, qualitative judgements about needs and priorities or formula?
- who will be responsible for the final decision about allocations – imposed by senior management or shared participatively among a wider group?

These choices are not unimportant. Not only will they determine the quality of resource allocation decisions; they will also contribute to understandings within the school about the wider management culture of which this particular decision-making process is a part. In particular, the process through which resources are allocated among curricular areas will be part of a wider set of arrangements through which those with responsibility for the strategic management of the school relate to those directly responsible for managing the delivery of the curriculum. We will return to this issue later.

There is little evidence currently about the ways in which budgetary processes in schools may be evolving in response to the demands of LM and GM. Levacic (1995) suggests that in secondary schools there may be some movement towards bidding systems, especially ones which require heads of department to be more accountable for their resource use through the establishment of departmental development plans, while in primary schools there may be some movement towards giving budgets to classroom teachers and establishing more explicit priorities which can be changed from year to year. The significance of such developments will depend very much on the broader strategic resource management framework within which they take place. This will be explored now.

STRATEGIC CHOICE

Despite the controls and constraints which were mentioned earlier, there is no doubt that LM and GM give schools much greater freedom to think creatively about resource deployment than was the case previously. However, the degree to which this is recognised within the school depends on two factors. The first is the financial situation within which the school finds itself: it may be difficult to see increased freedom of choice as much of a blessing if the school's budget is declining and its establishment contains a number of staff on high salaries who are unlikely to leave in the near future. The second factor, however, concerns the ways in which budgetary choices are viewed. Thomas and Martin (1996) emphasise the importance of what they call 'radical audit': the ability to think creatively and innovatively about the ways in which resources may be deployed in pursuit of a school's objectives. It can be argued that radical audit is facilitated by three particular perspectives, all of which are inter-related:

- 'whole-school thinking': the ability to look at the overall pattern of resource deployment in relation to key purposes, priorities and challenges rather than simply to focus on particular aspects of expenditure or areas of activity.
- 'zero-base thinking': the ability to question all aspects of current expenditure rather than simply to focus on changes at the margin. Linked to whole-school thinking this approach raises questions such as could we carry out this activity in a different way, or indeed do we need to do it at all?
- 'longer-term thinking': the ability to view choice not just within the constraints and pressures of the annual budgetary cycle, but in terms of a broader vision of where the school should be in 3, 5 or even 10 years' time, despite the uncertainties that such considerations involve.

Current evidence suggests that such strategic thinking is not well developed in many schools and in particular that the relationship between financial planning and curriculum planning is not always well developed. There are a number of reasons for this: the increased uncertainty of the resource environment resulting from LM and GM with the reduction of the 'cushioning' power of the LEA; the difficulties associated with thinking systematically and in depth about input–output relations in the school; and the fact that 'much of what concerns schools in operating delegated budgets does not impinge directly on improving learning unless the school makes a conscious effort to do this' (Levacic, 1995, p. 47).

Nevertheless, the powers granted to schools under LM and GM provide the opportunity to develop future scenarios which look critically at a number of key resource choices and the opportunity costs which these involve. As has been noted, prior to LM and GM the key trade-off was between the variables of class size and non-teaching time within a given establishment of teaching staff. Now the range of choice is much wider. The school itself must determine how many teaching staff it wishes to employ, subject to its curricular objectives and priorities and its overall budget. For the majority of schools this decision is probably still made on the basis of traditional judgements: about the desired pupil–teacher ratio and non-contact time for teachers in secondary schools and about maximum class sizes and the degree of tolerance for mixed-age classes in primary schools. However, the opportunity costs involved in decisions about the number of teachers to be employed can now be expressed in terms of *all* the other areas of expenditure which the budget might fund: numbers of support staff, the amount spent on allowances, staff development provision, management costs and so on.

Strategic choice, therefore, is much more complex than it used to be and, as Thomas and Martin (1996) argue, one of the most important potential consequences of delegation is 'to change the *perception* of school managers as to what is possible' (p. 162). There is now a good deal of evidence that schools are using the increased freedom provided by LM and GM to deploy resources in new ways (Simkins, 1994; Levacic, 1995).

First, schools have increasingly sought to save expenditure in areas such as premises and grounds maintenance and energy use. In part this has been done through taking advantage of the possibilities arising from provisions for compulsory competitive tendering, and in part it has been achieved through investment and changed practices, for example to encourage energy saving. Such strategies attempt to enhance economy and efficiency in the provision of these services and there is evidence that many schools have achieved this, often making substantial short-term savings which release resources for use elsewhere.

Secondly, there is evidence that schools are employing more support staff, both in the classroom (mainly teaching assistants in primary schools) and in administration. It is widely recognised that there is considerable potential for the more creative use of such staff (Mortimore *et al.*, 1994) both to undertake new tasks which LM and GM have generated and, perhaps more significantly, to enable teaching staff to be deployed in ways which make better use of their knowledge and skills. The latter reason is a good example of the ways in which increased discretion over the use of resources enables managers to achieve 'price efficiency' through deploying resources in ways which take account of relative costs.

Thirdly, there seems little doubt that, subject to legislative limitations, schools are employing more staff, both teaching and support, on part-time or temporary contracts. The most important reason for this is the need to cope with fluctuations and uncertainties in the school budget without the cushion which LEA staffing and redeployment policies typically provided previously. Such strategies do, of course, raise important value issues which are discussed in Chapter 2.5.

The evidence to date then suggests that some, probably most, schools are using their increased discretion over resource deployment to achieve increased economy and efficiency in the provision of operational services and to achieve further efficiencies through the greater use of support staff and more part-time and temporary contracts. What is less clear is how far schools are taking decisions which make explicit connections between choices about the use of resources and educational outcomes. In other words, how far are they using their increased powers to address explicitly the ways in which resourcing policies might be used to enhance effectiveness? The evidence that is available suggests that advances on this front to date have been limited. Certainly in a number of cases new patterns of staff deployment have been based 'on professional judgements that the most beneficial learning outcomes would result from this particular use of resources' (Levacic, 1995, p. 155), and development planning processes are tightening the linkages between curriculum and resource planning in some schools (see Case Study 12). However, such developments are probably still not widespread. For example, the annual report of HM Chief Inspector of Schools states that 'inspectors judged the evaluation of cost-effectiveness by governors and head teachers unfavourably in nearly two-thirds of the primary and nearly half of secondary schools' (Ofsted, 1995c, p. 24), a finding reiterated in other recent studies (Thomas and Martin, 1996; Levacic, 1995).

In a sense this is not surprising. One of the major characteristics of education as a process is how little we really know, to use the economist's jargon, about input–output relationships. Furthermore, our ignorance is not easy to dispel empirically and, partly as a result, discussions soon get tangled in political issues as the debate on the effects of class size clearly shows. We will return to this issue in the concluding section of this chapter.

ORGANISING RESOURCE MANAGEMENT

The demands of both budget management and financial administration have increased enormously in importance as a result of schools receiving block

Case Study 12:   Yellowstone School

Yellowstone School, is 450-pupil primary school situated in a medium-sized town in an area of socially mixed housing. The processes of resource management at Yellowstone had taken a good number of years to evolve and were still evolving. It is notable that they developed not because of the spur of local management, but through the initiative of the headteacher, who had been in post since the opening of the school in the mid-1970s, who seized on local management as a major opportunity to promote effective management and better resourcing. In order to emphasise that development planning is an on-going process, the plan is always referred to as a draft and is redone in full every three years.

Initially the staff, governors and LEA adviser spent an evening deciding which priorities should enter the reworked plan, drawing upon evaluative evidence gathered from a questionnaire to parents, staff and governors. The school development plan summarises the relationship between aims and resourcing objectives, which are placed in the separate categories of staff, premises and curriculum, each of which is overseen by one of the governors' sub-committees. This meant that it was referred to continually in decision-making. The fourth committee, finance, was responsible for drawing up the budget and did this by receiving bids from the other committees. The headteacher sat on all the committees and was thus the main integrator of all the information required for securing coherent planning. The finance officer, a member of the support staff and a governor, sat on all the committees as well, providing vital support to the headteacher. The chair of governors was a member of the premises and finance committees and the deputy head attended all committees regularly by invitation.

The curriculum committee met once a term to review and approve curriculum policies developed by teacher working parties. Certain areas of the curriculum were given priority in any one year, usually in response to national curriculum implementation. The development of a revised curriculum in science, say, was accompanied by a plan for its resourcing, in the case of science a central resource equipment centre. Thus science received a particularly large allocation of money in that year.

The headteacher described the budget planning process as follows:

> The broad budget planning is done by me, the chair of finance goes through it and then if necessary it will be redrafted, and that is what sees its way through to the other sub-committees, who are then working within what is possible and the best for the whole school rather than just a particular aspect. In the spring term, when budget-making takes place, each sub-committee reviews its own part of the school development plan and makes their proposals so that the budget is seeking to support and develop the SDP.

The budget-planning process at Yellowstone and its integration with school development planning is only one aspect, though an important one, of a well-integrated school culture, in which all staff were well aware of and supported the fundamental aims of the school. Staff participated in budget decision-making, but in a collaborative rather than a democratic school culture. The leadership of the headteacher and his primary influence on decisions were recognised and appreciated.

Source: Summarised with permission from R. Levacic (1995), pp. 92–4

financial budgets and all the additional responsibilities associated with LM and GM. Careful consideration therefore needs to be given to who carries out the roles of 'budget manager' and 'finance officer' (and the related role of 'site manager' in relation to premises) (Levacic, 1995), as well as how strategic leadership is to be provided for the resource management process. The key issues are:

- to ensure that the head and other senior staff *as well as governors* effectively exercise their responsibilities for strategic decisions about the deployment of resources in pursuit of the school's objectives and priorities. There is considerable evidence at present that most governing bodies exercise little more than a rubber-stamping function in relation to the school's budget;
- to ensure that the budget process itself is effectively and efficiently managed. In some schools, especially many primary schools, the head undertakes this task, but there is a strong case for delegating it to another senior member of staff provided the responsibility for budget strategy is not delegated. In the majority of schools where the head does not retain responsibility for budget management it will be delegated to a deputy, but a number of schools have created a new non-teaching post, such as that of bursar, to carry out these tasks (see Case Study 13);
- to ensure that the day-to-day tasks of financial administration are carried out by suitably qualified support staff and do not impinge unduly on the time of senior managers;
- to ensure a 'dialogue of accountability' (Thomas and Martin, 1996) and adequate delegation of responsibilities among all those responsible for resource management in the school – through which issues of resource management are explicitly linked to those of quality and standards.

This last issue is an especially important one. A common finding of recent research on the consequences of LM and GM is that in many schools they seem to have led to an increasing distancing of senior managers from other teachers. This has been expressed in a number of ways: 'schizoid schools' (Broadbent *et al.*, 1992, p. 67) which reflect 'a division of values and purposes' (Bowe and Ball, 1992, p. 159) between the increasingly 'corporatist' views of senior managers whose increasing concern is the school as a whole and its relationship with its external environment and the 'individualist' orientation of teachers

---

Case Study 13:   Whittaker School

Whittaker School is a grant-maintained 12–18 mixed comprehensive school with around 1,000 pupils serving a county town and surrounding villages. GM status has increased the administrative and managerial workload within the school, and in order to handle this with least disruption to existing staff a school administrator has been appointed. He has responsibility for developing efficient financial and administrative systems and for advising on expenditure plans. He attends Senior Management Team meetings and also acts as a clerk to the governing body, providing information and advice as an LEA officer might for an LM school, although as a member of staff he has a different perspective from such an officer.

The impact of this appointment had been felt most by senior management: not only through taking the administrative load from the Senior Management Team, but also through the financial and management information readily made available on which to base decisions. Thus it has been possible to redefine the roles of the deputy headteachers to allow them to focus on curriculum, staff development and pastoral matters respectively. While one deputy retains a brief for building matters, day-to-day administration is now taken care of by the administrator. However, the benefits of the post are not just seen by senior managers. Non-teaching staff are increasingly appreciating the creation of 'a ready point of contact for queries and concerns', while staff generally recognise the value of a much shorter chain of command in reporting and responding to minor repairs in the school. One head of department described this as having 'a major impact on my job'. The administrator himself maintains that the provision within the school of services previously provided by the LEA gives advantages of 'ownership and autonomy' as well as flexibility and speed in decision-making.

Source: Summarised with permission from Thomas and Martin (1996), Chapter 7.

---

whose prime concern is with the learning needs of individual pupils (Simkins, 1994). Perhaps the tension between these two perspectives has always been present, reflecting the differing perspectives of the 'managerial' and 'professional ' domains which were discussed in Chapter 1.2. For heads certainly, it makes it increasingly difficult to give continuing priority to the role of 'leading professional' over that of 'chief executive' (Hughes, 1985).

The important point is that the tension needs to be managed to ensure, as far as possible, that the two perspectives are reconciled so that the 'detachment of management' (Thomas and Martin, 1996) can be minimised. To achieve this, effective budget management has to balance a number of competing pressures:

- to ensure effectiveness and efficiency in resource use at the level of the school as a whole, while ensuring equity of treatment for different areas of work and for individual pupils and pupil groups;
- to prioritise and make difficult choices where necessary, while containing

conflict and maintaining a coalition of support where resources are insufficient to meet the legitimate expectations of different areas of the school's work;

- to respond flexibly to changing environmental demands, while maintaining a reasonably stable resource environment for those responsible for undertaking the core activities of the school, i.e. curricular and other provision for pupils;
- to encourage innovation and responsiveness among individual teachers and teams, while ensuring their accountability for their use of resources;
- to do all of these things under continuing pressure of limited time and information and without consuming too many resources (especially staff time) in the resource management process itself.

Given the complexity of these pressures it can safely be said that there is no ideal model of resource management. However, a number of broad characteristics of good practice can be identified. First, budgetary decisions should be based on adequate review along the lines suggested earlier, namely 'whole-school thinking', 'zero-base thinking' and 'longer-term thinking'. Secondly, there needs to be an appropriate pattern of involvement in resource management which balances the strategic perspective of senior managers with the knowledge and commitment of other staff to particular areas of work and groups of pupils. In particular the pattern of involvement chosen should enable middle managers, whether they be heads of secondary subject departments or primary year leaders or subject co-ordinators, to understand the kinds of difficult choices which need to be made at whole-school level when particular resource demands cannot all be met within available resources. It should also give them considerable delegated control over the resources they need to deliver those aspects of the curriculum for which they are responsible. Finally, whatever the particular criteria used to allocate resources, these should be explicable and defensible in relation to educational objectives and priorities. Resource management processes should strive constantly to link decisions about the use of resources to pupil achievement.

FUTURE POSSIBILITIES

If schools are to find ways of further improving their use of resources, their first need is for better information on, and greater attention to, the costs of the activities which they undertake, as Thomas and Martin (1996) argue. Traditional budget information emphasises what money is spent *on* (teaching staff, materials, energy, etc.) rather than what it is spent *for* (provision to meet particular curriculum objectives or the needs of particular pupil groups, resources for particular management tasks such as marketing or evaluation). Consequently it is of little use either for evaluation or for informing the process of choice at the strategic level. This is not to say that schools have not addressed the costs of what they do in the past. Indeed, since the major resource input into curriculum provision is staff time, this kind of analysis has always been possible. Useful questions can be asked about resource deployment without using money as a measure: curriculum or staff deployment analysis in secondary schools has been a good example of this. Now however, the availability of budgetary information should lead schools to ask questions such as the following:

- how far are the school's resources channelled to the direct support of teaching and learning?
- where resources do support teaching and learning, what aspects of the curriculum and which groups of pupils benefit most?
- what resources are devoted to management activities, such as planning, budgeting and 'marketing' in the widest sense?
- what resources are devoted to investment in the maintenance and quality of future provision, for example through improving the fabric of the school and, especially, staff development?
- what mixes of resources are used for particular areas of work, for example between teaching staff, non-teaching staff and materials of various kinds?

Various sorts of information can be used to explore these questions, including information on financial expenditure, on the deployment of staff time, and on other variables such as class sizes.

This raises a second point, however. It is difficult to make judgements about how effectively and efficiently resources are being used without having a basis for comparison. 'How are we doing?' is a meaningless question without the qualifier 'in relation to . . .'. This is why increasing attention is being given to the idea of 'benchmarking'. This is the process through which organisations compare their performance in key areas with similar or competitor organisations in a carefully structured way to explore where and how improvement may be possible. The benchmarking process is essentially a simple one, but needs to be carried out carefully. The stages are:

- identify suitable areas for analysis, preferably those which are critical to current performance and strategic objectives;
- identify forms of information, often but not necessarily quantitative indicators, which can be standardised among the organisations to be compared;
- gather data from the organisations, including one's own;
- identify significant differences between one's own organisation and others;
- explore the reasons for differences and draw conclusions.

Work in the school sector has been undertaken in a number of areas, including resource inputs (McAleese, 1996) and examination results (DfE, 1995).

Analysis of this kind can provide the basis for beginning to explore the difficult question of linking resource management to improved school effectiveness. However, a more thorough understanding of costs alone is clearly not enough. The challenge for the future is for schools to think more clearly about how particular strategies of resource deployment will impact on the learning outcomes of particular students. Some developments are taking place in this area: for example, the idea of targeting, i.e. 'identifying particular pupils or groups in order to focus attention, teaching resources and other support on them' is increasingly being advocated (DfEE, 1996, p. 5). In part this is occurring in response to pressure from government – for example, targeting those pupils who may just miss the 'magic' five A–C grades at GCSE – but there is clearly a wide range of other possibilities both more and less contentious than this.

Finally, and perhaps most important, serious attention has to be given to how creative resource management strategies can be used to contribute to school improvement. For many schools this is the greatest challenge of all, not least because:

> To carry out a change or improvement always involves an increment of *extra* resources – for training, released time, new materials and equipment, often new space, and staff time for coordination and management. Change, by definition, cannot be managed through the status quo level of resources. It makes new demands, creates unsolved problems, and is resource hungry.
>
> (Louis and Miles, 1990, p. 239)

In the financial circumstances faced by many schools, this could be seen as an insuperable obstacle to effective school improvement. However, it need not be so. As Louis and Miles go on to argue, 'above a certain floor the level of resources is less important than *how* resources are acquired and *where* they are applied' (Louis and Miles, 1990, pp. 239–40). Effective strategies for resourcing improvement are likely to include:

- proactive approaches to seeking and acquiring resources relevant to the improvement process;
- creative use of staff time to enable the establishment of effective task groups, of processes of data collection and feedback, of classroom observation and support, of staff development, and so on;
- the careful selection and use of relevant curriculum and support materials;
- the effective orchestration of relevant assistance which draws on expertise from both within and, especially, outside the school.

Perhaps most important in terms of this chapter is the need to devote adequate management effort to the difficult task of harnessing resources to the challenges of school improvement in what, for resource managers, are very difficult times. For, when all is said and done, the most important resources of all are the intangibles: energy, ideas, creativity and the ability to harness a variety of sources of power and influence in the interests of the school, its pupils and its community.

REFERENCES

Audit Commission (1985) *Audit Commission Handbook: A Guide to Economy, Efficiency and Effectiveness*, Audit Commission, London.
Audit Commission/Ofsted (1993) *Keeping Your Balance,* HMSO, London.

Audit Commission (1996) *Adding Up the Sums 4: comparative information for schools 1995/96*, HMSO, London.

Bennett, N. (1996) Class size in primary schools: perceptions of headteachers, chairs of governors, teachers and parents, *British Educational Research Journal*, Vol. 22, no. 1, pp. 33–55.

Bowe, R. and Ball, S. (1992) *Reforming Education and Changing Schools: case studies in policy sociology*, Routledge, London.

Broadbent, J., Laughlin, R., Shearn, D. and Dandy, N. (1992) 'It's a long way from teaching Susan to read': some preliminary observations from a project studying the introduction of local management of schools, in G. Wallace (ed.) *Local Management of Schools: research and experience*, Multilingual Matters, Clevedon.

Department for Education (1995) *GCSE to GCE A/AS Value Added: Briefing for Schools and Colleges*, Department for Education.

Department for Education and Employment (1996) *Setting Targets to Raise Standards: a survey of good practice*.

Hughes, M. G. (1985) Leadership in professionally staffed organisations, in M. Hughes, P. Ribbins, and H. Thomas (eds.) *Managing Education: the system and the institution*, Holt Education, London.

Levacic, R. (1995) *Local Management of Schools: analysis and practice*, Open University Press, Buckingham.

Louis, K. S and Miles, M. (1990) *Improving the Urban High School: what works and why*, Cassell, London.

Knight, B. (1993) *Financial Management for Schools*, Heinemann, London.

Knight, B. (1989) *Managing School Time*, Longman, Harlow.

McAleese, K. (1996) *Managing the Margins: a benchmarking approach to the school budget*, Secondary Heads Association, London.

Mortimore, P. and Blatchford, P. (1993) *The Issue of Class Size* (NCE Briefing 12), National Commission on Education, London.

Mortimore, P., Mortimore, J. with Thomas, H. (1994) *Managing Associate Staff: innovation in primary and secondary schools*, Paul Chapman Publishing, London.

Ofsted (1994) *Taught Time: a report on the relationship between the length of the taught week and the quality and standards of pupils' work, including examination results*, Ofsted, London.

Ofsted (1995a) *The Ofsted Handbook: Guidance on the Inspection of Secondary Schools*, HMSO, London.

Ofsted (1995b) *Class Size and the Quality of Education*, Ofsted, London.

Ofsted (1995c) *The Annual Report of Her Majesty's Chief Inspector of Schools*, HMSO, London.

Simkins, T. (1986) Patronage, markets and collegiality: reflections on the allocation of finance in secondary schools, *Educational Management and Administration*, Vol. 14, no. 1, pp. 17–30.

Simkins, T. (1989) Budgeting as a political and organizational process in educational institutions, in R. Levačić

c (ed.) *Financial Management in Education*, Open University Press, Buckingham.

Simkins. T. (1994) Efficiency, effectiveness and the local management of schools, *Journal of Education Policy*, Vol. 9, no. 1, pp. 15–33.

Simkins, T. (1995) The equity consequences of educational reform, *Educational Management and Administration*, Vol. 23, no. 4, pp. 221–32.

Simkins, T. and Lancaster, D. (1988) *Managing Schools: Block 5 – Managing School Resources*, The Open University Press, Buckingham.

Thomas, H. and Martin, J. (1996) *Managing Resources for School Improvement: creating a cost-effective school*, Routledge, London.

2.7

Managing Evaluation

SHEILA RUSSELL AND SYLVIA REID

EVALUATION AND SCHOOL IMPROVEMENT

The issues of evaluation have become more pressing and more complex as the restructuring of the education system following the 1988 Education Reform Act has unfolded. In the drive to improve standards of education in the late 1990s the government, and the main opposition party, have laid stress in their education policies on a school's ability to improve from within, encouraged by both support and pressure from outside the institution. This has been acknowledged by writers on school management. Hargreaves and Hopkins (1991, p. 106) argue for an alignment of external forces with the school's own strategy for development. They note, for instance, that a school may not easily move from a stable (one might even say stuck) pattern of self-maintenance without some pressure, such as that which comes from an external inspection. A key role for managers is to control the school's response to pressures and to minimise their adverse effects, while developing an element of self-evaluation in order to bring about school improvement.

Changes in the second cycle of Ofsted inspections have acknowledged the link between the school's self-evaluation procedures and statutory external inspection, and the *Framework for Inspection* (Ofsted, 1995) makes provision for inspectors to consider a range of evidence provided from a school's own internal review procedures. For there to be real benefit to the school there has to be an integration of the external and the internal evaluation processes, the one informing the other, and both informing subsequent action. Moon (1995, p. 166) suggests that 'school processes and procedures need to take account of the forms of evidence previously and necessarily left to inspection.' He lists these as performance measures: real routines for classroom observations, regular reported scrutiny of pupils' work, regular formal surveys of pupils' views on the quality of provision, regular surveys of parents, using criteria which allow indications of improvement to be revealed over time, and regular surveys of teachers' views. This chapter proposes a systematic and contextually sensitive approach to evaluation which gives attention to the forms of evidence that Moon identifies, in ways which develop individual and group powers of critical thinking.

This approach to evaluation would imply that external inspection may move closer to internal review, yet without losing its crucial role as a nationally applied accountability process. This can be achieved when inspection reports use qualitative as well as quantitative measures, and show a clear balance between identifying strengths and successes which can be built on, and identifying weaknesses where a key action for change is needed. The best use of this process requires collaboration between those responsible for external inspection and the managers in the school. It is possible to satisfy a legitimate demand for public accountability through a collegiate model of evaluation which can be used for internal development and also have public outcomes, giving an account of the school's work as in the examples provided by Bayne-Jardine and Holly (1994).

In this chapter two important features of evaluation in education are emphasised, first that it should be based on shared judgements, and secondly that it should lead to action for improvement. Consequently the management of evaluation should aim to create, support and sustain informal and formal processes that enable individuals and groups to participate actively in setting targets, in forming judgements, in making decisions and in taking action.

Evaluation will involve the examination of activities in relation to their 'functioning, efficiency and quality' (Hitchcock and Hughes, 1995, p. 31). Other chapters in this volume have explored the greater autonomy that schools have as institutions, and their greater accountability in terms of organisational effectiveness. Evaluation can assist in clarifying what is meant by the elusive concept of effectiveness, which would probably yield different interpretations for each school. Simply, evaluation is the process by which informed decisions are made about the worth of an activity, policy or practice. One view is that these decisions are informed by the systematic, open collection and analysis of information related to explicit objectives, criteria and values (Aspinwall, et al., 1992, p. 2). In this chapter it is argued that the three elements of setting objectives, criteria and the underlying values all involve judgement and need to be agreed in collaboration with the different parties involved, in order to gain insight in to how to best achieve meaningful and tangible improvements as outcomes of evaluation. It is possible and regrettable, for criteria to be applied narrowly and rigidly, for objectives to be poorly understood, or the conflicting nature of values to be left unrecognised.

'Man (sic) is an evaluating animal' and therefore it seems that it is impossible 'for man to escape from choice based on value judgements' and these values must be recognised as the 'building blocks of culture' (Hofstede, 1984, pp. 19–21). Schein (1985, p. 50) defines culture as: 'the shared patterns of thought, belief, feelings, and values that result from shared experience and common learning'. A school's culture will reflect the values which have been established over a period of time, and will be based on the assumptions that a group of people has made and applied when encountering problems in relation to surviving as an entity.

A school's culture both determines the means by which evaluation is conducted, and is itself influenced and altered by the outcomes of evaluation, in essence a truly reciprocal and significant relationship. The culture will influence, and be influenced by the evaluation process; how the outcomes are made public, the means by which improvements are made. Ultimately this interaction will contribute to creating a climate for subsequent evaluations. Hopkins, Ainscow and West (1994, p. 103) emphasise the attention that managers need to give to a school's culture:

> School *culture* is the vital yet neglected dimension in the improvement process . . . The types of school culture most supportive of school improvement efforts . . . are those that are collaborative, have high expectations for both students and staff, exhibit a consensus on values (or an ability to deal effectively with differences), support an orderly and secure environment, and encourage teachers to assume a variety of leadership roles.

Teachers, support staff and managers in schools constantly evaluate, albeit often intuitively, their own actions as well as those of others, in relation to the culture of the school, or a sub-group within the school, as well as in relation to their own individual value systems. Yet, the intuitive judgements that are regularly made are not always appropriate, and often not explicitly shared. As schools and the environments they operate within become increasingly more complex and, in today's world, simultaneously more ambiguous and fragmented, individuals may choose to play safe in decision-making. A school's culture can reinforce inappropriate behaviours and inhibit the explicit sharing of intuitive judgements, or can do the reverse. In some cultures the acceptable, or more apparently reasonable, courses of action or solutions are preferred, in what could be described as some sort of 'default' mode. It is rare for the widest range of alternatives to be considered, because 'decision-makers satisfice' (Bazerman, 1994, p. 5), in other words tolerate a merely 'acceptable' level of performance. Evaluation is a means of exploring alternatives, re-educating and re-forming judgements and consequently a means by which the decision-making processes and activities can be improved.

It is helpful to consider briefly how judgements are generally applied. As Bazerman (1994) indicates, individuals and groups often apply judgement by using rule-of-thumb simplifying strategies. Such strategies, while helpful in enabling people to cope with uncertainty and complexity, have hidden dangers and may conceal bias. Unawareness of bias can lead to inadequately informed and inappropriate decisions. There is a variety of ways that bias can be overcome. These include developing experience and expertise, and using accurate and immediate feedback in order to learn from the outcomes and consequences of action. In order to minimise the impact of individual and collective biases evaluation should:

- use both formative and summative approaches;
- use a wide range of means of collecting data;
- involve as many varying individuals and groups as is appropriate to its focus;
- provide feedback.

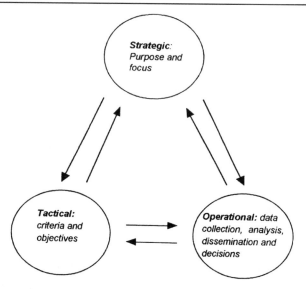

Figure 2.7.1   Evaluation triangle

Evaluation will inform a school's development and may subsequently demand change. It is the feedback gained through the evaluation process that can inform the management of change. Hargreaves and Hopkins (1991) stress that evaluation is central to the notions of accountability and school development, but, as Hargreaves (1995) later reports, leaders in schools appear not to monitor development planning closely enough, nor respond to changing circumstances. If leaders in schools use the range of multiple intelligences (professional, personal and management (Whitaker, 1993, pp. 35–8)), and value the informed confidence effective evaluation processes and practices can provide, development planning for improvement may begin to become a reality.

In any institution evaluation is underpinned by explicit and implicit value judgements. 'Evaluation is a critical activity. It involves not only analysis and judgement concerning the object of criticism, but also analyses and judges the process itself' (Rowland, 1993, p. 127). Figure 2.7.1 presents what is here termed the evaluation triangle, a term intended to capture the interdependence of three stages of evaluation: strategic, tactical, and operational. These stages are crucial in the design and application of any evaluation. The strategic stage relates to purpose and focus, and the tactical stage to the identification and agreement of success criteria and objectives. The operational stage involves deciding the means by which information will be collected, analysed and reported to inform decision-making. Figure 2.7.1 emphasises that value judgements have an effect across and throughout these three stages, and should be made as explicit as possible, through relating them to a school's aims and purposes, as well as allowing for that implicit sharing and modifying of values that occurs when a school works on changing its 'conditions' (Hopkins, Ainscow and West, 1994).

From his observations on evaluation within a higher education setting Rowland (1993) expresses concern about the trend towards the 'technicist' approach to evaluation:

> A technicist outlook in course provision (and hence evaluation) casts the student as merely a means to a managerial end . . . The objectivity that technicism claims to celebrate is bought at the cost of humanity of those it seeks to control. If course evaluation is to be free of technicism it must . . . acknowledge the subjectivity of the participants and enquire into the ways in which this subjectivity is shaped by the course and wider contexts.
>
> (Rowland, 1993, p. 135)

MacDonald and Walker (1974) view 'democratic' evaluation as a means by which a community can be given information on the attributes of an educational activity. Although this perspective on evaluation was developed over twenty years ago, in a very different context to that existing today, there is much to be gained from applying it, and recognising that a 'democratic' evaluator aims to:

> value pluralism and seek to represent a range of interests in his issue formulation. The basic value is an informed citizenry, and the evaluator acts as a broker in exchanges of information between groups who want knowledge of each other. . . . the evaluator has no concept of information misuse. . . . The criterion of success is the range of audiences served. The key concepts of democratic evaluation are 'confidentiality', 'negotiation', and 'accessibility'.
>
> (MacDonald and Walker, 1974, pp. 17–18)

A form of democratic evaluation is perhaps the most appropriate way forward for the educational institutions which serve such a wide range of interests and which has been experiencing significant imposed change.

EVALUATION IN PRACTICE

The accountability measures put in place by the Education Acts of 1992 and 1993 require that a school manages its responses to, and its use of, externally applied measures such as performance tables, and external judgements on the school such as Ofsted, which are publicly reported. These features have to be seen within a framework of self-evaluation and continuing review as implied by both the government agency Ofsted (1995), and the Secondary Heads Association (1996). The following sections deal with the practical issues of managing internal evaluation and review. It has been argued in this chapter that the responsibilities of undertaking evaluation in a school can be shared and owned by different interested parties, in order to gain a wide perspective on the work of the school. Managing evaluation therefore requires considerable co-ordination, and should rely on liaising and facilitating functions as much as on controlling ones.

Leaders in schools have the opportunity to adopt an attitude of mind which seeks to listen, observe and learn through developing and sustaining meaningful relationships internally and externally. It is important to identify what partnerships already exist, and what further partnerships should be developed within the school and with those outside the school. It is also helpful to identify what evaluation already occurs, both formally and informally. In some ways this process can be likened to conducting an audit on the climate for evaluation. The climate for evaluation should attempt to promote the qualities of interdependence, respect, trust, consistency and fairness. Creating and nurturing such a climate is a continuous key function for all leaders in schools and provides the foundations and working context for evaluation. The climate permeates the formal and informal strata of a school's organisation. The management structure, policies, management styles and practices need to support and sustain these five notions, because a healthy climate will ease and support the processes of evaluation and assist in achieving resulting improvements. The health of a school's climate can alter quickly, often due to external forces or factors, or because of changes in key personnel in the school. Leaders are therefore well advised to observe and identify potential factors and sensitively manage their likely impact on the organisational climate. Although external factors may initially pose challenges and problems and even be viewed negatively, they also provide potential opportunities for people collectively to identify issues, to resolve difficulties and conflict and to work collaboratively together in the best interests of the school.

The example below describes how the introduction of evaluation processes sustained and developed a climate and ultimately a culture that supported change in a primary school.

USING PEER PARTNERSHIPS TO ESTABLISH A CULTURE

The headteacher of a first school described the first years of introducing monitoring and peer partnerships in this way: 'It's taken about 3 years for me to establish a culture whereby staff really can understand why we monitor. We used to call it the m-word. I think we are about 75% there now. People say things like 'we've got to check up on this to see that it is happening'.

The school uses peer partnerships in several ways. When the idea was first introduced teachers each chose a 'learning partner'; they selected a focus and observed each other's lessons, giving feedback and planning action which they reviewed again. The headteacher remembers that they first had to be clear about the difference between appraisal and the partnerships – it was important to explore and establish, for the whole staff, levels of trust, honesty, openness and confidentiality.

They used planning sheets to record what they planned to do together, what they found out as a result of observation and discussion, and what they decided to do next. The headteacher found a variety of ways to cover classes so that these pairings of teachers could occur. On the second cycle each teacher was required to work with a different learning partner, and this has now been repeated four times.

After learning partnerships were well established the school introduced peer observations of a different sort (with different partners) called 'checking partnerships'. In this sort of partnership there was an agreed whole-school focus and a teacher would ask a colleague for specific feedback about things she or he was endeavouring to change. Each of the two teachers chose three targets to meet, and these were checked on three times with the same partner.

During the course of the year the school now provides time for staff to explore their own learning, as well as time for 'checking partners' with a focus on agreed school policy and practice.

Teachers reported that both sorts of partnerships had been useful; 'long term benefits for my classroom practice'; 'the benefits for me are sharing problems, pressures and workload'; 'the possibilities of change are stimulating — sometimes worrying, but challenging too'.

As well as the peer partnerships the school uses a system of 'school management monitoring' which arises from the identification of 'critical incidents'. Most recently this has led to a whole school focus on improving the teaching of reading. A staff development day on this topic generated 14 different issues (which were used as evaluation features. On the headteacher's visit to a classroom both she and the teacher know that these are issues that she might be looking at. This arrangement has elements of formality and informality. The criteria are implicit but nevertheless shared, because of the joint planning which has identified this as an important area for improvement. The headteacher feeds back to individual teachers immediately (at break, at lunchtime, or after school) or makes time for a longer session if the observations need more discussion in depth. She summarises what she has seen in several visits (say five or six) at senior management team meetings (headteacher, deputy and key stage co-ordinators). The school will also report in a different way to governors about the reading initiative, and has commissioned an external consultant's report on literacy in the school.

Even with this variety of initiatives the headteacher acknowledges that what is most difficult is to evaluate whether what a teacher is doing makes a real difference to the progress of an individual child. The school is working on improving their methods to ensure that review partnerships really shift attitudes and make things change.

(Russell, 1996, pp. 153–5)

The fundamental questions that must be asked about any evaluation in schools are as follows:

- Why evaluate?
- How can evaluation be resourced?

- What should be evaluated?
- How should quality be judged?
- By whom should the evidence be collected and analysed?
- To whom should an evaluation report be made and when?
- What will be done with the information gathered?

The first question relates to the purpose and aim. There are three underlying and symbiotic functions of evaluation which should be considered when selecting a focus in the strategic phase. These three functions, to *improve*, to *prove* or to *learn* are always present to some degree, but for different evaluations different purposes will seem more significant, as Figure 2.7.2 indicates. For instance looking at the behaviour of pupils in order to develop a behaviour policy might have the primary aim of improvement; an investigation of Key Stage 2 Maths attainment results might be primarily intended to prove something to the general public; getting involved in team-teaching with systematic reflection built in to the work might initially seek to bring about learning. It is maybe not always as simple as Goddard and Leask (1992) claim, when they write that 'The first purpose of evaluation is to inform the subject: evaluation for improvement. The second is to inform others.' (p. 81). Goddard and Leask refer to the aspects of improving and proving, which have to be held in balance, and the interconnected circles in Figure 2.7.2 show how these aspects are also closely linked to learning and growth. Evaluation provides a means for individuals and organisations to learn and grow as Leithwood and Aitken (1993) highlight in their definition of a learning organisation: 'A group of

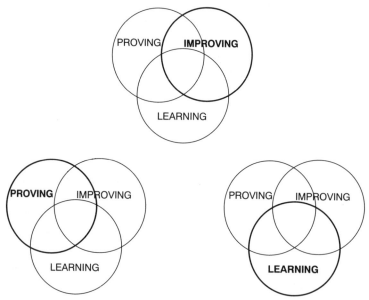

Figure 2.7.2   Relative significance of the three functions of evaluation

people pursuing common purposes (individual purposes as well) with a collective commitment to regularly weighing the value of those purposes, modifying them when that makes sense and continuously developing more effective and efficient ways of accomplishing those purposes' (p. 63).

The question of how evaluation can be resourced clearly relates to the limitations on the resources available. Conducting any formal evaluation implies a conscious commitment of resources such as time, money, and goodwill and may require the access to critical friends. It is therefore useful to take on the responsibility of limiting evaluation to what can be afforded and what is really significant. Ambitious evaluations which fail and result in no tangible progress are demoralising, provide disincentives for future evaluations and are more often than not demotivating. A cautious cynicism is perhaps helpful, as this headteacher suggests:

> You cannot help but salute these new Ofsted inspectors. In their first year of existence they have discovered the educational equivalent of turning lead into gold. To listen to them for any length of time it becomes blindingly obvious why so many of our schools are under-performing. Headteachers are just not up to scratch when it comes to monitoring and evaluation. . . . Many of us would welcome it with open arms if we could be shown the value of all the time and effort that would be involved.
> (Mooney, 1995, p. 10)

In the light of an acknowledgement of the resources available, a focus for evaluation can be selected, knowing what is affordable. Finding the focus is best achieved through open consultation with a range of interested parties in the light of three possible purposes for an evaluation. In general the number of areas of the school's work that are subject to formal evaluation in any one year should be limited in order to be effective. It is sometimes necessary to choose a limited focus for an evaluation in order to practise evaluation skills, to initiate a change or to test the climate and expectations of staff.

Once the purpose and focus of an evaluation are decided a consensus regarding the tactical stage needs to be sought. The objectives that are aimed for and the criteria to be applied can be discussed and agreed, or, if imposed from outside, should be made public and understandable. This stage may take time in listening to a range of perspectives and finding consensus, however it can provide valuable opportunities for learning about others' perspectives, their hopes and fears for the work of the school, as shown in the work of MacBeath *et al.* (1996).

A collaborative approach to choosing criteria

A team from the University of Strathclyde (MacBeath et *al.*, 1996) was asked by the National Union of Teachers (NUT) to develop a self-evaluation framework for schools. The team piloted an approach that involved parents, pupils, teaching and non-teaching staff in generating lists of what was important for them about a school. These researchers refer to the criteria generated as 'indicators' and their aim was to create a framework based on the indicators of effectiveness defined by different interest groups. The project was aimed at identifying criteria and, ultimately, instruments for collecting evidence, but it also crucially recognised the need for the framework for self-evaluation to be workable and user-friendly.

The team reported that they first asked all groups (pupils, parents, teachers and other staff) in all the schools to list individually their own five key factors of an effective school This was done as a brainstorming exercise where there were language or writing difficulties. Secondly, a card sort exercise was used with 23 criteria drawn from OFSTED guidelines for school inspection and two blank cards for people to add their own. In small groups people were asked to agree on the five most important criteria for them and then to do the same with the three criteria which they considered to be least important. With very young pupils variations of these approaches were used, for example they were asked to draw the things they liked best about schools and their teachers, and this was followed up with questioning and discussion.

This approach acknowledges that different interest groups may have different values and expectations. The researchers argue that 'it is possible to start the process of building an indicator set with one group and one set of perspectives and then to overlay this with the perspectives of other groups in order eventually to arrive at a common set that is school-specific, a common set that accomodates differences' (MacBeath et al., 1996, p. 22). Despite the existence of a rich body of evidence about effective schools they demonstrate the benefits of a 'people-centred' exercise in creating ownership, in exploring the dynamic inter-relationships between factors, and in testing the findings of outside researchers.

As in the Strathclyde research, it may be valuable for a school to involve outsiders in determining standards of judgement. There are illustrations of successful evaluation practice involving LEA, Higher Education institutions and schools in the work of Bayne-Jardine and Holly (1994). Useful, meaningful and manageable criteria can be found if the school has a method for the task. Criteria selected as standards in evaluation should be few in number, specific, clearly expressed, relevant to the focus and capable of being investigated. Wherever possible they should include measures of pupils' achievements.

Collecting and analysing data

The operational stage, as do the tactical and strategic stages, needs to be based on agreed basic principles which ensure people maintain trust and respect for each other during the collection of data and analysis stages. Decisions about methods for collecting data should be based on consideration of three key factors: ethical factors; appropriateness; and variety. Ethical considerations are far reaching. Some data schools currently hold, if released, could breach codes

Table 2.7.1 Methodology matrix

Aims	Resourcing	Focus of evaluation	Data and methods	People involved	Timescale	Reporting audience	Planning responsibility
Prove	Management duties	Standards	Tracking pupils	Headteacher	Within a term	Whole staff	Headteacher and SMT
Improve	Directed time	Teaching	Questionnaires	Deputy	At regular intervals	Senior management team	Governing body
Learn	GEST funding	Curriculum	Observations	Coordinator	Over a year	Headteacher	Governing body with LEA/DFEE
	Volunteers	Discipline	Reflection	Outsiders (LEA, HE)	Continuous	Pupils and staff	Key stage team
	INSET days	Support for staff	Survey of views	Governors	At infrequent intervals	Governing body	
	Supply cover	Home-school	Interviews with pupils	Teachers	Within a week	Parents	
		Leadership	Interviews with parents	Pupils		Community	
		Relationships	Group discussion	Parents			
		Environment	Peer observations	School review teams			
		Equipment					
WHY?	**HOW RESOURCED?**	**WHAT?**	**HOW?**	**BY WHOM?**	**WHEN?**	**TO WHOM?**	**WHAT NEXT?**

of confidentiality. Gathering certain forms of data could also breach codes of confidentiality and it needs to be remembered that data stored on computerised systems fall within the provisions of the Data Protection Act. Clearly if existing data are to be accessed or new data collected then the collection methods, uses and applications of the data require negotiating with individuals, and should not set precedents which counter legislative requirements. Additionally, data collected for one audience should not be used in a different context without further negotiation. Issues of anonymity, relevance and accessibility of data also require negotiation with interested and involved parties. Appropriateness relates to the means by which data is collected, its use and the application that will be made of the data. Appropriateness also affects the timescale of data collection and reporting back procedures, as well as the ability to find approaches which are suitable to the purpose of the evaluation in question. Thirdly, variety must be considered, for instance, how best to collect a range of quantitative and qualitative information, and how best to gain a range of perspectives in order to capture and share the variety of viewpoints that exist on the subject under examination. Data should be gathered in a disciplined manner and analysed and reported so that people feel they have some sense of beginning to own and appreciate the whole picture of the issue under examination.

Co-ordinating and planning

As organisational structures are adapting to the changes in the education system, the activities of co-ordinating and planning become ever more significant. The new responsibilities of schools promote the need for effective co-ordination and greater confidence in planning. Effective evaluation requires both.

The co-ordinating function is implicit now within all leadership roles within schools. Co-ordinating involves liaising between individuals and groups with the aim of ensuring that there is effective communication both vertically and horizontally across the organisation's structure, and externally. This is a key issue in evaluation, where information and its handling is so important. Management information systems need to be established, maintained and monitored with the aim of ensuring information is both accurate and appropriately accessible. An additional aspect of the co-ordinating function is the ability to identify, but not always solve, problems, and support individuals and groups in confronting and ultimately resolving their own problems. For co-ordinating a whole school approach and avoiding overload what is needed is a map, identifying what has to be done, who will be involved, when and what will be the outcomes. A methodology matrix such as Table 2.7.1 presents a practical basic planning aid enabling a school to make a number of choices in relation to the key questions.

Table 2.7.1 shows a partially completed matrix, where a school has first generated lists of options and then made some choices for a particular evaluation activity. The jagged line illustrates the choices selected in this situation:

A primary school agrees to evaluate reading standards, with the principal aim of improving the progress and achievement of pupils. It is decided to resource this activity from GEST funding, and to employ a researcher from the initial teacher training department of an HE institution to observe pupils at intervals over a term, in order to monitor their progress and to observe how far the styles of teaching used meet individual needs. At the end of the term a report is made to the whole staff, and the key stage teams are given the responsibility of planning action in classrooms to build on the recommendations of the report.

The methodology matrix serves a range of purposes. It assists in identifying possible approaches to conducting the evaluation. It can act as a means of recording approaches and, over time, highlight aspects which may have been overlooked in conducting evaluations. It can act as a vehicle to initiate and support the brainstorming and idea generation of developing new evaluation methods. The matrix should be viewed as a means of ensuring that the operational stage of evaluation, whilst disciplined, is capable of being thought about creatively and flexibly.

Skill development

Schools as organisations are beginning to recognise the need to develop confidence in evaluating their work. All aspects of institutional evaluation demand that those involved learn new skills, and apply those that they already have in different ways. The opportunity to use the evaluation process to practise and extend skills is an important one. Some evaluation skills are learned collaboratively in the school, but the support of outsiders, whether as advisers, researchers or trainers may be beneficial. Specifically in the collaborative model recommended in this chapter teachers and others need the skills and commitment to:

- identify a subset of questions which need the closest consideration at any given time;
- generate a set of qualitative indicators relating to each of these questions;
- define the methods that will be used to collect evidence about these indicators;
- decide how to move from the evaluative stage to action for change;
- set targets;
- monitor the effects of the action.

Clearly, the training needs for evaluation could be considerable. It is important to allocate resources for staff development in evaluation and to identify training needs as the process takes place. The following list of relevant skills offers an initial starting point for identifying needs:

negotiating access to collect data;   communication skills;
designing evaluation instruments;   networking;
interviewing skills;   observation skills;
problem identification skills;   analysing and interpreting
                                                    information;

feeding back;
presenting an evaluation report.

CONCLUSION

Evaluation provides a means of recording success and controlling the pace of change. Such features are particularly important for educational institutions, which are distinctive in nature.

> Education is the sum of formal and informal structures and arrangements instituted by society to ensure its renewal . . . Formal education exhibits a major paradox. On the one hand, it developed in a time of rapid industrial expansion to serve the needs of a factory based society . . . Generally speaking, it has subjects which look back but none which look forward . . . change in the real world over the last two centuries has been rapid, profound and structural. . . . Yet schools have no systematic way of monitoring, describing or even noticing this fact directly and clearly.
>
> (Slaughter, 1995, p. 24)

If the problems inherent in the nature and process of evaluation are ignored by managers, evaluation can become a strait-jacket and constrain the search for improvement. It can even inhibit individuals and schools from taking a positive approach to the future. Evaluation has its roots in the values and aims of the school based on the past and present, yet it can offer the means to provide for the unknown and uncertain future. The responsibility for evaluation lies within the many different leadership roles taken on in schools: classroom teachers; curriculum co-ordinators, heads of departments, heads of year, senior managers. If evaluation is to be effective, those with leadership responsibility will need to address the complex yet significant task of managing evaluation through consultation, collaboration and planning in order to ensure that it results in improvements and in individual and collective confidence.

In practice new strategies of evaluation will only become accepted if they lead to perceived benefits in people's lives. Conversely it is unlikely that an evaluation strategy will be sustained if no improvement ensues. In most schools a self-evaluation approach linked to action can be of benefit if, on a day to day basis teachers' lives are affected, they can see a measurable benefit and they see that pupils are getting something out of it, if on a day to day basis teachers' conditions of work are improved, and if all can see a measurable increase in the success of pupils. The highest aspiration is that a managed approach to evaluation can be successful in enabling a school to become a learning organisation for staff and for pupils.

REFERENCES

Aspinwall, K., Simkins, T., Wilkinson, J., McAuley, M., (1992) *Managing Evaluation in Education*, Routledge, London.

Bayne-Jardine, C., Holly P., (1994) *Developing Quality Schools*, The Falmer Press, London.

Bazerman, M. H., (1994) *Judgement in Managerial Decision Making*, (3rd edn), John Wiley & Sons, USA

Goddard, D., Leask, M., (1992) *The Search for Quality*, Paul Chapman Publishing, London.

Hargreaves, D. H., Hopkins, D., (1991) *The Empowered School: the management and practice of development planning*, Cassell, London.

Hargreaves, D. H., (1995) Self Managing Schools and Development Planning in *School Organisation*, Vol. 15, no. 3, p. 226.

Hitchcock, G., Hughes, D., (1995) *Research and the Teacher, A Qualitative Introduction to school-based Research*, (2nd edn), Routledge, London.

Hofstede, G., (1984) *Culture's Consequences*, Sage, USA.

Hopkins, D., Ainscow, M., West, M., (1994) *School Improvement in an Era of Change*, Cassell, London.

Leithwood, K., Aitken, R., (1993) *Making schools smarter: a system for monitoring school and district progress*, Corwen, Newbury Park..

MacBeath, J., Boyd, B., Rand, J., Bell, S., (1996) *Schools Speak for Themselves*, NUT, London.

MacDonald, B., Walker, R., (1974) *Information Evaluation Research and the Problem of Control*, SAFARI. Working Paper, no. 1, Centre for Applied Research in Education, University of East Anglia, Norwich.

Moon, B., (1995) Judgement and evidence: redefining professionality in a new era of school accountability in T. Brighouse and B. Moon (eds) *School Inspection*, Pitman, London.

Mooney, T (1995) Paying attention to ME in *Education*, Vol.185, no. 17 p. 10

Ofsted (1995) *The Handbook for the Inspection of Schools*, HMSO, London.

Rowland, S., (1993) *The Enquiring Tutor: Exploring the Process of Professional Learning*, The Falmer Press, London.

Russell, S., (1996) *Collaborative School Self-Review*, Lemos-Crane, London.

Schein, E. H., (1985) *Organizational Culture and Leadership*, Jossey-Bass, USA.

Secondary Heads Association (1996) *Towards More Effective Schools*, Secondary Heads Association.

Slaughter, R. A., (1995) *The Foresight Principle*, Adamantine Press, UK.

Whitaker, P., (1993) *Managing Change in Schools*, Open University Press, Buckingham.

PART 3
LOOKING TOWARDS THE FUTURE

3.1

Leadership: a Model of Cultural Change

HUGH JENKINS

The view put forward in this chapter is that leadership over the last 15–20 years has undergone a radical change both in the language used to describe it and in the way it is practised. There seems to be a remarkable consensus in studies of leadership both inside and outside the field of education management about the key principles that underpin effective leadership behaviour. To a person, writers on leadership describe it as transformational not transactional, as a source of empowerment not the centre of power, as post heroic where the workers and not the leaders are the heroes, as facilitating and enabling not directing and ordering. These leaders care for and value staff, and build the 'right' sort of culture in which staff can flourish in their new state of empowerment. Staff are therefore highly motivated and this type of leadership inevitably leads to better outcomes with increased productivity and improved performance.

The physical manifestation of the new leadership behaviour is the creation of the post-bureaucratic organisation in which bureaucratic processes disappear. There is delayering and flat structures with a reduction in the levels of hierarchy, staff are working in functional and cross-organisational teams, individuals and teams are empowered at the point of delivery and there are open networks of information. The result is lean, flexible organisations pervaded with the entrepreneurial spirit that allows the challenges of change to be met head on. These organisations too are in this sense led by visionaries in that the leaders have enunciated and encapsulated in an easily repeatable form – the organisational vision.

Above all, however, these organisations are externally not internally focused. They have a fixation on customer satisfaction and an obsession with listening to the customer. Their leaders create constructive alliances with stakeholders and set up powerful stakeholder partnerships. High levels of local accountability are their mark. Finally, leaders in these organisations have a preoccupation with quality and high performance. While 'loose' in terms of their approach to staff autonomy they are 'tight' in terms of their insistence on continuous evaluation and measurement of performance.

This oversimplistic summary of the key components of effective leadership is given, not because they always lead to success but because the language used in the descriptions is starkly indicative of changed perceptions of what leadership is all about. The 'new' language is about power sharing, openness, collaborative working, stakeholder partnerships and the creation of flexible, responsive, innovative organisations. Far removed from rational positivist attempts to build principles of leadership based on a belief in power, control and order, new leaders use language that has turned notions of power on its head. To argue as Gronn does (1996, p. 24) that in leadership studies 'there have been no big breakthroughs which justify the idea of a new paradigm, watershed or quantum leap' is seriously misguided; it fails to take into account a new understanding of leadership in terms of 'cultural transformation, social integration and inspiring (literally to 'breath life into') the vision of learning organisations' (Senge, 1990, p. 340).

The view is therefore taken in this chapter that leadership is about changing the organisation by building collaborative cultures. It is argued that such cultures are the most appropriate for schools (indeed for all organisations) in a social and political context of constant change. The growth of the belief in collaborative cultures is outlined below and definitions offered of what is meant by such cultures. Models of leadership for cultural change are discussed. Examples are then given, from recent research into schools, of how heads are succeeding (or sometimes failing) in their attempts to build empowerment cultures within the context of school-based management.

It should be noted that it is not intended to make any differentiation between managers and leaders. Leadership is considered as an integral part of management. Effective managers are effective leaders (or the other way about). Little difference was also found in the research quoted later, in the language and perceptions of leadership between leaders inside and outside education. In practice, most effective leaders in all types of organisations are committed to the concepts and practice of collaborative or empowerment cultures.

LEADERSHIP THEORY AND THE PROCESS OF CULTURAL CHANGE

Post-modern society is marked by constant change and unpredictability. There are in society and the organisations that inhabit it, many sources of substantial disorder and chaos – not chaos in the sense of anarchy but in the sense of considerable uncertainty and complexity. However, in spite of the unpredictability associated with post-modern society, Bergquist (1993) contends that we have moved away from a traditional society, based on dominance, to a society based on partnership and collaboration. Certainly there is now severe questioning of divisions caused by hierarchies and status:

> Leaders, of this edgy postmodern world must somehow navigate a turbulent 'white water' environment, one filled with unpredictability and requiring both short-term survival tactics and long-term strategies based on broad visions and deeply embedded

values. Leaders must be sources of integration in postmodern organisations. They perform this integrative role through the creation and sustenance of community and through acting in the role of servant to those with whom they work.

(Bergquist, 1993, p. 13).

Leadership in this view is about creating a culture of empowerment which in turn creates collaborative systems which are the safe spaces which allow individuals to be led to a deeper understanding and where they 'can deal productively with the critical issues they face' (Senge, 1990, p. 345).

Models of leadership such as the structural functionalist model and the systems model (Busher and Saran, 1994) which in essence build on organisational roles and positions (Ball, 1987; Bush, 1986), are considered to be of limited value at a time of rapid change and lack of adherence to traditional hierarchies. Managers, in spite of themselves, are now postmodernist because their practices, and the concepts which underlie these, are 'permeated with the same confusions, assumptions and concerns that define postmodernism in society at large' (Moult, 1990). Leaders have to help create a culture which can accommodate rapid change and considerable uncertainty and the best way forward proposed in this chapter is the building of a collaborative culture.

As long ago as 1978, Burns drew a distinction between what he called transactional and transformational leadership. Transactional leadership is concerned with the necessary activities in getting things done and sorted out within the organisation through people and systems; the transformational leader builds on people's need for meaning and purpose and inspires followers to higher levels of motivation and morality. Leadership in this context is a visionary and moral activity which offers a vision that transforms the existing situation and which is concerned with ethical values such as freedom and equity (Foster, 1986; Bennis and Nanus, 1985).

Closely linked to the idea of transformational leadership is that of the role of leader in establishing the organisational culture which determines the practices and behaviour of individual members within the organisation (Schein, 1992). The shaping of culture is 'one of the prime tests of the leader through the establishment of norms and values, a clear communication of a philosophy and the creation of symbols, ceremonies and myths which create and re-inforce the culture' (Jenkins, 1991, p. 25). Sergiovanni and Corbally (1984), in considering a hierarchy of the tasks of educational leadership, conclude that the creation of organisational culture is at the top of the pyramid. Educational leaders express and embody the symbolic and cultural dimensions of the values shared by others both inside and external to the school.

Bate (1994) offers a strong warning, however, against the use of culture as an independent variable which can be manipulated by the leader. Culture in Bate's view is not a separate sub-system but is synonymous with organisation. Taking an anthropological view, he argues that we need to think of organisations as being cultures rather than having cultures. Changing cultures, therefore, is the same as changing the organisation. A further complication is the issue of the strong integrative culture as the goal of leadership. The belief that a unitary monolithic culture is necessary to drive everyone in the organisation forward on a unified basis of agreed values is strongly held by many involved in organisational development. However, a pluralistic culture which gives free-dom to the organisational sub-units with the centre playing a coordinating role may be more effective in achieving the organisation's goals.

By bringing together a number of theorists who support what can be called a critical theory perspective it is possible to see how far thinking on leadership has broken away from conventional rationalistic views. In this critical reap-praisal, views of leadership as value free are rejected, so that Greenfield (1986), for example, in his view of organisations as invented social realities, asserts that we have under-estimated the part that values play in leaders' views of the world and their actions. This, in turn, implies key ethical and moral consider-ations which the leader must take into account. Duignan (1990) has pointed out that leaders now find themselves embroiled in conflicts of values, goals, purposes and interests and that the rapidly changing uncertain and unstable nature of the educational policy framework has compelled leaders into a new focus on the subjective and adaptive aspects of organisational process. As a response to the need for constant adaptation, it is argued that the role of leadership is primarily educative in nature. By using a cultural and value based paradigm an educative leader can challenge 'others to participate in the vision-ary activity of identifying what is worthwhile' (Duignan, 1990, p. 338). This process is seen as both enlightening and empowering if educative leaders take responsibility for creating organisational cultures that enhance the growth and development of all involved in teaching and learning (Macpherson, 1995). Educative leadership implies challenging both policy and structural elements which suppress critical and creative education, while maintaining an effective inquiry and problem solving climate to ensure freedom for staff to participate in the process of learning and development. However, this is a demanding view of school leadership in that 'leaders in schools now require coherent knowl-edge and skills in philosophical, strategic, political, cultural, managerial and evaluation realms if they are to boost the quality of teaching and learning' (Macpherson, 1995, p. 174)

Summary – a model of leadership for cultural change

From the ideas on leadership summarised above, it is clear that cultural leader-ship has multiple dimensions which go beyond the technical activities of man-agement. It has political, philosophical and ethical dimensions in addition to practices associated with action and implementation. Bate (1994) in analysing the role of the leader in cultural, and therefore in his view, organisational change, offers us a multi-dimensional model of leadership as follows:

1 *An aesthetic dimension:* the leader assists in the creation, expression and communication of a new idea or system of ideas.
2 *A political dimension:* the leader assists in 'writing' or inscribing those

ideas into a body of socially agreed meanings – fitting into or supplanting existing frames of reference.

3.   *An ethical dimension:* the leader assists in developing and imparting to others a framework of moral standards governing the expression and development of these meanings and ideas.

4.   *An action dimension:* the leader assists in the process of transmuting the agreed cultural meanings into concrete cultural practices.

5.   *A formative dimension:* the leader assists in structuring these meanings and practices into some kind of rationale or framework.

Bate goes on to argue that given this multi-dimensional characteristic, we may need different leaders for different parts of the cultural change process and that leadership is a collective and not an individual activity. Leaders are therefore required at all levels of the organisation and not just at the top.

If we accept the model of leadership as essentially one of cultural change, then in the multiple cultural dimensions of any organisation, leadership activity can be carried out by multiple leaders. What also emerges from this analysis is that leadership is a two way social construct which is continuously negotiated and renegotiated by leaders and followers. It is a form of social influence which has ethical purposes and is carried out in a collaborative and not a hierarchical manner. Its ethical base supports the development of moral values and sound standards. It adopts a critical and self-reflective stance in order to expose underlying issues such as the nature of power and its use. It is essentially to do with collective group activities building on agreed meanings about the organisation's vision and direction.

We now discuss these issues in relation to the practice of school leadership.

CULTURAL CHANGE AND SCHOOL-BASED MANAGEMENT

This section examines the extent to which school leaders are succeeding or failing in fulfilling a model of leadership which embraces cultural change into collaborative cultures. More specifically we ask to what extent cultural change towards increased collaboration is affected by the introduction of school-based management and in which ways leadership is affected by the introduction of school-based management (SBM). For example, now that schools have greater autonomy, does the collaborative model of leadership hold good, or is increased autonomy resulting in a retreat into more functionalist modes of leadership behaviour? Does SBM make any difference? In SBM school leaders are working within new decision making parameters with wider responsibilities, without the traditional protection of the broader educational control frameworks. Will closer forms of accountability to governors, parents and the community (the stakeholder phenomenon) encourage leaders to employ controlling or liberating mechanisms? And what about anxieties about OFSTED visits, performance levels and league tables – will they seduce leaders into centralising and instrumental attitudes?

To give at least some answers to these questions evidence is offered from research studies of educational leaders carried out in South East England during which 34 heads of Secondary Schools were interviewed over a period of three years. A quarter of the heads interviewed were women, but the study did not examine in detail differences between men and women heads. In reality, there appeared little difference between the styles adopted by men and women heads (Coleman, 1996). These studies sought to update major studies on school leadership carried out in the 1980s (Jenkins, 1985, 1991) and were particularly concerned with changes in leadership behaviour in key areas such as staff empowerment, instructional leadership, school improvement, the creation and implementation of strategy and entrepreneurial behaviour (Jenkins and Evans, 1992). A further study using the same research criteria was carried out as an international comparative study of school heads in South East England and in Sri Lanka (Evans, 1995).

Leadership models in schools and industry

Much of the author's writing has concentrated on the similarities and differences between the leadership of educational and commercial/industrial organisations. In the eighties, divisions were pronounced between the two groups of managers both in terms of the language of leadership and also in the way they carried out their main activities as managers. School heads were especially suspicious of the model of management used in industry which they perceived as instrumentally concerned with profits rather than with values and ethical issues, lacking a professional dimension and operating with totally different forms of accountability. The fact that research showed that in many cases heads behaved in more autocratic ways than their industrial counterparts, were also more instrumental in their dealings with staff and had little concern for a wider client or stakeholder base did nothing to dissuade school leaders that they were limited in their managerial perspective. Strangely when leaders in schools, faced with government pressure for better management, began to adopt new management practices, they began to employ Taylorist or managerialist approaches which led to less staff autonomy, increased hierarchies and generally to the introduction of out of date management ideas (Jenkins, 1991). However the research described in this chapter indicates that school leaders have begun to understand and implement a range of practices which displays a new understanding of leadership and that the language and constructs of leadership used by school leaders are those also used by leaders outside education.

We found that there was general acceptance of what leaders consider to be 'business' models of management. The terminology of financial management, marketing and stakeholder partnerships came as easily to the lips of school leaders as to those of any leader in a commercial or industrial organisation. Although one or two heads bemoaned the change in the model of leadership from instructional leader to corporate manager, none disagreed that their leadership task was to manage their resources effectively including the management of teaching and learning.

There was no evidence that leaders were ambivalent about their managerial as opposed to their educational role. They saw them as inextricably interlinked. Nor did they resent reductions in time spent on learning activities, such as curriculum development, because of the time spent dealing with administrative and managerial business. The models of business management and educational development have become fused in the minds of school leaders and the debate is no longer about which model is more appropriate, but about what the 'new' integrated model means in terms of leadership behaviour in practice. This view was accepted equally by heads of Grant Maintained and LEA schools. There were one or two heads who dissented from this general viewpoint: not so much in resisting the responsibility of the leader to manage effectively, but in terms of a belief that the 'business ethic' was too predominant and too powerful in determining leadership behaviour. It had led according to one head of a large Catholic secondary school to a 'secular' approach which had distorted values through an over-concentration on cost efficiency and performance review. He saw the last five years as a failure of leadership in that school heads had lost sight of the promulgation of clear ethical values for schooling which underpinned beliefs about society and social justice.

Staff empowerment

A belief in staff empowerment is strongly expressed by school leaders as the cornerstone of a collaborative culture. The diminishing hierarchical and status constraints, the lessening of differentiation between managers and other staff, the confirmation of devolved decision making, the creation of empowered staff teams were all cited as indicative of the 'new' leadership. Collaborative and shared approaches were the norm. School leaders claimed to have bridged the gap that existed previously between SMT and the rest of the staff. They asserted that they now led from behind and had become enablers, coaches, counsellors, facilitators and consultants within their own school. A number of structural solutions to empowerment were described by the heads ranging from flattening the organisation through reducing the number of senior staff, creating self managing teams, rotating the leadership teams and creating opportunities for staff at all levels to contribute to decision making.

However, in practice considerable variation was observed in different heads' interpretations and perceptions of empowerment. The range of collaborative management activities observed varied from almost total empowerment to 'mock' empowerment where processes of consultation existed but staff power over decision making was restricted to mundane and unimportant issues. In these schools, in reality, the power of the head was undiminished and the empty gestures toward collaboration further alienated staff, although even these heads genuinely believed that they were empowering staff and that they had shed power.

When interviewed, staff at these schools expressed a deep disillusionment about the collaborative processes and considered that the leader was either paying lip service to conventional thinking or had little understanding of the meaning of empowerment which the leader had confused with inadequate forms of consultation. One middle manager in one of the schools visited claimed that:

> The Head has recently introduced a new management structure with the aim of involving more staff in decision making. Despite the time-consuming consultation about the elaborate changes in staff responsibilities it has largely been a sham – the Head continues to make all the key decisions. The whole process and its outcomes have made the staff even more frustrated than they were before.

There was a strong feeling among staff that these heads did not have the leadership skills to put into practice the processes and structures of empowerment. They lacked not only the will but the skill to empower staff.

Collaborative cultures and school improvement

The leaders interviewed also believed that the collaborative approaches to management which they had introduced had led to school improvement and better pupil outcomes. Although there are well documented difficulties about determining the causal effects of leadership on organisational outcomes, nevertheless the heads believed that staff empowerment and collaborative processes brought about organisational improvement. Their experience is in line with the results of a research project described by Russ (1995), which explored the features of management within 'improving' schools. This study found that a common feature of such schools was 'collaborative management' which revealed itself in terms of 'collaborative leadership' and through a 'collaborative culture of professional development'. Russ concludes: 'It is suggested therefore that the schools in the research sample were improving because they were successful at empowering staff and pupils to work collaboratively within the organisation. In short, these schools were operating as learning institutions' (Russ, 1995, p. 6) with collaborative cultures that are considered 'transformational in effect' (Leithwood, Begley and Cousins, 1992, p. 144).

SBM and collaborative cultures

Without exception, the heads interviewed considered that SBM had increased their ability to change the culture of their school. Although, as stated above, there were marked differences in their understanding of what could be considered a collaborative culture, they believed that the enhanced autonomy created under SBM made it easier to be innovative and to build a new culture of partnership with staff and with the community. They had no fears about the increased accountability to governors and parents because they sought to incorporate stakeholders into the partnership and they saw a collaborative

Case Study 14:   The Effects of a Collaborative Culture

One of the schools visited demonstrated an openness and friendliness from the helpful guidance offered by young pupils in finding the head's room to the pleasant and efficient reception staff.

The head, in his second headship, had seen significant changes in the context in which he operated. The self-managing school, initially an LM school and for the last three years a GM school, had enabled him to set up a different kind of organisation. Grant Maintained status immediately moved his training budget from £5,000 to £50,000, which transformed the way in which staff could be developed. He was now able to target his resources more effectively on school priorities. However, self-management brought with it not only autonomy but also a new focus on accountability, through GM requirements for annual audits, management reports and OFSTED efficiency and value for money audits.

According to the head, before the early 1990s power came from the LEA straight to his office and the school's bureaucracy aped that of the LEA. The school as an organisation has now fundamentally changed. A commercially trained bursar has been appointed who is a member of the senior management team together with the two deputies, three senior teachers, director of the Technology Centre, director of the 6th Form and the head, making a team of nine. The governing body takes the key strategic decisions and the SMT sets the overall direction and targets.

Middle managers are proactive and growing in effectiveness as they assume more power to take initiatives in their own sphere of activity. There is a total recognition on the part of the head that he can't do it all. 'I used to think I knew more about the curriculum than anyone else in the school, but I have come to realise that I have experts all around me. We must allow them to develop their strengths and be responsible for their own areas'. Curriculum conferences are organised periodically, led by the head, and outside speakers are invited to make contributions. In a recent conference it was generally agreed that there was too much teaching and not enough learning. This resulted in middle managers designing a common lesson planner. The November league tables demonstrate that pupil achievement is being raised year-on-year.

There is much evidence in the school of open leadership which transforms, inspires, facilitates and empowers staff. The traditional role of the head has changed: he has become an internal consultant, largely engaged in advising and supporting staff. 'Organisations are dynamic and when staff know they count, they simply take over and make it happen,' he said with some passion. He recounts with clear pride the story of a group of staff who felt that they were not as involved as they wanted to be in what was going on in the school. They were invited to do something about it and they set up a 'suggestion box' in the staff room. However, instead of passing the suggestions up the line, they established themselves into a group and gave coherent form to unrelated suggestions and submitted them to the SMT. This has now become a recognised and effective channel of communication between main scale teachers (and others who have now joined them) and the SMT.

At the heart of this open approach is the head's vision of the school which, he repeats constantly to staff, will be one of the best comprehensive schools in England in the next three years. Clarity of vision for him is the essence of leadership. The mission statement provides a package of commitments. 'It starts with quality teaching through which the highest quality of learning can be achieved to fulfil the potential of every pupil in the school – but it must be based on strategic planning which has to involve pupils, staff, governors and parents and must be open to the influences of all these stakeholders and attuned to their aspirations'.

The head claimed that 'things have changed in secondary schools during the last four years, and it's happening not only to me but to so many other people in the school'. Middle managers have really become leaders of curriculum and pastoral activities where they act as internal advisors to empower other colleagues. This freedom to take and act upon initiatives is not confined to staff; it is evident too in the voluntary involvement of pupils. One example is the anti-bullying mentor scheme set up by Year 11 pupils. In each Pastoral House area, photographs of Year 11 mentors are displayed giving times when they can be consulted if any pupil encounters difficulty. Every facet of school life seems to be permeated by a quality of care and a sense of satisfaction that comes from doing the right things well.

Central to this phenomenon is the way that all members of the school community are treated both informally and formally. The success of staff, for example, in gaining promotion to other schools is celebrated; the achievement of pupils becomes the focal point in the morning assembly. The school has been awarded the Investors in People Charter which is underpinned by a transparent process of appraisal and staff development with a direct relationship to the Institutional Development Plan. The school has established a partnership with a London university where currently twelve members of staff are engaged in a school-based Masters programme, 50 per cent of which is achieved through experiential learning so that the theoretical and knowledge based learning has immediate utility for their work as practising senior and middle managers. 'School based management,' the head summed up, 'has released an energy which is transforming the school.'

culture as embracing not only the internal but the external partners in the school enterprise. They saw agreement about the values for which the school stood as fundamental to the collaborative culture, with an agreed statement of values giving them legitimacy to act.

The heads of GM schools in the sample were particularly adamant about the benefits of SBM. There are some who argue that SBM has made little difference to the culture of schools (Sackney and Dibski, 1995), while others argue that increased school effectiveness is not contingent on SBM (Caldwell, 1994). This was not the view of the heads interviewed: in their view the claims that SBM makes no difference are not true. Case Study 14 illustrates the way in which a collaborative (and innovative) culture has been built in a GM school.

Leaders as followers

Another finding from the research is the increased expectations of staff within these schools. They too are keenly aware of their own 'followship' needs. Followers believe, for example, that they have the right of access to decision-making and to all relevant information within the school and the right to discuss with senior management their concerns about 'weak' leadership. As part of the critical reflectivity involved in developing more effective leadership, it is right that followers too are trained in 'followership' skills (Thody, 1996). The problem with re-opening the old debate about followers is that the promotion of followship as a concept begins to undermine a key tenet of collaborative management, namely that leadership is spread throughout the organisation and that sources of leadership are constantly changing. A true culture of collaboration will absorb 'followers' into processes of learning and development which will in turn create leaders all through the organisation to be responsible for changing and building organisations 'where people continually expand their capabilities to understand complexity, clarify vision and improve shared mental models – that is they are responsible for learning' (Senge, 1990, p. 340).

Collaborative models in different contexts

What is also clear from our findings is that the creation of a collaborative culture does not mean an identical approach to cultural change in each school. The processes and outcomes of creating a collaborative culture were different in all cases. Teams were used in different ways, decision-making had no set pattern, vision and focus varied considerably. What was apparent however was that staff knew when the culture was not collaborative, and, as we have seen, some heads' understanding of the context of collaboration was very limited and nowhere near satisfied the aspirations of the staff. The research also found that in some environments the process of cultural change is much more difficult than in others. Perhaps we would expect a less easy model of change in schools in deprived areas where crises and pressures such as fear of staff redundancies, bad pupil behaviour and lack of community support continually subvert the building of a coherent culture. These schools reveal the depth and complexity of leadership skills which have to reside throughout the school before it can build a culture of learning where assumptions and values are commonly created and owned.

CONCLUSIONS

The research has confirmed that many heads are committed to changing the culture of their schools into collaborative learning cultures. Any residual belief that ideas of empowerment, collaborative decision making, improving performance and responding to stakeholders are alien imports from industry and commerce has now disappeared. The building of collaborative cultures is increasingly seen as the most creative way of coping with the unpredictability of postmodern organisations and the rapidly changing context in which they operate. The heads interviewed, particularly those in GM schools, believed that SBM had given them the autonomy and the confidence to build collaborative systems. A number were very close to the model suggested by Bate described earlier for cultural leadership. These heads in pursuing a collaborative culture brought about the creation of a new idea or vision for the school (the aesthetic dimension), they were politically adept at getting the vision accepted with a commonly agreed frame of reference (the political dimension), they promoted the ideas within an ethical framework (the ethical dimension), they were able to put the vision into practice by transforming cultural meanings into cultural realities (the action dimension) and finally they set the ideas and actions into an agreed rationale (the formative dimension). Unlike those who assert that SBM makes no difference, they were clear that SBM had given them a new freedom to work with their staff towards new cultures in their schools: they had clearly taken on board the powerful movement within the leadership agenda towards collaborative management.

Interestingly, the idea of a 'strong' and 'weak' leader has been turned on its head. The 'strong' leader is now perceived as the person who has the skills and abilities to create a collaborative culture which, in effect, diminishes autocracy and extends leadership to others in the organisation. The 'weak' leader is the person who is unable to create the culture which stakeholders are looking for, although these leaders often give the appearance of being 'strong' through their autocratic stances. Heads are judged on their ability to create the culture which draws all the stakeholders into a coherent integrated organisational process where all have their part in promoting the organisational vision. To achieve this, they require a wide range of creative leadership and managerial competences which make collaborative cultures work (Jenkins, 1991).

FOOTNOTE

The author would like to thank his colleague David Evans for his help with the research described in this chapter.

REFERENCES

Ball, S. J. (1987) *The Micro-Politics of the School*, Methuen, London.
Bate, P. (1994) *Strategies for Cultural Change*, Butterworth/Heinemann, London.
Bennis, W. and Nanus, B. (1985) *Leaders*, Harper and Row, New York.
Bergquist, W. (1993) *The Postmodern Organisation*, Jossey Bass, San Francisco.
Burns, J. M. (1978) *Leadership*, Harper and Row, New York.
Bush, T. (1986) *Theories of Educational Management*, Harper & Row, London.
Busher, H. and Saran, R. (1994) Towards a model of school leadership, *Educational Management and Administration*, Vol. 22, no. 1, pp. 5–13.
Caldwell, B. J. (1994) Australian perspectives on leadership: the principal's role in radical decentralisation in Victoria's Schools in the Future, *Australian Educational Researcher*, Vol. 21, no. 2. pp. 45–62.

Coleman, M. (1996) The management style of female headteachers, *Educational Management and Administration*, Vol. 24, no. 2, pp. 167–74.

Duignan, P. (1990) School-based decision-making and management: retrospect and prospect, in Chapman, J. (Ed.) *School-Based Decision-Making and Management*, Falmer Press, London.

Evans, D. (1995) Managerial Behaviour and School Effectiveness: An International Perspective. Unpublished Paper, Anglia Business School.

Foster, W. (1986) *Paradigms and Promises: New Approaches to Educational Administration*, Promethius, Buffalo NY.

Greenfield, T. B. (1986) The decline and fall of science in educational administration, *Interchange*, Vol. 17, no. 2, pp. 57–80.

Gronn, P. (1996) From transactions to transformations: a New World Order in the study of leadership, *Educational Management and Administration*, Vol. 24, no. 1, pp. 7–30.

Jenkins, H. O. (1985) Job perceptions of senior managers in schools and manufacturing industry, *Educational Management and Administration*, Vol. 13, no. 1, pp. 1–11.

Jenkins, H. O. (1991) *Getting it Right: A Handbook for Successful School Leadership*, Blackwell, Qxford.

Jenkins, H. O. and Evans, D. (1992) School principals and the entrepreneurial organisation, *European Conference on Educational Research*, University of Twente, Netherlands.

Leithwood, K., Begley, P. T. and Cousins, J. (1992) *Developing Expert Leadership for Future Schools*, Falmer Press, London.

Macpherson, R. J. S. (1995) Educative school executive teams in Wong, K. C. and Cheng, K. M. (eds) *Educational Leadership and Change*, Hong Kong University Press.

Moult, G. (1990) Under new management, *Management Education and Development*, Vol. 21, Part 3, pp. 171–82.

Russ, J. (1995) Collaborative management and school improvement, *International Studies in Educational Administration*, Vol. 23, no. 2.

Sackney, L. and Dibski, D. (1995) School based management: Will it fly?, in Wong, K. C. and Cheng, K. M. (eds) *Educational Leadership and Change*, Hong Kong University Press.

Schein, E. H. (1985) *Organisational Culture and Leadership: a Dynamic View*, Jossey Bass, San Francisco.

Senge, P. (1990) *The Fifth Discipline*, Doubleday, New York.

Sergiovanni, T. J. and Corbally, J. E. (Eds) (1984) *Leadership and Organizational Culture: New Perspectives on Administrative Theory and Practice*, University of Illinois Press, Alabama and Chicago.

Thody, A. (1996) Leadership in Teaching and Learning: Exploring Controversies. Paper presented to New Zealand Administration Society, International Conference, Christchurch.

Powerful Learning, Powerful Teaching and Powerful Schools

DAVID HOPKINS

Powerful learning does not occur by accident. It is usually the result of an effective learning situation created by a skilful teacher. Such learning and teaching engagements are commonplace in schools that have an ethos characterised by high expectations, collaboration and innovativeness. These schools, powerful schools, are designed and organised to support powerful teaching and learning. Effective schools throughout the world – those schools whose students progress further and faster than one would expect on the basis of their prior learning histories – share very similar characteristics.

In this chapter however, I do not wish to recite the knowledge base related to school effectiveness, as helpful as that knowledge is (for a recent review see Sammons, Hillman and Mortimore, 1995). On this occasion I prefer to describe some aspects of powerful learning and teaching, those school level conditions necessary to sustain effective teaching and learning, and the role school leaders play in creating them. I will also attempt to locate the substance of this chapter within the themes of the book. In particular, the ways in which school leaders can use the new 'freedoms' creatively to manage change, both at classroom and school level. The final section of the book which focuses on innovative ways of working is an appropriate place for a chapter that explores issues such as the:

- creation of a climate that enables teachers to use powerful teaching to bring about powerful learning;
- involvement of teachers and pupils in strategies for school improvement with a classroom focus;
- ways in which schools work on their internal conditions as well as on their priorities and strategies for student learning.

When I begin to reflect on these issues my vision is of students engaged in compelling learning situations, created by skilful teachers in school settings designed to promote learning for both of them. At the same time, however, I am also reminded of some Australian research that I recently discussed with its authors, in particular, the graph in Figure 3.2.1. The graph depicts the reading scores for school age children in the State of Victoria, Australia in the early 1990s (Rowe, Holmes-Smith and Hill, 1993). I do not believe that it reflects a very different situation from that pertaining in many other 'western' educational systems. The recent OFSTED report on reading standards in Inner London Primary schools suggests a similar picture (OFSTED, 1996). Aside from the 'S' shape of the curve (which is the topic for another discussion), there are two distinctive features to the graph which continue to concern me. The first is the widening of the gap between the best and the poorest readers over time. The second is the flattening of the curve for the less able readers as they move into secondary school. Indeed some of the young people represented in this graph are reading virtually no better at the age of fifteen than they were at age ten.

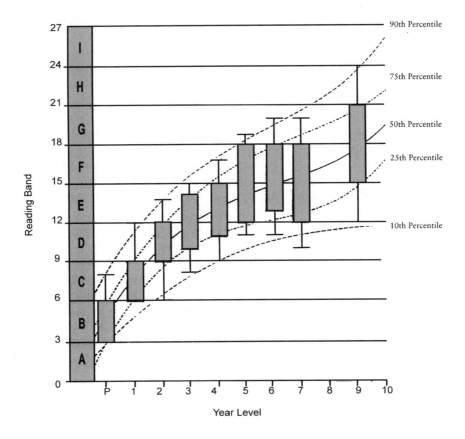

Figure 3.2.1   Progression in reading in the state of Victoria, Australia.

I do not wish to get into a debate about the technical detail of this research. I am using it heuristically to make a point. The point is that I can find little justification for the state of affairs depicted by the graph. The increasing variance and the flattening of the curve for the lower achieving readers simply cannot be explained away by ability or background. Consider for a moment what it is like to be one of those children who are struggling to learn to read. Year by year they are falling behind and becoming increasingly unable to exert control over their lives. Think of the result this will have on their behaviour in school, the effect of the inevitable 'labelling' by their teachers and peers that would occur as a result, the downward spiral of low expectations, and the impact on their self esteem. I suggest with Robert Slavin (1996), that the difficulty these young people experience in learning to read adequately is a reflection of the quality of their learning experiences within school.

However predictable this scenario may be, we now have considerable evidence to suggest that powerful learning experiences enable students to draw information, ideas, and wisdom from their teachers and use learning resources effectively (Joyce and Showers, 1991, p. 10). 'Thus a major role of teaching is to create powerful learners. The same principle applies to schools.' 'Outstanding schools', as Joyce and Showers also note, 'teach their students ways of learning. Thus, teaching becomes more effective as the students progress through those schools because, year by year, the students have been taught to be stronger learners.'

The challenge for school leaders of course is to manage the ways in which teachers create powerful learning experiences for students within the school. To return to the title of the book, these are the crucial choices that school leaders make. The strong implication from the research is that it is the attitude to teaching and learning on the part of the Heads, and the way it is managed that makes the difference to the learning outcomes of students (e.g. Stringfield and Teddlie, 1991). The Heads of the high achieving schools realise that how teachers teach is probably more crucial than what they teach. Because they know that teaching can make a significant difference to students both at the classroom and school levels they are prepared to do something about it.

I hope it is now evident that there are important relationships operating between learning, teaching and the organisation of the school. In the remainder of this chapter I will discuss the nature of quality teaching, and then the variety of conditions at school level that enable teachers to create powerful learning experiences for their students.

QUALITY TEACHING

Of all the variables under the control of the school and its teachers, teaching has the most demonstrable impact upon student learning. Successful teachers are not simply charismatic, persuasive, and expert presenters. Rather, they create powerful cognitive and social tasks for their students and teach the students how to make productive use of them.

The quality of teaching is at the heart of school improvement. There are at least three aspects to quality teaching that have their own literature and research tradition:

- the research on teaching effects;
- the acquisition of a repertoire of 'models of teaching';
- the 'artistry' of teaching.

There is an extensive research literature on *teaching effects*. Consistently high levels of correlation are achieved between student achievement scores and classroom processes (*vide* Brophy and Good, 1986; Walberg, 1990; Creemers, 1994). This is very complex territory, the intricacies of which are beyond the scope of this chapter. One general conclusion however, stands out: 'The most consistently replicated findings link achievement to the quantity and pacing of instruction' (Brophy and Good, 1986, p. 360). It is naive to assume that the amount of time spent teaching is in itself a sufficient condition for student achievement. The literature on teaching effects is replete with descriptions of the behaviours necessary for effective teaching. However, although the research may have identified correlations between individual teacher behaviours and student achievement, it is when the elements are combined that we begin to access powerful teaching. Powerful teaching is a strategic rather than tactical response to the learning needs of students.

The second issue here that needs highlighting is the lack of a language with which to talk about teaching in the educational system of England and Wales as compared with other industrialised countries. Although I applaud HMCI Chris Woodhead's commitment to focus the educational debate on the quality of teaching, I am convinced that this will not lead to enhanced levels of student achievement unless at the same time we as an educational community expand and define more precisely our vocabulary of teaching.

The relationship between these two issues can be seen for example in the current discussion about the relationship between 'whole class teaching' and student achievement. To begin with, the supporters of 'whole class teaching' infrequently specify what they mean by the term. As a consequence there is a perception among some that 'whole class teaching' implies something similar to 'chalk and talk'. Nothing could be further from reality! The form of 'whole class teaching' that is best associated with gains in student achievement is 'direct instruction'. Direct instruction, however, comprises a far more complex range of teaching skills than the rather reductionist and singular view of 'whole class teaching' currently being advocated by a wide variety of politicians and their advisers. Doyle (1987, p. 95) provides a useful summary. From his perspective, a teacher promotes student learning by being active in planning and organising his or her teaching, explaining to students what they are to learn, arranging occasions for guided practice, monitoring progress, providing feedback, and otherwise helping students understand and accomplish work.

Despite the impressive gains associated with 'direct instruction' neither it nor the series of teaching skills described in the previous section are a panacea.

There is a strong body of research to suggest that student achievement can be further enhanced by the consistent and strategic use of specific *teaching models* (Joyce and Weil, 1996). As Joyce and Weil (1996) point out, there are many models of teaching designed to bring about particular kinds of learning and to help students become more effective learners, of which 'direct instruction' is but one example. Powerful teachers have at their disposal a repertoire of teaching models that they can use at different times, with different students, with different curriculum content to achieve a range of learning outcomes. There is no implication that one model is better than another. It is just that one may be more appropriate than another at any point in time given the learning outcomes desired.

It is also worth noting that models of teaching are really models of learning. As students acquire information, ideas, skills, values, ways of thinking, and means of expressing themselves, they are also learning how to learn. In fact, the most important long-term outcome of instruction may be the students' increased capabilities to learn more easily and effectively in the future both because of the knowledge and skill they have acquired, and because they have mastered learning processes. How teaching is conducted has a large impact on students' abilities to educate themselves.

Bruce Joyce, Emily Calhoun and I are currently adapting the 'models of teaching' approach for teachers in British schools. In 'Models for Learning' (Joyce *et al.* 1997) we describe, with examples, eight complementary teaching strategies drawn from Joyce's original four families of teaching models, viz. the information processing, the social, the personal, and the behavioural. When these models and strategies are combined, they have even greater potential for improving student learning. This, as Joyce and Showers (1991, p. 12) argue, 'is the core of effective teaching, because effective teachers are confident that they can make a difference and that the difference is made by increasing their own teaching repertoires and the learning repertoires of their students.' Thus, imagine a school where the variety of models of teaching is not only intended to accomplish a range of curriculum goals, but is also designed to help the students increase their power as learners. As students master information and skills, the result of each learning experience is not only the content they learn, but the greater ability they acquire to approach future learning tasks and to create programs of study for themselves.

There is another set of factors that characterise quality teaching which are related to the *teachers' 'artistry', personality or ability to reflect upon practice*. For example, the teacher 'who made a difference' is a common topic of conversation following one's admission that 'I am a teacher'. To many educators a prime indicator of the 'effective' school is one in which a high proportion of pupils 'have a good or "vital" relationship with one or more teachers'. The ability to generate and sustain this good or vital relationship is a fundamentally important aspect of teaching quality.

I have recently completed for the OECD a comparative study of policies aimed at improving teacher quality (Hopkins and Stern, 1996). The key characteristics of high quality teachers highlighted by the study are: commitment, love of children, mastery of subject didactics and multiple models of teaching, the ability to collaborate with other teachers, and a capacity for reflection. Although it is convenient to group teachers' desired capacities and behaviours into categories, these attributes all interact in practice. For example, one French teacher elegantly defined teacher quality as '*savoirs, savoir-faire, et savoir-être*', this is translatable perhaps as 'knowledge, knowing how to do, and knowing how to be'. Similarly, a highly accomplished teacher in New Zealand explained, 'Other people have rationalised these things into a set of steps and put them into boxes, but really you must work more holistically.' It is this capacity that defines the quality or artist teacher.

These three perspectives on quality in teaching are not exclusive. Fine teachers create their own personal style through testing out the research on teaching 'effects', acquiring a customised repertoire of models of teaching, and infusing them both with their own personality and commitment to the education of children. It seems that the somewhat technical aspects of teaching integrate with the more personal through a process of reflection. So much so that 'reflection' may be a necessary condition for quality teaching. Donald Schon (1983) has coined the term 'The Reflective Practitioner' to describe the way in which professionals learn. Schon stresses the importance of what he calls professional artistry as a basis for the improvement of practice. This leads him to seek approaches to professional development that encourage practitioners to reflect upon the taken-for-granted knowledge that is implicit in their actions. It is through reflection that the teacher harmonises, integrates and transcends the necessary classroom management skills, the acquisition of a repertoire of models of teaching, and the personal aspects of her teaching into a style that has meaning for her students.

TEACHER DEVELOPMENT

This brief review of research about effective teaching has indicated how different perspectives on teaching can be used to inform the development of practice. This is important because the issue of teacher development is at the heart of school improvement efforts.

I use the term 'teacher development' deliberately, as opposed to the more familiar 'in-service training'. This is part of an attempt to conceptualise an approach to the improvement of practice that is analogous to the one I would recommend in connection with the learning of children. Just as successful classrooms provide conditions that support and encourage all children's learning, so a successful approach to teacher development must address contextual matters in order to create the conditions that facilitate the learning of adults.

The research evidence that is available on the effectiveness of teacher development initiatives is far from encouraging. Despite all the effort and resources that have been utilised, the impact of such programmes in terms of improvements in teaching and better learning outcomes for pupils is rather

disappointing (Fullan, 1991; Joyce and Showers, 1988). What is the explanation for this sad state of affairs? What is the nature of the mistakes that have
been made?

As a result of his review of available research evidence, Fullan (1991, p. 316)
provides the following summary of the reasons for the failure of in-service
education:

- One-shot workshops are widespread but are ineffective.
- Topics are frequently selected by people other than those for whom the in-
  service is provided.
- Follow-up support for ideas and practices introduced during in-service pro-
  grammes occurs in only a very small minority of cases.
- Follow-up evaluation occurs infrequently.
- In-service programmes rarely address the individual needs and concerns of
  participants.
- The majority of programmes involve teachers from many different schools
  and/or school districts, but there is no recognition of the differential impact
  of positive and negative factors within the system to which they must return.
- There is a profound lack of any conceptual basis in the planning and implementation of in-service programmes that would ensure their effectiveness.

This analysis presents a picture of in-service initiatives that are poorly conceptualised, insensitive to the concerns of individual participants and, perhaps
critically, make little effort to help participants relate their learning experiences
to their usual workplace conditions.

Recognising the strength of these arguments, successful schools build infrastructures for teacher development within their day-to-day arrangements.
Such infrastructures involve portions of the school week being devoted to staff
development activities such as curriculum development and implementation,
discussion of teaching approaches, regular observation sessions and on-site
coaching. Integral to these activities is a commitment to reviewing one's performance as a prelude to development. To use the language of this book, these
are some of the management choices made by those who lead successful
schools.

Bruce Joyce and Beverly Showers' (1988) work on staff development, in
particular their peer coaching strategy, has in recent years transformed thinking about staff development. Joyce and Showers identified a number of key
training components which when used in combination have much greater
power than when they are used singly. The major components of training are:

- presentation of theory or description of skill or strategy;
- modelling or demonstration of skills or models of teaching;
- practice in simulated and classroom settings;
- structured and open-ended feedback (provision of information about
  performance);
- coaching for application (hands-on, in-classroom assistance with the transfer of skills and strategies to the classroom).

Based on this analysis Joyce and Showers (quoted in Hopkins, 1993, pp. 183–4), summarised the 'best knowledge' we have on staff development like this:

- The use of the integrated theory–demonstration–practice–feedback training programme to ensure skill development.
- The use of considerable amounts of practice in simulated conditions to ensure fluid control of the new skills.
- The employment of regular on-site coaching to facilitate vertical transfer of teaching skills.
- The preparation of teachers who can provide one another with the necessary coaching.

Joyce (1992) has also distinguished, helpfully in my opinion, between the two key elements of staff development: the workshop and the workplace. The workshop, which is equivalent to the best practice on the traditional INSET course, is where we gain understanding, see demonstrations of the teaching strategy we may wish to acquire, and have the opportunity to practise them in a non-threatening environment.

If however we wish to transfer those skills that the workshop has introduced us to back into the workplace – the classroom and school – then merely attending the workshop is insufficient. The research evidence is very clear that skill acquisition and the ability to transfer vertically to a range of situations requires 'on-the-job-support'. This implies changes in the workplace and the way in which we organise staff development in our schools. In particular, this means the opportunity for immediate and sustained practice, collaboration and peer coaching, and studying development and implementation. We cannot achieve these changes in the workplace without, in most cases, drastic alterations to the ways in which we organise our schools. Yet we will not be able to transfer teaching skills from INSET sessions to a range of classrooms without them. As is seen in the following section, successful schools pay careful attention to their workplace conditions.

SCHOOL DEVELOPMENT

In the rhetoric surrounding the professional development of teachers we frequently hear that 'there is little school development without teacher development.' Much of our educational research, policy and practice is based on that premiss. Although I have no wish to argue against the established convention that to improve schools one needs to improve teachers, we are finding in our current work that sustained teacher development is difficult to achieve without reference to a whole school context. This points to the corollary, that 'there is little teacher development without school development.' Indeed, in order to cope with the demands of a radical national reform agenda, such as we are currently experiencing in England and Wales, school leaders are increasingly searching for practical ways of bringing teacher and school development together.

During the past six years or so we have been working closely with some forty schools in East Anglia, North London, and Yorkshire, on a collaborative school improvement project known as Improving the Quality of Education for All (IQEA) (Hopkins, 1994; Hopkins, Ainscow and West, 1994, 1996, 1997). The overall aim of the project is to strengthen the school's ability to provide quality education for all its pupils. In so doing, we are also producing and evaluating a model of school development, and a programme of support.

At the outset of IQEA we attempted to outline our own vision of school improvement by articulating a set of principles that provided us with a philosophical and practical starting point. Because it is our assumption that schools are most likely to provide quality education and enhanced outcomes for pupils when they adopt ways of working that are consistent with these principles, these were offered as the basis for collaboration with the IQEA project schools. In short, we were inviting the schools to identify and to work on their own projects and priorities, but to do so in a way which embodied a set of 'core' values about school improvement. These values represent the expectations we had of the way project schools would pursue school improvement, serving as an *aide-mémoir* to the schools and to ourselves.

The five principles of IQEA are:

- School improvement is a process that focuses on enhancing the quality of students' learning.
- The vision of the school should be one which embraces all members of the school community as both learners and contributors.
- The school will see in external pressures for change important opportunities to secure its internal priorities.
- The school will seek to develop structures and create conditions which encourage collaboration and lead to the empowerment of individuals and groups.
- The school will seek to promote the view that monitoring and evaluating quality is a responsibility which all members of staff share.

We feel that the operation of these principles creates synergism – like the research on teaching effects – they are greater than the sum of their parts. The intention is that they should inform the thinking and actions of teachers during school improvement efforts, and provide a touchstone for the strategies they devise and the behaviours they adopt. They characterise an overall approach rather than prescribing a course of action.

One of the great fallacies of educational change is that policy directives, from any level, have a direct impact on student achievement. What we do know from experience, and as we have seen in the discussion of the research on student achievement and classroom effectiveness, is that the greatest impact on student progress is achieved by those innovations or adaptations of practice that intervene in, or modify, the learning process. Changes in curriculum, teaching methods, grouping practices, and assessment procedures have the greatest potential impact on the performance of students.

The key to our linking of teacher and school development is found in our contention that school improvement works best when a clear and practical focus for development is linked to simultaneous work on the internal conditions within the school. Conditions are the internal features of the school, the 'arrangements' that enable it to get work done. We have found that without an equal focus on conditions, even development priorities that directly affect classroom practice quickly become marginalised. It is this dual focus, on strategies for enhancing the quality of student learning whilst strengthening the schools capacity for change, that characterise our approach to school improvement in times of change.

The central point for those involved in school improvement is that if we take the enhancement of pupil outcomes seriously, then work on the internal conditions of the school has to complement that on development priorities related to classroom practice, all of course within the context of a national reform agenda. I have attempted to express this idea in Figure 3.2.2 by representing the three main contributors to the enhancement of student progress – national reform, internal school conditions, and modifications to classroom practice – as a series of concentric rings. All three need to be in a reciprocal relationship if student achievement is to be enhanced. When all three elements are pulling in the same direction, then school improvement has much more chance of success.

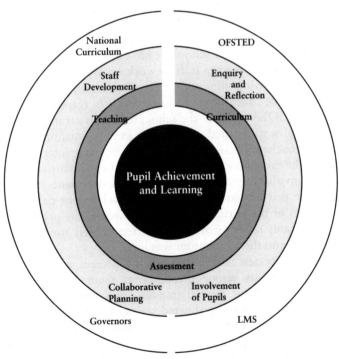

Figure 3.2.2   The 'layers' of school improvement

CREATING THE CONDITIONS FOR SCHOOL IMPROVEMENT

In the IQEA project we have begun to associate a number of 'conditions' within the school with its capacity for sustained development. At present, our best estimate of these conditions which underpin improvement efforts, and so therefore represent the key management arrangements, can be broadly stated as:

- a commitment to staff development;
- practical efforts to involve staff, students and the community in school policies and decisions;
- 'transformational' leadership approaches;
- effective co-ordination strategies;
- proper attention to the potential benefits of enquiry and reflection;
- a commitment to collaborative planning activity.

For those interested, we have described the conditions necessary for school improvement in detail elsewhere (Ainscow *et al.*, 1994; Hopkins, Ainscow and West, 1994; Hopkins and West, 1994; West, Fielding and Beresford, 1995).

We could illustrate this key idea with many examples from schools involved in IQEA. Some, sadly, would show how lack of attention to what we refer to as 'conditions' eventually means that potentially excellent school improvement initiatives disappear without trace. On the other hand, there are plenty of positive examples that illustrate the importance of our argument.

In one large, urban secondary school we have seen a series of developments that have attempted to encourage staff to work on aspects of their classroom practice. Early on, following some negative feedback from inspectors, the main focus was on the 'pace of learning' during lessons. In response to the inspectors' comments the IQEA cadre in the school set up an arrangement whereby volunteer groups of staff assisted one another in experimenting with alternative teaching approaches. These activities led to some very interesting developments which, at the same time, fostered a degree of enthusiasm amongst those teachers directly involved. Eventually some of these experiences were reported to the rest of the teachers as part of a staff development day. Despite the enthusiastic efforts of the participating staff, however, the project seemed to lose its way. Inevitably other priorities arose that needed attention, some key staff left the school and the momentum was lost.

At a meeting to review the two years of project activities the head teacher and some of his senior management team expressed their disappointment at the lack of overall impact upon classroom practice and learning outcomes. After a rather heated series of exchanges, the argument was made and accepted that insufficient attention had been given to providing the organisational support necessary to move forward an initiative that was regarded by many staff as being rather marginal. In our terms the school was attempting to achieve significant modifications to its practice within an organisation that was structured around maintenance rather than development tasks.

In the light of this analysis it was decided that a survey should be carried out of staff perceptions. Using a variety of data collection techniques developed as part of IQEA (Ainscow *et al.*, 1994a, 1994b), a review of school conditions was undertaken. In general this indicated that many staff felt that insufficient leadership was given to support innovation; that they were not consulted about the nature of the school improvement activity being attempted; and that there was a need for forms of staff development that would provide time and technical support for classroom experimentation.

During the following year the cadre designed and introduced a school-wide initiative to raise reading standards across the curriculum. Their initiative, which is now in its second year, included specific strategies that were designed to provide more effective leadership, greater involvement of staff in decision making, and regular opportunities for teachers to have time for group planning and partnership teaching. In short, changes in organisational conditions have been introduced in order to support development activities.

We are continuing to refine our understanding of the 'conditions' in light of our ongoing work with schools, and are currently developing a set of 'classroom conditions' to complement our original set of school level conditions briefly described above (Hopkins *et al.*, 1997).

Our initial conceptualisation of classroom conditions are as follows:

- Authentic Relationships – being the quality, openness and congruence of relationships existing in the classroom.
- Rules and Boundaries – being the pattern of expectations set by the teacher and school of student performance and behaviour within the classroom.
- Planning, Resources and Preparation – being the access of teachers to a range of pertinent teaching materials and the ability to plan and differentiate these materials for a range of students.
- Teacher's Repertoire – being the range of teaching styles and models internalised and available to a teacher dependent on student, context, curriculum and desired outcome.
- Pedagogic Partnerships – being the ability of teachers to form professional relationships within and outside the classroom that focus on the study and improvement of practice.
- Reflection on Teaching – being the capacity of the individual teacher to reflect on his/her own practice and to put to the test of practice specifications of teaching from other sources.

Although space precludes further description of the classroom conditions, the following example of developing classroom conditions in the area of 'Authentic Relationships' conveys something of the spirit of classroom focused improvement activities which have been taking place within our recent work on the IQEA project. The notion that the relationships between pupil and teacher is at the centre of the learning process is by no means new.

Certainly, within the IQEA project schools there have been extended programmes of classroom observation related to this theme. As a consequence, we have identified as a 'condition' the need to establish authentic relationships within the classroom. By this we mean establishing the classroom as a safe and secure learning environment in which pupils can expect acceptance, respect and even warmth from their teachers, without having to earn these – they are intrinsic rights which are extended to pupils because they are there. But beyond this, of course, the security and the mutual trust within the relationship will mean that the teacher is able to make demands on the pupils, because there is also support.

As might be expected, within the project schools the extent to which this condition is established varies between schools, between classes within the same school, between teachers and even with the same teacher when paired with different teaching groups. Nevertheless, there has been a general accept-ance that the schools and the teachers should attempt to extend the authen-ticity of relationships to as many teacher-pupil groups as possible, and several initiatives have been targeted at the development of classroom relationships. The following example is drawn from an 11–18 secondary school.

The school identified the quality of teaching and learning as the main pri-ority within the 1994–95 School Development Plan. Supported by the IQEA cadre group within the school, each department was invited to select its own classroom focus for development. Two departments (Technology and Science) decided to look at the quality of pupil/teacher interactions within their subject area. Both departments selected Year 9 as the target for enquiry, and after discussion within the departments it was agreed that both would look at pupil–teacher interaction using an observation schedule derived from the work of Marzano *et al.* (1992).

The schedule was designed to investigate the extent to which teacher com-ments and behaviours contributed to the quality of classroom climate and relationships. Specifically teacher actions which:

- increased pupils' sense of acceptance;
- increased pupils' sense of comfort and order;
- helped pupils to see the value of tasks and activities;
- helped pupils understand what was expected of them in terms of tasks and activities;

were logged, using a schedule which identified 20 different teacher actions/behaviours. The observations were carried out by a member of the IQEA team.

There was slight variation between the two subject areas, but in both cases approximately two-thirds of teacher behaviours related to administrative or disciplinary matters, and only one-third of behaviours which were likely to create greater authenticity in the relationships between teacher and pupil. This 'balance' may of course be typical, certainly it compares with other studies which have looked at positive and negative feedback to pupils.

But the investigations were not carried out in order to see whether practice was satisfactory or not, but to establish what practice was. Now there is a base-line against which changes can be measured, as the two departments embark upon a range of measures aimed at increasing the quality of pupil–teacher interactions over time. There is also a clearer appreciation of the need to work at the development of appropriate classroom relationships, rather than assuming that this is something which teachers can establish intuitively.

The example from this particular facet of our research activity provides a useful example of how research within the IQEA project proceeds, and on how a specific research activity contributes to our more general aim of elaborating a theory of school development and the enhancement of school improvement practice.

One of our major concerns is to explicate how the focus on the internal conditions of the school contributes to an emerging theory of school development (Hopkins, 1996). The next major step in this process is to attempt to find some relationship between the school level and the classroom level conditions. Because we know from experience that the two operate in parallel, it is tempting to push this coincidence too far in order to get a correspondence between school and classroom level conditions. There is no space for such speculation here!

CODA

Successful school improvement efforts engender a language about teaching and cultural change

The general approach to school improvement described in this chapter is highly consistent with Joyce's analysis of the characteristics of effective large scale school improvement initiatives (Joyce, Wolf and Calhoun, 1993, p. 72):

- All have focused on specific student-learning outcomes. None have had only general goals of the 'to make exam results go up' variety.
- All have employed strategies tailored to their goals and backed by rationales grounded in theory, research, good practice, one's own experience, or a combination of these.
- All have employed substantial amounts of staff development in recognition that any development involves teacher and student learning.
- All have monitored learning outcomes on a regular basis; they have not left evaluation to a yearly examination.

There are two respects in which these characteristics are particularly relevant to the theme of this chapter. First they provide an example of how a developmental focus on teaching and learning (the first two points) links together with simultaneous work on the school conditions (the second two points). The second is the emphasis on specifications of teaching and learning. A major goal for school improvement is to help teachers become so professionally flexible that they can select, from a repertoire of possibilities, the teaching approach most suited to a particular content area, their students' age, interests and aptitudes.

One of the characteristics of successful schools is that teachers talk about teaching. School improvement strategies should as a consequence help teachers create a discourse about, and language for, teaching. Within the context of development work this is best achieved through:

- teachers discussing with each other the nature of teaching strategies and their application to classroom practice and schemes of work;
- establishing specifications or guidelines for the chosen teaching strategies;
- agreeing on standards used to assess student progress as a result of employing a range of teaching methods;
- mutual observation and partnership teaching in the classroom.

This is however easier said than done. Many research studies have found that without a period of destabilisation, successful, long lasting change is unlikely to occur (Fullan, 1991). Yet it is at this point that most change fails to progress beyond early implementation. In these cases, when the change hits the 'wall' of individual learning or institutional resistance, turbulence begins to occur and developmental work begins to stall. This is the cycle of educational failure, the predictable pathology of educational change.

I have already suggested that many of the schools that we have been working with survive this period of destabilisation by either consciously or intuitively adapting the internal conditions to meet the demands of the agreed on change or priority. We encourage schools to diagnose their internal conditions in relation to their chosen change before they begin developmental work. They can then begin to build these modifications to the school's internal conditions into the strategies they are going to adopt. When this happens, we begin to see changes occurring to the culture of the school. For example, classroom observation becomes more common in many schools as a result of development work, teachers also begin to talk more about teaching, collaborative work outside of the particular project increases, and management structures are adapted to support the work. When taken together, these changes in attitudes, practice and structure create a more supportive environment within the school for managing change. The school's 'change capacity' is increased and the ground-work is laid for future change efforts. A virtuous circle of change begins to be established.

Many of the school leaders we work with and have interviewed, adopt, albeit intuitively, such an approach to the management of change. They seem to agree with Schein (1982, p. 5) when he wrote, 'the only thing of real importance that leaders do is to create and manage culture'. They realise that the impact of successful change in teaching and learning needs to be on the culture of the school, for it is culture that sustains change and consequently enhances the achievement of students. The link between setting priorities for teaching and learning and the culture of the school is therefore of crucial importance. Powerful school cultures result in the creation of opportunities for teachers to feel more powerful and confident about their work. It is in this way, as Judith Little once remarked, that 'teachers teach each other the practice of teaching'. When this occurs we not only begin to meet the real challenge of educational reform, but we also create classrooms and schools where both our children and their teachers learn.

REFERENCES

Ainscow, M., Hargreaves, D. H., Hopkins, D., Balshaw, M. and Black-Hawkins, K. (1994b) *Mapping the Process of Change in Schools*. Cambridge: University of Cambridge Institute of Education.

Ainscow M., Hopkins D., Southworth G. and West M. (1994a) *Creating the Conditions for School Improvement*. London: David Fulton.

Brophy J. and Good T. (1986) Teacher Behaviour and Student Achievement, in Wittrock, M. (ed) *Handbook of Research on Teaching* (3rd edn). Macmillan, New York.

Creemers B. (1994) *The Effective Classroom*. Cassell, London.

Doyle, W. (1987) Research on teaching effects as a resource for improving instruction, in M. Wideen and I. Andrews (eds.) *Staff Development for School Improvement*, Falmer Press, Lewes.

Fullan M. (1991) *The Meaning of Educational Change*. Cassell, London.

Hopkins D. (1993) *A Teacher's Guide to Classroom Research* (second edition), Open University Press, Buckingham.

Hopkins D. (1994) The Yellow Brick Road, *Managing Schools Today*, Vol. 3, no. 6. March, pp. 14–17.

Hopkins D. (1996) Towards a Theory for School Improvement in Gray J., Reynolds D., Fitz-Gibbon C. (eds) *Merging Traditions: The Future of Research on School Effectiveness and School Improvement*. Cassell, London.

Hopkins D. (1997) *Creating the Conditions for Classroom Development*. David Fulton, London.

Hopkins D., Ainscow M. and West M. (1994) *School Improvement in an Era of Change*. Cassell, London.

Hopkins D., Ainscow M. and West M. (1996a) Unravelling the Complexities of School Improvement in Harris A. *et al. Organisational Effectiveness and Improvement in Education*, (Open University Course E838 Reader), Open University Press, Buckingham.

Hopkins D., Ainscow M. and West M. (1996b) *Improving the Quality of Education for All*. David Fulton, London.

Hopkins D. and West M. (1994) Teacher Development and School Improvement in D. Walling *Teachers as Learners*. PDK, Bloomington, Ind.

Hopkins D. and Stern D. (1996) Quality Teachers, Quality Schools *Teaching and Teacher Education* Vol. 12, no. 5, pp. 501–517.

Joyce B. (1992) Co-operative Learning and Staff Development: teaching the method with the method *Co-operative Learning*, 12(2), pp. 10–13.

Joyce B. and Showers B. (1988) *Student Achievement Through Staff Development*. Longman, New York.

Joyce B. and Showers B. (1991) *Information Processing Models of Teaching*. Booksend Laboratories, Aptos, CA.

Joyce B. and Weil M. (1996) *Models of Teaching* (Fifth Edition). Prentice-Hall, Englewood Cliffs, New Jersey.

Joyce B., Wolf J. and Calhoun E. (1993) *The Self Renewing School*. ASCD, Alexandria, VA.

Joyce, B., Calhoun, E. and Hopkins, D. (1997) *Models for Learning – Tools for Teaching*, Open University Press, Buckingham.

Marzano R. J. *et al.* (1992) *Dimensions of Learning.* Teacher's Manual, ASCD/McREL, Aurora.

OFSTED (1996) *The Teaching of Reading.* Office for Standards in Education, London.

Rowe K., Holmes-Smith P. and Hill P. (1993) The Link between School Effectiveness Research, Policy and School Improvement. Paper presented at the 1993 annual conference of the Australian Association for Research in Education, Fremantle, Western Australia, November 22–25, 1993.

Sammons P., Hillman J. and Mortimore P. (1995) *Characteristics of Effective Schools,* OFSTED, London.

Schein E. (1985) *Organisation Cultures and Leadership: a Dynamic View.* Jossey-Bass, San Francisco.

Schon D. (1983) *The Reflective Practitioner.* Basic Books, New York.

Slavin, R. (1996) *Education for All.* Swets and Zweitlinger, Lisse.

Stringfield S. and Teddlie C. (1991) Observers as predictors of schools' effective status. *The Elementary School Journal,* 91 (4), pp. 357–76.

Walberg H. (1990) Productive Teaching and Instruction: Assessing the Knowledge Base, *Phi Delta Kappan,* Vol. 71, no. 6, pp. 470–78.

West M., Fielding M. and Beresford J. (1995) *Using Mapping Techniques in IQEA Schools,* paper presented at the Eighth International Congress for School Effectiveness and School Improvement at Leeuwarden, Netherlands, 3–6 January 1995 (mimeo).

3.3

Schools as Learning Organisations

KATH ASPINWALL AND MIKE PEDLER

School improvement has proved an elusive goal partly because we have tended to back the wrong horse – the individual teacher.

(Reid, Hopkins and Holly, 1987, p. 162)

Acceptance of the fact that developing individuals will never of itself be enough, has increasingly led to a search for systems, processes and approaches which might have greater impact on the whole school. This chapter explores the relevance for schools of one of these, that of the learning organisation. Fullan is unequivocal about the current situation: 'The school is not now a learning organization. Irregular waves of change, episodic projects, fragmentation of effort, and grinding overload is the lot of most schools' (Fullan, 1993, p. 42). Yet, as Revans points out, learning is exactly what is needed in such circumstances. As the rate of change increases, so must the pace of learning: 'For an organisation to survive, its rate of learning must be equal to or greater than the rate of change in its external environment' (see Garratt, 1987, p. 26). Schools have been facing an unprecedented rate of change, of which increasing autonomy is only one facet. Is the rate of learning increasing fast enough to keep up? What is known about how schools learn? Why is it that, as Rosenholtz found, it is: 'Far easier to learn to teach, and to learn to teach better, in some schools than in others' (Rosenholtz, 1989, p. 104)?

This chapter will consider the answers to these questions and attempt to identify the factors that enable schools to engage in the kind of learning necessary to survive in turbulent times. It explores some of the recent literature on organisational learning and considers what this concept can contribute to this process. It then looks in some detail at two particular ideas, the concept of Energy Flow (Pedler, Burgoyne and Boydell, 1996) and the issue of Organisational Learning Styles (Pedler and Aspinwall, 1996) giving examples of how these have been or might be used to increase organisational learning in schools. The chapter concludes with a summary of the key characteristics of a learning school.

WHAT IS A LEARNING ORGANISATION?

Organisational learning is a relatively new concept. However, references to the term can be dated back at least to the late 1960s and rapidly expand from the late 1980s. The terms 'learning organisation' and 'learning company' stem from the notion of a 'learning system' discussed by Revans in 1969 and Schon in his Reith Lectures of 1970 *Beyond the Stable State.*

A significant contribution to the literature is Argyris and Schon's first chapter of their book on organisational learning 'What is an organisation that it may learn?' In this they recognise that no amount of individual development will alone produce an organisation able to change itself as a whole:

> it is clear that organizational learning is not the same thing as individual learning, even when the individuals who learn are members of the organization. There are too many cases in which organizations know *less* than their members. There are even cases in which the organization cannot seem to learn what every member knows.
>
> (Argyris and Schon, 1978, p. 9)

This reification of organisation into an entity that is more than the sum of its parts pervades the relevant literature. The development of learning individuals and learning teams is crucial, but they are not sufficient in themselves to achieve the status of a learning organisation

The concept of the learning organisation can be seen as one of the latest in a long line of management 'solutions'. It may be the necessary successor to the 1980s 'search for excellence' led by the realisation that after only five years many of Peters and Waterman's (1982) excellent organisations had already lost their place in that particular league table (see for example Pascale, 1990). Achieving excellence at one time is clearly not enough to guarantee it in perpetuity.

Some of the writing on learning organisations draws attention to the commercial advantages. For example, Garratt argues that 'learning has become the key developable and tradable commodity of an organisation' (1987, p. 10) However, there is a quite different emphasis to be discerned, a more idealistic or philosophical commitment to a notion of learning. Fullan constantly reminds us that 'education has a moral purpose . . . to make a difference to the lives of students regardless of background' (1993, p. 4). He quotes Sarason (1990, p. 163):

> Should not our aim be to judge whatever we do for our children in our schools by the criterion of how we are fostering the desire to continue to learn about self, others, and the world, to live in the world of ideas and possibilities, to see the life span as an endless, intellectual and personal quest for knowledge and meaning.
>
> (In Fullan, 1993, p. 45)

Unlike most of the other processes attracting attention in schools, for example, TQM (Total Quality Management) and IIP (Investors in People) there is no readily available, importable, accredited system leading to the award of a Learning Organisation 'kitemark'. This may be perceived to be a difficulty or as an advantage, depending on your inclination. Some schools and colleges have spent a great deal of time and effort trying to translate quality processes derived from manufacturing industry into workable systems for their institutions. It is not, for example, quite as straightforward to deal with a 'non-conforming product' when it is a pupil in year 10 as it is on a production line.

Writers on the learning organisation provide a variety of models, disciplines (see Senge, 1990) and characteristics (see Pedler, Burgoyne, and Boydell, 1996). The latter use the term 'company' (often a difficult one for those in schools and the public sector) because of its connotation of being 'in company' or a 'company of learners'. According to them, the Learning Company is 'an organisation that facilitates the learning of all its members *and* consciously transforms itself and its context' (p. 1). Senge describes 'organisations where people continually expand their capacity to create the results they truly desire, where new and expansive patterns of thinking are nurtured, where collective aspiration is set free, and where people are continually learning how to learn together' (1990, p. 3) and emphasises that achieving this means 'destroying the illusion that the world is created of separate, unrelated forces'. He identifies the five *Disciplines of the Learning Organisation*. The 'cornerstone' and integrating fifth discipline is that of *Systems Thinking* which he describes as:

- seeing inter-relationships rather than linear cause–effect chains, and
- seeing processes of change rather than snapshots.

(Senge, 1990 p. 73)

This capacity is of fundamental importance. At the micro level Senge proposes that systems thinking leads to the development of understanding and purpose rather than feeling helpless in the face of 'the system'. At a macro level it is essential for our survival: 'We are literally killing ourselves because of our inability to understand wholes' (Senge, 1991, p. 42).

The other four disciplines are as follows:

- *Personal Mastery*: the discipline of continually clarifying and deepening personal vision thus focusing our energies.
- *Mental Models*: deeply ingrained assumptions, generalisations or even pictures or images that influence how we understand the world and how we take action – what we perceive can or cannot be done.
- *Shared Vision*: that binds people together around a common identity and sense of destiny, because they want to not because they have to.
- *Team Learning*: through team learning the whole become greater than the parts, 'teams, not individuals are the fundamental learning unit' (Senge, 1991, p. 40).

It may be difficult for those engaged in the daily busy-ness of schools to engage in systems thinking. Understanding connections and seeing underlying patterns requires the space and time for reflection. The current climate of hyperactivity is unlikely to be helpful. Increasing autonomy may in itself add to the problem. If autonomous schools become self-protective, self-seeking, self-sealing this will affect both their own potential for learning and growth and the society which they serve. This is not inevitable. Autonomy need not lead to disconnection and fragmentation.

WHAT KIND OF LEARNING IS NEEDED?

The term learning organisation is to some extent metaphorical, perhaps akin to the notions of organisations as 'organisms', as 'brains' and as 'cultures' in Morgan's *Images of Organization* (1986). Learning organisations are more than the sum of their parts, and are able to integrate individual and team learning into some kind of a whole. One way of understanding how this can happen is to break learning into different types:

1 Knowledge **or** learning *about* things.
2 Skills, Abilities, Competences **or** learning to *do* things.
3 Personal Development **or** learning to *become ourselves, to achieve our full potential.*
4 Collaborative Enquiry **or** learning to *achieve things together.*

The first two of these types – Knowledge and Skills, Abilities, Competences – are the most familiar. Learning *about* things covers a wide spectrum from the memorising of simple facts to the deep understanding of complex ideas and ranges from knowing 'this or that' to knowing 'why'. Learning to *do* things includes mental and manual skills and competence in certain situations. These two conceptions of learning have great significance for schools. The development of the National Curriculum in the UK was an attempt to define what knowledge should form the basis of schooling and, as such, has been a matter of dispute since its inception. The two types of learning are seen as relatively discrete by some who place importance on maintaining an academic/vocational divide.

Personal development has also long been valued in schools and in adult education. It is about achieving full potential and moves beyond intellectual and competency development to questions of purpose and identity, echoed in Murdoch's 'learning is moral progress' (1992). This type of learning has, perhaps, been in retreat in recent years. The school curriculum has become crowded. Courses for teachers have increasingly emphasised gaining the knowledge and skills relevant to the imposed changes. Schools are learning how to conform to an imposed framework of inspection. Harrison discovered the levels of exhaustion and burn-out amongst public sector participants in his workshops in Australia and New Zealand, people similarly suffering from 'mandated change' with little room for manoeuvre:

> Their organizations were in retreat, their clients and colleagues were in shock, and they were feeling inadequate as they tried to drum up enthusiasm for upbeat, forward looking programmes in organizations reeling from one imposed change after another. My discussions with the participants convinced me that it was time to reframe the work of organizational development, making a shift from the idea that organizations needed *agents of change* to the idea that they needed *facilitators of healing.*
> (Harrison, 1995, p. 166).

Knowledge, skills and competence, meeting inspection requirements are clearly necessary to teachers but are not enough in themselves. To quote the head-teacher from a primary school who had found the inspection of her school to be a useful, developmental and stabilising experience: 'I have only one reserva-tion. If the framework becomes dominant in our thinking, and if the inspectors spend all their time inspecting, where will the new ideas and creativity and the "magic" come from in the future?'

The fourth type of learning is less often recognised. Learning is most often seen as something which individuals do on their own, happening somehow inside them. Collaborative Enquiry is more than group work. It is about learn-ing to achieve things together, cooperating in collective learning. Interesting historical precedent can be found with Samuel Hartlib (1600–1662) and his associates who proposed an early sort of learning community with the 'Office of Addresses' for the spreading of scientific knowledge during the ferment of the Commonwealth parliament. They often published anonymously or collab-oratively under one name because their work was 'all in a knot of one an-other's labours'. Collaborative Enquiry, where outcomes cannot be fully measured in terms of what individuals take away but by what is created together, can form the bridge from individual learning to the learning organ-isation.

MAKING USE OF MODELS OF ORGANISATIONAL LEARNING

In order to explore this concept in more detail, we will take two particular models of organisational learning and apply them to schools. The first is that of the Energy Flow which is designed to explore how energy, information and learning flow around an organisation when it is working as a whole. A school will need to balance four key functions:

Policy (**P**) or the underpinning purpose including values and vision: 'What does this school stand for?'
Operations (**O**) or the structures, systems and approaches that enable this purpose to become a reality: 'How does this school work?'
Action (**A**) or the action in which individuals are engaged: 'What are individ-uals actually doing?' and
Ideas (**I**) or the ideas and beliefs which individuals bring their work: 'What do individuals think and believe?'

In this model:

- the continuous flow between Policy and Operations and back again is the *collective* or corporate learning cycle;
- the continuous flow between Ideas and Action and vice versa is the *individ-ual* or personal learning cycle.

Together these produce four double-feedback loops representing four different types of energy, information and learning (see Figure 3.3.1).

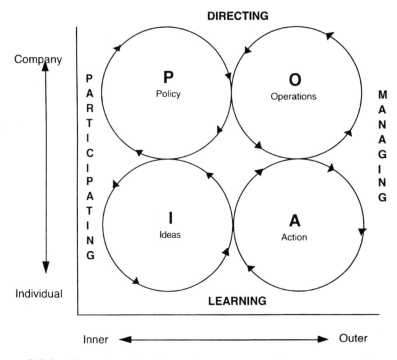

Figure 3.3.1   The energy flow diagram
Source: Pedler, Burgoyne and Boydell, 1996

For an organisation to work and learn effectively, energy must flow through and link all of these functions. Otherwise, for example, individuals may be pulling against each other and structures and systems may impede rather than promote the purposes of an organisation. The process is interrupted and prevented by:

- *biases*, when any one, two or three of these processes predominate to the exclusion or disadvantage of the others, and
- *blocks* where a function exists but is disconnected from, and uninfluenced by, the others.

For example, if a school was biased towards just two of these functions **I** (individual ideas) and **A** (individual actions), teachers would tend to work alone in their classrooms pursuing their own interests. Any time together would be spent on non-educational matters such as fundraising, gossip, practical matters. Examples of three way biases would be:

pO   the lack of a policy dimension which would leave a school lacking in any
IA   real sense of direction or purpose

Po   a school lacking any collective organisational function This might suit a
IA   group of autonomous, dynamic and creative people happy to work
     around a set of policies or principles but might prove confusing and

disconnected for the pupils. Perhaps some primary schools in the UK were able to carry on quite comfortably in this way before the advent of the National Curriculum.

pO   allowing no room for the influence of individual ideas (perhaps appropri-
iA   ate for a cult or an army engaged in conflict) might serve in a moment of crisis but would be unlikely in the longer term to attract committed professionals to work in a school.

PO   because of the nature of schooling it is hard to envisage the absence of
Ia   any individual action except in the context of a proposed new develop-ment. In this case ideas, structures and processes might be designed and redesigned by a team but never be put into action and become a reality.

Identifying the blocks to the the smooth flow of energy between the four functions is also illuminating. For example:

- Two education officers from Zimbabwe realised that in many instances the policy function felt quite disconnected from the other three. This was be-cause many initiatives were funded from abroad and therefore reflected the policies and priorities of the funders rather than of the Zimbabweans.
- Tutors from a College of Nursing realised that, because the operations func-tion was by far the dominant bias in their organisation, individual ideas tended to be blocked from influencing both individual action and the de-velopment of policy.
- A primary teacher realised that her school was still in the process of learning how to develop the policy function and to link it to individual ideas. The initial response of her headteacher to the need to produce a School Develop-ment Plan had been to write one single handed. However, now there was a real attempt being made to involve all staff and bring their individual ideas into the process.
- A different form of block emerged in a secondary school when the emphasis on cross-curricular issues in TVEI revealed the barriers and lack of means or systems to enable communication between the operational tunnels of subject departments. When the teachers began to audit the existence of the cross curricular themes across the school they found that some were covered several times in different subject areas while others were nowhere to be found.

A further use of this model is to consider the balance of the four functions below:

Policy (P) + Operations (O) = *Directing*
Operations (O) + Action (A) = *Managing*
Action (A) + Ideas (I) = *Learning*
Ideas (I) + Policy (P) = *Participating*

Directing is akin to leadership providing the steer and sense of purpose. Managing ensures that purpose become reality and that reality feeds back and influences policy and purpose. Ideas and actions link together to bring about learning. Individual ideas both influence and are influenced by the development of policy. These processes are needed at all levels within an organisation. A school that is divided into those who direct and those who do not will not be effective at organisational learning. The four functions are often not equally well developed. For most organisations participating seems to be the most problematic. Bottery draws a distinction between 'pseudo participation', where we are persuaded to accept decisions already made by management, 'partial participation', where we can genuinely influence decisions, and 'full participation' where each person has equal power to determine the outcome. Perhaps not surprisingly, he describes full participation as the exception (Bottery, 1992, p. 51).

While this model is particularly useful as a framework for examining the effectiveness of internal processes it is also necessary to consider the organisation in its wider context. The world outside the school will impinge on each of the four functions in different ways. For example, Government policy in the UK has increasingly affected the way in which schools work. Schools are required to put specified policies into action. The National Curriculum has strongly influenced the operational function. Individual teachers may live and take action in their local communities or bring in ideas from national bodies or their own developmental activities. These and many other influences come in and contribute to the flow of organisational energy and learning.

Here too there may be biases and blocks. For example, teachers often express frustration and disappointment when new ideas and fresh energy gained from courses fall upon stony ground on their return to school. Policies in themselves change little and are often undermined or 'translated', particularly when they are imposed from outside and there can have been no participation in their creation. In these situations, far from external influences increasing the energy flow, precious energy is wasted on resistance.

Making use of the Energy Flow model requires setting it into context. The four functions may be influenced by the size of a school and the age group served. However, checking the flow of energy, identifying biases and blockages, and developing strategies to overcome these can lead to a significant growth in both energy and learning within a school.

FIVE ORGANISATIONAL LEARNING STYLES

The second model we want to introduce is that of organisational learning styles. We want to suggest that just as individuals have preferences about the ways that they like to learn so have organisations. The learning styles we are using are:

• Habits

- Memory
- Imitation
- Experiment
- Critical awareness

A questionnaire, the *Organisational Learning Styles Inventory*, designed to help to diagnose the learning preferences of an organisation can be found in Pedler and Aspinwall (1996, pp. 96–9). The key characteristics of each of the learning styles are as follows.

Habits might be described as standard operating procedures, rules, ways of working, methods of teaching that continue regardless of changes of staff or in the external environment. Habits are useful and can provide a crucial sense of stability. Change is disturbing for pupils as well as staff. There must be some certainties. Familiar events such as sports days or school concerts may have considerable symbolic importance and form part of the rhythm of the school year.

Of course there is a down side to habitual behaviour. It often outlives its usefulness or becomes inappropriate. It is (sadly) not unknown for the population of a school to change quite dramatically, as its neighbourhood flourishes or declines, and yet for teachers to continue to teach in the same old way. They have learned to survive by repeating behaviour but without any emphasis on change or improvement. They are likely to take accountability to mean adhering to external requirements without too much reflection. Such organisations may function quite well in stable times or in protected corners of a less stable general environment.

One problem with habits is that disturbing them or even questioning their validity can threaten some core belief or sense of self. Schools can find themselves caught up in some kind of collective romanticism, required to hold on to a better past, symbolised perhaps by 'the gold standard of A levels' or school uniforms that would not have looked out of place in the 1950's, while at the same time being asked to prepare their pupils for the 21st century.

Memory represents the stored experience in an organisation. Some of this may be in record systems but much is in the heads of individuals, largely invisible, not easily accessible and uncollected. Sometimes important aspects of a school's memory, of past pupils and of the wider community, is held primarily in the heads of non-teaching staff, secretaries, caretakers, cleaners who often live in the community themselves and have a long term commitment to this particular school.

Memory differs from habit in that it does not merely reproduce the past. However, the past exerts a powerful influence over present action. In the context of accountability, a school committed to building up its memory might be keen to build up an evaluation 'archive' rather than to take action in the light of new evidence. It might be very good at monitoring, keeping records, building databases. However, an interesting aspect of memory is how much crucial knowledge about how to teach remains unspoken and unshared in schools. Little suggests that the ability to engage in 'frequent, continuous and increasingly concrete and precise *talk* about practice' is a key factor in school improvement (Little, 1981, p. 12). Secondary teachers involved in mentoring student teachers found they had to learn how to be clear and explicit about practice in order to help their students (Aspinwall, Garrett, and Owen-Jackson, 1994, p. 100).

The downside of memory is that it can become too past-oriented and render a school strongly, and unhelpfully, resistant to change. The balance of staffing may be crucial. Sometimes individuals seek early retirement when change seems to be coming full circle and they realise that they are feeling unable to summon up any enthusiasm. Conversely a rapidly changing staff or one that constantly moves on to something new may be in danger of developing no useful memory at all. A school that has great difficulty in retaining staff would be an example of this.

Imitation involves modelling best practice, benchmarking and learning from elsewhere. This practice has long been a feature of in-service education through presentations and workshops provided by experienced practitioners. The opportunity to share information and ideas is often cited by teachers as the most helpful aspect of a programme. Some schools may have become more cautious about sharing information in this way but, in our experience, the introduction of a more competitive climate between schools has had remarkably little impact so far in this context.

Local authority advisers (and in the past HMI) have seen the dissemination of good practice as a key part of their role. Visiting other institutions has also been a long established practice with some schools attracting perhaps more attention than they can cope with. Working alongside colleagues in the same school can also provide insight into other ways of teaching or relating to particular pupils. Educationalists have also been encouraged, through grants and secondments to spend time in the commercial sector. A preference for imitation is likely to lead a school to look for ways to compare itself with others in holding itself to account. The ability to look outside and learn from others' experience is clearly an important skill. Fullan suggests that it is the schools that think they are self-sufficient that learn least: 'Time and time again we find that seeking external support and training is a sign of vitality. It is the schools that act self-sufficiently that are going nowhere' (Fullan, 1993, p. 86). However, imitation too has its downside. There is always the danger of rushing from one flavour of the month to another or of adopting yesterday's ideas just before their inadequacies are discovered. Processes that work well in one situation do not always transpose easily or are simply inappropriate in a different situation. Perhaps the most serious danger of all is that an institution that develops a preference for looking outside for inspiration may lose confidence in its own ability to innovate and learn.

Experiment involves learning through innovation and trial and error. There is an emphasis on trying new ways of doing things, getting feedback, reflecting and further experimentation. Experiment and innovation can be life giving particularly when carefully paced and accompanied by reflection and evaluation. The term 'ownership' is perhaps most often linked to this kind of learning and development. Sometimes more than one school may be involved in an experiment. TVEI encouraged schools and colleges to work together. Primary pyramids of schools may link up with the local secondary school. This kind of experimenting can be very creative, building on a mix of school cultures, building in ongoing review activity and checking for evidence of effectiveness.

However, unless experimentation is firmly rooted and arises out of questions relating to the fundamental purposes of a school, enthusiasm can be dangerously undirected and become mere hyperactivity. Tight budgets can make it very difficult to resource a change properly and, as one new development is overwhelmed by the next, very few reach any sort of maturity. This may suit the 'change junkies' but before long most staff cease to take new initiatives seriously.

Critical awareness, the fifth of these learning styles, is perhaps the most wide ranging. It requires an open and questioning attitude to the organisation itself, to the wider field of education, to the community and beyond. Everything is open to critical questioning and analysis. This kind of learning is akin to Senge's systems thinking. Connections, underpinning values and ultimate purposes are explored in a serious attempt to understand the whole. It may also reflect Argyris and Schon's concept of double loop learning. As opposed to single loop learning, when errors are detected and corrected without any real challenge to the status quo, double loop learning requires the error or difficulty to be viewed in the wider context and may result in more fundamental changes. For example, rather than asking 'How can we do this just a little bit better?', we may have to ask 'Should we be doing this at all?' (Argyris and Schon, 1978, p. 3).

There is, of course, a downside. Raising awareness can sometimes make decision-making difficult. There are so many possibilities to consider. It may lead to a loss of focus or even to interest moving so far away from the day to day business of the school that it becomes neglected. An important element of critical awareness is to include the immediate and the here and now in the field of awareness.

Critical awareness requires holding on to more than one perspective at a time, being aware of short, medium and longer-term objectives. A teacher will need to hold in his or her consciousness the immediacy of the classroom, within a sense of the relevant department, the whole school and the wider community. Personal needs should not be ignored; neglect of self can lead to illness and stress. Of course, a total awareness of all these levels simultaneously is difficult, if not impossible, but remaining cocooned in a single perspective is not a viable alternative. Fullan recognises that linking schools with the wider world:

> requires a prodigious and mobilised effort and collaboration amongst a number of constituencies – parents and community, business and industry (labour and management) government and other social agencies, and the education system. The educa-

tion system cannot do it alone, but it must help break the cycle of disjuncture by helping to lead the way in its own right and through alliances.

(Fullan, 1993, p. 136)

Accountability in this context would mean engaging in thoughtful and open dialogue with all those with a stake in the school and reaching agreement about what is necessary – choosing particular priorities in the light of discussion.

All of these styles of learning are needed at different times. Some may be more essential than others at particular times or in particular situations. As with individual learning preferences, the broader and more balanced the repertoire the more learning skills a school will have to draw upon.

CREATING THE LEARNING SCHOOL

Fullan is a particularly rich source of information, ideas and models of the ways in which schools are developing their capacity to learn. In *Change Forces* (1993), and in earlier books written with Hargreaves, he draws together examples from a number of educational writers and researchers (Little, Rosenholtz, Nias, Southworth, Yeomans, Louis and Miles and many others) who all, in one form or another, stress the importance of creating collaborative, integrative, developmental and learning cultures. Schools may be autonomous but they are part of a neighbourhood, a wider community, a region, a nation and ultimately the world. This is important as: 'The societies that appear to be adapting most successfully are those that have historically placed a very high value on learning, and regard it as a lifelong process' (CIAR, 1992, p. 22).

Fullan speaks of 'transforming the school from a bureaucratic organization to a thriving community of learners' (1993, p. 42) and, writing with Hargreaves, places great emphasis on the value of interdependency, describing the dangers of a 'balkanised teacher culture – a culture made up of separate and sometimes competing groups, jockeying for position and supremacy like loosely connected, independent city states'. This leads to 'poor communication, indifference and to groups going their separate ways' (Fullan and Hargreaves, 1991, pp. 71–2) and is, therefore, unlikely to promote organisational learning. They identify collaborative working as the way to create an open and learning climate and quote Nias, Southworth and Yeoman's finding (1989) that in highly collaborative schools 'the individual and the group are simultaneously valued'.

This learning climate needs to extend to all those in the school. Non-teaching staff have a serious part to play. A school adviser once reported that she visited an infant school shortly after the LEA had provided a course for cleaning and caretaking staff on young children's learning needs. This had been provided in response to complaints about the amount of 'mess' in the classrooms at the end of the day. The caretaker asked to speak to her as a matter of urgency. He wanted to report his anxiety about the lack of sand, clay and water in the reception class.

This example may not portray a learning organisation but it does demonstrate a potential for learning that had not been tapped within the school. Senge places great value on team learning and 'colleagueship':

Treating each other as colleagues acknowledges the mutual risk and establishes the sense of safety in facing the risk. Colleagueship does not mean that you need to agree or share the same view. On the contrary, the real power of seeing each other as colleagues comes into play when there are differences of view. It is easy to feel collegial when everyone agrees. When there are significant disagreements it is more difficult. But the pay off is much greater'.

(Senge, 1990, p. 245)

Rosenholtz (1989), in explaining why learning occurs more easily in some schools than others, identifies two categories of school. *'Stuck'* or *'learning impoverished'* schools are characterised by:

- teacher isolation/privatism;
- lack of positive feedback;
- uncertainty;
- avoidance of risk taking;
- a sense of powerlessness.

In contrast *'moving'* or *'learning enriched'* schools are characterised by:

- collaboration and sharing;
- continuous teacher talk about practice;
- a common focus;
- a sense of efficacy;
- a belief in life-long learning;
- looking out as well as in.

The contrast between being 'stuck' and 'moving' is a powerful one. Isolation and fragmentation dissipate energy. Practical action is indicated. Teachers must talk to each other, plan together, identify a sense of common purpose.

Where the energy to move is absent it has to be created. Some years ago a headteacher took over a primary school after it had been run by an autocratic head for many years. The staff in the school were truly stuck. They preferred it that way. The head was able to appoint two new staff but they had little immediate impact against the prevailing culture. She was, however, an enthusiastic learner herself and was taking an Open University Diploma which focused on the teaching of reading. She would frequently go into the staffroom at breaks to discuss what she was learning: 'Do you know, I have been teaching reading for years and yet I had not realised . . . Have any of you noticed this? Look out for it and please let me know.' For the first time people began to find it possible to acknowledge their own learning. It became 'normal' to discuss what was going on behind those closed classroom doors. They were encouraged to go on courses. The new staff were the first to take up this opportunity but the idea began to catch on. The school began, slowly at first but with increasing energy, to move.

No one in this school had heard of the learning organisation and there was little discussion within it of the school's relationship with the outside world. Nixon *et. al.* conceive the learning school as having a more sophisticated sense of awareness as it 'becomes self aware about the cycles of learning and conditions for learning. It becomes proficient at asking questions, developing ideas, testing them and reflecting on practice' (1996, p. 128).

THE FOUR KEY CHARACTERISTICS OF A LEARNING SCHOOL

The concept of the learning organisation must surely be relevant to teachers and schools. If schools are not truly committed to learning in the widest sense, something must be wrong. It is perhaps a matter for serious thought that the proponents of organisational learning have not rushed to schools as a sure and certain reservoir of good practice in this area. Yet none of the characteristics, skills, attitudes and relationships explored in this chapter are revolutionary or unfamiliar to teachers. Many groups of staff work to attain them, and many prospective headteachers speak of their intention to foster just such cultures at their interviews.

From this chapter it is possible to identify the four key characteristics of a learning school:

- A commitment to lifelong learning for all those within the school.
- An emphasis on collaborative learning and the creative and positive use of difference and conflict.
- A holistic understanding of the school as an organisation.
- Strong connections and relationships with the community and world outside the school.

This is clearly not an easy route offering formulaic, standardised, externally assessed procedures to work through. However, the broadness of the concept leaves room for less confident schools to choose such approaches as a starting point if they wish. Developing the characteristics of a learning school will require time and effort but the rewards are potentially great and may be very relevant for schools at this time. Increasing autonomy for schools offers an opportunity for independence and growth but also holds the threat of the kind of fragmentation and balkanisation between schools that has proved so damaging within them.

The fourth of the key characteristics is particular relevant in this context. Schools that develop the learning potential of individuals and teams, have an understanding of the whole school as an organisation and are also aware of their place in, and responsibilities to, the wider community will have much to contribute. Schools have a crucial role to play in society; almost every one of our future citizens goes to school. There is potential for the purpose, energy and learning within them to spread across the educational community, thus benefiting all children, and beyond schools towards the creation of a learning society.

REFERENCES

Argyris, C., and Schon, D. (1978) *Organizational Learning: A Theory of Action Perspective*, Addison-Wesley, Reading, Mass.

Aspinwall, K., Garrett, V. and Owen-Jackson, G (1994) In at the beginning, in Reid, I., Constable, H and Griffiths, R. (eds.) *Teacher Education Reform: The Research Evidence*, Paul Chapman Publishing, London.

Bottery, M. (1992) *The Ethics of Educational Management*, Cassell, London.

Canadian Institute of Advanced Research (CIAR) (1992) *The Learning Society*, CIAR, Toronto, Ontario.

Fullan, M. (1993) *Change Forces: Probing the Depth of Educational Reform*, The Falmer Press, London.

Fullan, M. and Hargreaves, A. (1991) *What's Worth Fighting For in Your School?* Open University Press, Buckingham.

Garratt, R. (1987) *The Learning Organisation*, Fontana London.

Harrison, R. (1995) *Consultant's Journey*, McGraw-Hill, Maidenhead.

Little, J. (1981) The power of the organizational setting. Paper adapted from final report, *School Success and Staff Development*, National Institute of Education, Washington DC.

Morgan, G. (1986) *Images of Organization*, Sage, London.

Murdoch, I. (1992) *Metaphysics as a Guide to Morals*, Chatto & Windus, London.

Nias, J., Southworth, G. and Yeomans R. (1989) *Staff Relationships in the Primary School*, Cassell, London.

Nixon, J., Martin, J., McKeown, P. and Ranson, S. (1996) *Encouraging Learning: Towards A Theory of the Learning School*, Open University Press, Buckingham.

Pascale, R. (1990) *Managing on the Edge*, Penguin, Harmondsworth.

Pedler, M., and Aspinwall, K. (1996) *'Perfect plc?' The Purpose and Practice of Organisational Learning*, McGraw-Hill, Maidenhead.

Pedler, M., Burgoyne, J. and Boydell, T. (1996) *The Learning Company: A Strategy for Sustainable Development*, (2nd edn), McGraw-Hill, Maidenhead.

Peters, T. and Waterman, R. (1982) *In Search of Excellence*, Harper & Row, New York.

Reid K., Hopkins, D.and Holly, P. (1987) *Towards the Effective School*, Blackwell, Oxford.

Revans, R. (1969) The Enterprise as a learning system, in his *The Origins & Growth of Action Learning*, Chartwell Bratt Ltd, Lund, Sweden.

Rosenholtz, S. (1989) *Teachers' Workplace: The Social Organisation of Schools*, Longman, New York.

Sarason, S. (1990) *The Predictable Failure of Educational Reform*, Jossey-Bass, San Francisco.

Schon, D. (1971) *Beyond the Stable State*, Random House, New York.

Senge, P. (1990) *The Fifth Discipline*, Doubleday Currency, New York.

Senge P. (1991) The learning organisation made plain, *Training and Development*, October, pp. 37–64.

PART 4
OVERVIEW

4

Overview

SHEILA RUSSELL, TIM SIMKINS AND BRIAN FIDLER

AUTONOMY CONSTRAINED

Self-management offers many opportunities to schools. What it cannot do, however, is free them and those who manage and work in them, from the constraints associated with working in an economic and political climate which presents major challenges for public sector organisations of all kinds. New forms of institutional government in the schools sector (and not just there) have been accompanied by new, and perhaps more varied, constraints on the way in which institutional powers may be exercised. These constraints derive primarily from three sources: the *legal framework* within which the school system operates, the *resource environment* relating to both the financial context within which schools must work and the nature of the market pressures which impinge on individual schools, and the *social/political pressures* to which all public sector organisations are subject. These three sets of pressures are not easily separable: each influences the others in complex ways. Furthermore, while some constraints are universal and apply equally to all schools, the majority have a differentiated effect in different localities and may indeed be a direct result of the choices that schools themselves legitimately make. These issues were explored in some detail in Chapters 1.1 and 1.2. Nevertheless it may be useful to commence this final chapter with a short summary of the main themes.

Legal constraints

The principal constraints on a school that derive from statute are in the area of the curriculum, testing and the consequent definition of sets of performance measures relating to academic achievement. The extent of these constraints is explored in more detail in Chapter 2.3. The legal determination of a national curriculum has led to a more unified approach to classroom practice, to planning and to pedagogy, and has had a wider influence in bringing about an orientation to management that implies more control of teachers' work, and more attention to targets for individual pupils and classes as well as for schools.

Further constraints derive from the diverse characters of schools and their governance, determined by the 1988 Act, and discussed in this volume in Chapters 1.1 and 2.1. In some schools the increased power of governors may be more apparent than real, yet the tension between governor power and responsibility and management decision making and planning is still to be explored and worked through in the system.

Finally, as schools take on powers of staff management they become more aware of developing employment legislation. Case law clarifies legislation and increasingly schools are subject to EC directives which affect the rights of, among others, those in temporary appointments.

Resource constraints

There is a national concern to limit funding of public services, which is shown acutely in the funding of health services, social services and education. Schools have received the freedom to manage their budgets at a time when there have been real constraints, if not cuts, in the resources available to them to manage. There is a cynical view that increased delegation of decisions about spending to a local level simply serves to mask the effects of reduced spending. Certainly there have been protests and organised governor movements against cuts in education spending, and even mass resignations when faced with a budget allocation that does not appear to meet needs. Yet the reality for managers is that they must make the hard decisions within the resources they are allocated.

While there are apparent opportunities for schools to increase their income through attracting more pupils or through generating extra income these are limited by local contexts. As is pointed out in Chapter 2.6, schools do not have the freedom that commercial organisations do, to enter new markets or to determine pricing strategies. Realistically the degree of choice is locally determined, by the nature of local arena and schools' position within it.

Political/social constraints

A further real set of constraints relates to 'the art of the possible'. The human resource, the staff of a school, is a significant determinant of the potential for school development, and because of employment legislation cannot rapidly be altered in composition. This group of people will have their own ideas of professionalism, and expectations about degrees of individual freedom of action within the organisation. Changing educational pressures over such issues as teaching methods will impinge. Managers have to consider what is possible with the people involved and what they can be persuaded or successfully instructed to do.

Similar political and social constraints exist in relation to those outside the school, not only the governors but the wider community in the locality and beyond. There will be expectations of the school which constrain its ability to make certain decisions – particularly evidenced when a school's governors might wish to adopt GM status, but be frustrated by a parental 'no' vote. There are also the hidden 'steering forces' of government, which, through mechanisms such as inspection, can persuade a school of the value of certain management practices, or certain definitions of effectiveness. These broader constraints are not unimportant. Indeed, Glatter (1996, p. 3) argues that 'we in "mainstream" educational management have become too pre-occupied with what might be called the institutional side of leadership and management to the extent of disregarding or at least underemphasizing policy and con- textual factors'.

Whatever the source of constraint, perhaps the worst situation for a school is to be unwittingly constrained, to be steered into ways of acting and thinking without reflection. There is a description derived from the work of Habermas (1984) that characterises such steering forces as colonising the lifeworlds of the school and the education system. When this happens people are not able to communicate as equals but come, under the pressures of money and power, to adopt externally defined measures of effectiveness and success, thus limiting their areas of choice. This process is well described as 'steering'. It can be done with so light a touch that those involved believe that they have made their own choices – hence the use of the word 'colonisation' (Wilcox, 1996). Perhaps the greatest challenge for those who are responsible for schools and their work is to prevent their perceptions of the choices which are available to them being constrained in these ways.

CHOICE FOR WHOM? CHANGING ROLES

The discussion so far makes an implicit assumption that it is 'the school' which must assert its freedom within a world of constraints. But who or what exactly is the school in this context? As was demonstrated in Chapter 1.2, a major consequence of the educational reforms has been a reconfiguration of power relationships both within schools and between schools and the outside world. In part these have been *de jure* changes: legal powers, duties, rights, and responsibilities have been redistributed, with the particular consequence of empowering, among others, the Secretary of State, school governing bodies, headteachers and parents and disempowering teachers and local education authorities. However, formal powers and duties – while important – do not fully determine the behaviour of individuals and groups. The *de facto* distribu- tion of power – and consequently the amount of autonomy and effective choice – within a system may be very different from that which appears to follow from the system's legal framework. There are three reasons for this.

First, however tightly formal powers and duties may appear to be specified, there will remain major areas where choice may legitimately be exercised. This has been a major theme of this book. Second, as has been suggested above, the degree to which and the ways in which actors choose to exercise such choices depends to a considerable degree on their interpretations of the amount of freedom with which they can operate. Is the national curriculum for example to be treated as a strait-jacket, or as a set of constraints which nevertheless leave considerable opportunities for the exercise of creative curriculum management? Finally, even where considerable freedom is perceived to exist, the actors may choose to utilise this freedom to a greater or a lesser degree. Choices and opportunities may be perceived, but the national curriculum may provide an excuse for not trying out new ideas, especially risky ones.

Viewed in this way autonomy and accountability become problematic concepts: changes in either variable in relation to 'the school' may mean very different things in different local circumstances. Three themes may be identified to illustrate this point. The first concerns the relationship between the school and the outside world. Given the complexity of even the formal accountability relationships described in Chapter 1.1 and 1.2 it is helpful to consider this in terms of the currently fashionable concept of 'stakeholders' (Hutton, 1996). Whatever the legal position, the reality is that the choices about which stakeholder groups are to exert a major influence on the school are made at school level. In part this will depend on the assertiveness of particular stakeholder groups: for example parents are more likely to exercise their powers of choice and 'voice' in schools whose catchment areas are more advantaged. Whatever the relative power of particular groups, however, key gatekeepers within the school have considerable influence over the terms on which the various groups may exercise their powers. To a considerable degree they have the power to determine which groups are to have influence and over what.

Ironically the 'voice' of pupils is one that has scarcely been heard. Research on school choice has shown that pupils exercise a measurable impact on the choice of school which is ostensibly made by their parents. However, once they have joined a school they are often assumed to have no worthwhile views about their conditions of learning and other choices made by the school.

Many individuals and groups may play gatekeeping roles within the school. There can be little doubt, however, that within the self-managing school the key gatekeepers are the governing body and the headteacher. Recent debate about the exclusion from school of children with behavioural difficulties is an excellent illustration of the issues at stake. In part this is a legal question: who has, or should have, the power to determine decisions about exclusion – the head, governing body, the local education authority or the Secretary of State? Underlying this, however, is a more fundamental question. How are a number of conflicting legitimate interests to be reconciled: the rights of the individual child to receive an adequate and appropriate education; the rights of other children in the school to receive an undisturbed education; the rights of parents in relation to their children; and the rights of teachers to work in safety? Whatever the legal technicalities, critical issues are raised at the level of the school concerning how its governance system is to balance these rights. And these lead back inevitably to a more fundamental questions still: who is to determine these decisions and how, and what is the values base on which this is to be done?

To pose these questions is to raise a second issue about roles and power. This is the relationship between the senior management of the school, especially the headteacher, and the governing body. Chapter 2.1 demonstrates that, whatever the legal position, the determination of major issues of school policy involves negotiation between the headteacher and the governing body. This issue is illuminated through Peter Newsam's (1994) distinction between three possible roles for governing bodies: as part of the school authority structure rather like a board of directors; as semi-detached group of people which provides support to the school when it is needed; and as a body essentially separate from the work of the school but to which the school, through the head, is clearly accountable. Like all typologies, this analysis has its limitations. Nevertheless it captures an important truth about the ambiguity of governing relationships in the real world and it demonstrates that the choice and implementation of effective and agreed ways of working at this level is one of the most fundamental issues which self-managing schools must address.

If relations between the head and the governing body, and consequent decisions about the empowerment of external stakeholder groups, are two critical areas in the micro-politics of self-managing schools, a third is the relationship between the senior management of the school and the staff as a whole. There seems to be a good deal of agreement among commentators that, whatever else they may have done, one of the most important consequences of the reforms has been to empower heads and to disempower teachers. This has occurred for a number of reasons. First, the development of the national curriculum and its associated testing arrangements have significantly constrained the ability of teachers at school level, individually and collectively, to exercise discretion over key aspects of their work. Secondly, the emphasise which the reforms give to the performance of schools *as whole organisations,* whether this be assessed in terms of measured achievement in tests and examinations, the judgements of inspectors or success in market place of parental choice, means that the accountability of the head for the school's overall performance is re-emphasised. It is difficult to separate the performance of the school from that of its headteacher, especially if he or she has been in post for some time.

Finally, while the educational reforms may have centralised criteria power (see Chapter 1.2), school self-management has delegated to the school major areas of operational power, especially in the areas of personnel and resource management. These new powers require senior managers – directly or with the approval of their governing bodies – to make difficult choices, for example about staff appointments, deployment, remuneration and discipline, which are not only critical to the strategic direction of the school but may impinge on the conditions of service and careers of their colleagues. As is pointed out clearly in Chapter 2.5, this produces 'an uncomfortable agenda in relations between school managers and their colleagues' which highlights, sometimes painfully, the potential tension between new types and levels of managerial responsibility and ideals of collegial management which are advocated in much of the literature on education management. Clearly this is an area where self-managing schools have important choices to make, and we will return to it later. First, however, we need to address a wider issue, that of the character of the school itself.

THE PURPOSE AND CHARACTER OF THE SCHOOL

Despite the constraints discussed earlier and the centralising tendency in legislation over the last ten years, there is still a place for the school to affirm an organisational commitment to certain values about the purposes of education and the place which the school seeks within the wider system. There are variations between institutions not only in the values they hold, but in the extent to which these are explicitly stated, examined and debated. However conscious or unconscious these beliefs about the purpose of education and the roles of schools as providers may be, they form the basis for the choices that schools make within the limited freedoms they have. A school's values about education will determine its attitude to the market, to its client group, to its deployment of resources and to its choice of performance measures to demonstrate effectiveness and to inspire improvement.

This point can be well illustrated by the debate about school effectiveness (see Chapter 1.4). Much of the literature in this area sidesteps the point that terms such as effectiveness, efficiency and economy are value laden so that the apparently neutral notion of 'school improvement' also comes with hidden values (Elliott, 1996). The different attitudes to improvement and to the effects of choosing and publicising certain measures of performance can be illustrated by the story of one small village school which had a good Ofsted inspection report. In the year following the report the school had 14 applications from out-of-village families. The head was worried that such an influx could destroy the advantages of being a village school and the very distinctive ethos they had created. She was also concerned that this development was 'inadvertently alienating other schools locally, upsetting the delicate relationship between heads, who prefer to be collaborative rather than competitive' (Brimblecombe, Ormston and Shaw, 1996). She was faced, as are many heads and schools, with a dilemma about purpose within an environment which encourages parental choice and inter-school competition.

To some extent a school can choose the model it adopts as a description of its main purpose. This may be embodied in a mission statement or statement of aims as described in Chapter 2.2, but it is often implicit in the way that the school publicises its success or identifies the parents whose children it wishes to attract. The metaphors described in Chapter 1.2 provide a means of making some of these choices more explicit. For instance, should the school function as a local outlet for products determined centrally by the DFEE and SCAA? Or does it seek to act as a participatory community where stakeholders are involved in ways which reflect and respond to local concerns? Such an approach might also imply acting as one of a community of partnership schools who seek to maximise resources for the good of all – an attitude that has been adopted by clusters of primary and secondary schools in some London boroughs which have even pooled some of their respective financial allocation and redistributed it. Alternatively does the school see itself as a separate business operating in a competitive market, where it has to aim for success or go under, and consequently cannot afford to consider the effects its success in attracting pupils may have on the dynamic of other local schools?

The choice of metaphor or style will be determined by values that members of the school community have, not just in relation to the meaning of 'effectiveness', but also about equity and interpretations of equity, and the ways in which these values are transformed into school policy. What values do school communities espouse? Indeed can these values be determined unless individuals are able to express differing views, in an atmosphere that permits a consensus to emerge or differences to be acknowledged openly and some compromises made. There are no simple, right answers to some of the hard questions posed by equity issues. We might ask, for example, whether the school interprets equity as 'levelling', requiring resources to be distributed so that the least advantaged are favoured most and variances in achievement are minimised. Is it the job of the school to compensate for circumstances of disadvantage which are beyond the individual's control? Or is the shared interpretation of equity more to do with competition and efficient use of resources, distributing resources in proportion to the pupils' ability to benefit and so, supposedly, maximising the total learning gain from resources which appear to be increasingly scarce (Simkins, 1995)? Such considerations will underpin choices a school makes in relation to aspects of its character beyond those established centrally, and in particular its attitude to selection. It can, for instance use its admissions policy to select a percentage of pupils on criteria related to perceived ability to benefit from education. This percentage is higher for GM schools, but whether or not to use and advertise this opportunity is a real choice for all schools. Ironically schools can select in order to make up a 'balanced' intake from one otherwise skewed to lower abilities. The local situation will determine the appropriateness or viability of such a choice, as well as the values about equity discussed above.

CHOICE ABOUT HOW? LEADERSHIP STYLE AND SCHOOL CULTURE

The central section of this book identifies and explores a number of areas where choices need to be exercised within the self-managing school. That of governance has been briefly revisited earlier in this chapter. The others areas, however – strategic management, curriculum management, the management of the relationship between the school and its environment, the management of people, resource management and the management of evaluation – attempt to establish a 'menu' of areas where self-managing schools need to consider afresh the areas of freedom which are now available to them, the constraints under which these freedoms must be exercised, and consequently the choices which will need to be made in pursuit of their goals and values within an increasingly unpredictable environment.

This is not the place to revisit the substantive questions which these chapters explore. It is important to note, however, that each of these areas can be seen as providing a number of policy *levers* or *mechanisms* which leaders and others can use to influence the process of change and development. Choices about *which* levers to use and *how* to use them must not be seen simply as instrumental ones embodying ideas and assumptions about cause and effect. Such choices also carry powerful expressive meanings: they embody values – and, more importantly, are *seen* to embody values – which are often of much deeper significance than may at first sight appear to be the case. In this context it is worth re-emphasising three key areas within which such levers may be exercised.

First, there are real choices to be made about resource deployment. Managing scarce resources means making decisions about the rival claims to need of different groups, and about their ability to benefit. For example, which groups of children and which aspects of the curriculum are to be resourced more favourably, through smaller classes or other forms of discriminatory resourcing? What factors will determine the ways in which teachers are allocated amongst groups? How are special educational needs to be defined and resourced? The answers to such questions make important statements about the ways in which the concepts of effectiveness and equity discussed earlier are to be operationalised in school policy: about how effective learning can best be achieved and how learning opportunities are to be distributed.

Second, in making choices about the curriculum there is more freedom, since the Dearing review, than appeared to the early critics of the control implied by introduction of the national curriculum. Yet there is emerging a new 'steering' control over how the curriculum is taught, through the alliance of SCAA, Ofsted reports on effective teaching and TTA programmes for the development of teachers. Choices about styles of teaching and pedagogy may be reduced over the next few years. The extent to which the hopes for 'powerful teachers' expressed in Chapter 3.2 can be realised will depend on national attitudes to teacher professionalism.

Finally, the management of staff embodies important choices, many of which are heavily value laden. A good example here is that of decisions about the employment of part-time and temporary staff. Chapter 2.6 suggests that the employment of staff on such terms is increasing as schools seek ways to increase their ability to respond flexibly to an uncertain environment. However, Chapter 2.5 reminds us that such decisions can embody different values:

> When they are based on a recognition of all employees' needs for flexibility, particularly women combining work and family, then they have a humanistic as well as a pragmatic basis. When flexibility is synonymous with casualisation, then people and their rights as employees are under threat.

In its choices about staff recruitment, deployment and development the school will demonstrate its views of professionalism and the importance of personal growth for employees as well as pupils. Burgess (1992, p. 5) argues for a view of professionalism that is based on the notion that education is a personal service which succeeds or fails with individuals, not with systems. He believes that teachers 'have knowledge, experience and qualifications which they place at the client's service, and . . . exercise individual judgement in the solution of a client's problems'. The ways in which teachers are treated will say much about the interpretation of professionalism which the school espouses.

Such examples serve to underline some common themes which emerge from these chapters and which are dealt with in more depth in Part 3. These themes can be summarised in terms of the importance for self-managing schools of effective leadership, the management of culture and the ways in which these in turn can impact on the capacity of the school to be a 'learning organisation' in two senses: a place where, in David Hopkins' words, 'powerful' teaching and learning takes place and where individuals, groups and the organisation as a whole grow and change in response to a changing and challenging environment.

Questions of leadership and culture are inherent in the point about the relationships between senior management and other staff discussed above. The issue is alluded in a number of chapters. For example, Chapter 2.5 refers to research which suggests a distancing of senior managers from other staff in the school with a 'division of values and purposes' (Bowe and Ball, 1992, p. 59); a division between the concern of teachers with the classroom and the needs of individual pupils and that of senior managers with the performance of the school as a whole and its consequences for the organisation's survival and growth. In stark contrast to this scenario, Hugh Jenkins in Chapter 3.1, suggests that school-based management is leading to more collaborative and 'transformational' leadership styles with flatter structures and a much greater emphasis on shared leadership than has been the case in the past. Empirically the jury is still out on the issue of the impact of self-management on the structure, culture and management styles exhibited by self-managing schools. It is not clear yet how far schools which are subject to the kinds of external pressures described in Chapters 1.1 and 1.2 are, and will be, free to adopt the kinds of collegial approaches to management advocated by so much of the education management literature; and the issue is further complicated by the view that such approaches were relatively rare anyway before schools were subject to the kind of pressures they are under today (Ball, 1987; Jenkins, 1991).

Nevertheless, a common theme throughout this book is the importance of school culture and its management. There is more than one allusion to Edgar Schein's dictum that 'the only thing of real importance that leaders do is to create and manage culture' (Schein, 1985, p. 2). This powerful quotation, of course, begs two important questions: first whether culture *can* be managed, and second whether its management *should* be given the highest priority by school leaders. These are large questions, but the leaders of self-managing schools must take a position on each of them.

The final chapters of the book should help in this and their powerful arguments should stand on their own. However, it may be useful to re-emphasise some of their key points. These can, perhaps, be summarised as follows:

- The core activity of schooling takes place in the classroom, and school improvement is a process that focuses on enhancing the quality of students' learning.
- While the school should have a strong external focus – for its *raison d'être* lies in the wider community and society – external pressures for change must be used as opportunities to secure the school's internal values and priorities.
- The school needs to be understood as a whole, embracing all its members as both learners and contributors. It should seek to develop structures and create conditions which encourage collaboration and lead to the empowerment of individuals and groups.
- There should be a commitment to learning at all levels within the school – individual, group, and whole school – and a recognition that improvement will only occur through a combination of internal processes of monitoring and evaluation and reflection on the best practice to be found elsewhere.
- The educative and moral nature of the leadership role in educational organisations needs constantly to be reaffirmed.

The promise of the self-managing school is that it is free, at least in part, to determine how it is led and managed and hence to seek ways of putting ideas such as these into practice. The pessimistic view that funding constraints and increasing centralisation have reduced decision making to a merely operational level is belied by the opportunities that these types of choices present. Yet it will take strength of purpose on the part of school leaders to resist, if they so choose, the reductionist stress on measurable efficiencies, and the prevailing tendency to treat the complexities of defining effectiveness in a simplistic way.

On these issues there can be no final choices. Schools will need periodically to reappraise their choices in order to ensure that they have taken account of current external pressures in a way which has the best chance of securing a successful future for the school and its learners.

In conclusion, schools have moral decisions to make about ends and means, both in terms of teaching and assessment and in terms of management practices. These decisions will derive from and embody the values of the school. As Chapter 2.3 suggests, schools have a special position in relation to their ethical stances, for they are expected to give a moral education to pupils; it surely follows a school's strategic and operational decisions should be consonant with the values it endeavours to transmit to its pupils. If the exercise of opportunities and choices is to take place within a moral framework, overt discussion of values seems essential. Perhaps the most important moral imperative is to consider carefully whether there are options, and if there do not appear to be any, to check out the validity of this perception. This will imply questioning the culture of the school as well as the force of legal and financial constraints. It is important not to accept apparent constraints without testing out their limits. It has been demonstrated by changes in the national curriculum how far the pressures from within schools can be influential. Baumann (1994) argues for a society which can make ethical decisions through collective debate, and his model and his hopes could well be applied to schools. We need both more autonomy for *individual* moral selves and more vigorous sharing of *collective* responsibilities . . . Choices are indeed choices, and that means that each is to some extent arbitrary and that uncertainty as to its propriety is likely to linger long after the choice was made. We understand that uncertainty is not a temporary nuisance . . . it is a permanent condition of life. A society that engages its members . . . in the . . . imperative task of caring for, and running common affairs . . . requires neither disciplined subjects nor satisfaction-seeking consumers of socially provided services, but rather tenacious and sometimes obstinate, but always responsible, citizens . . . [S]uch responsibility makes the citizen into that basis on which can be built a human community resourceful and thoughtful enough to cope with the present challenges. (pp. 44–5)

REFERENCES

Ball, S.J. (1987) *The Micro-politics of the School: towards a theory of school organisation*, Methuen, London.

Baumann Z. (1994) *Alone Again: Ethics After Certainty*, Demos, London.

Bowe, R. and Ball, S. (1992) *Reforming Education and Changing Schools: case studies in policy sociology*, Routledge, London.

Brimblecombe, N., Ormston, M. and Shaw, M. (1996) What Role does Ofsted Inspection have in Meeting the Government's Aims for Parents and Schools? Paper presented at the British Educational Research Association Annual Conference, September 1996, University of Lancaster.

Burgess T. (1992) Accountability with confidence, in T. Burgess (ed) *Accountability in Schools*, Harlow, Longman.

Elliott, J. (1996) School effectiveness research and its critics: alternative visions of schooling, *Cambridge Journal of Education*, Vol 26 no. 2, pp. 199–224.

Glatter, R (1996) Context and capability in education management. Paper presented at the British Educational Management and Administration Society Annual Conference, September 1996, Coventry.

Habermas, J. (1984) *The Theory of Communicative Action: Reason and Rationalization of Society*, Polity Press, Cambridge.

Hutton, W (1996) *The State We're In*, (Revised edn.), Vintage, London.

Jenkins, H.O. (1991) *Getting It Right: a handbook for successful school leadership*, Blackwell, Oxford.

Newsam, P. (1994) Last bastion against the mighty state, Governors Guide, *Times Educational Supplement*, 30th September.

Schein, E. (1985) *Organizational Culture and Leadership*, Jossey-Bass, San Francisco, CA.

Simkins, T. (1995) The equity consequences of educational reform, *Educational Management and Administration*, Vol 23 no. 4, pp. 221–32.

Wilcox, B. (1996) Inspection: Common Sense or Conceptual Melange? Paper presented at the British Educational Research Association Annual Conference, September 1996, University of Lancaster.

Index